Reporting:

The Tulsa Riot, 1921

Immigrants, 1802 - 1931

Pandemic, 1918 - 1920

Fascism, 1914 - 1928

The Archive
of American Journalism

Lincoln Steffens/Henry Stanley

Theodore Roosevelt/Richard Harding Davis

Ida Tarbell/Ray Stannard Baker

Nellie Bly/H.L. Mencken

Ambrose Bierce/Stephen Crane

O.O. McIntyre/Dorothy Thompson

Annie Laurie/Ring Lardner

Jack London/Mark Twain

Damon Runyon/Ernest Hemingway/Westbrook Pegler

www.historicjournalism.com

Reporting:
Fascism

Vol. 1: 1914 - 1928

The Archive of American Journalism
St. Paul, MN
2024

Note on Sources

All articles are complete and unabridged, with headlines, subheads and formatting that match those of the original publication. Note that minor edits have been made to correct obsolete spelling and punctuation. Students and researchers: these are "public domain" texts that can be freely copied, reproduced and distributed without permission or cost. Please credit The Archive of American Journalism as your source.

The Archive LLC
9269 Troon Court
Woodbury, MN 55125.

Article selection and original Introduction
Copyright ©2024 by Tom Streissguth
Cover Image:

ISBN: 979-8-9899409-0-5
Printed in the United States of America

Acknowledgments

For their encouragement and suggestions, sincere thanks to Mark Lerner, Gordon Hagert, Pier Gustafson, Phil Gapp, Jonathan Peacock, John Hatch, Marian Streissguth and our original founding supporters: William F. Zeman, Phil Gapp, Walter Crowley, Adele Streissguth, Richard Prosser, Abhilash Sarhadi, James McGrath Morris

Contents

Introduction

American reporters in Europe had much to observe, and explain, in the 1920s.

The continent was still recovering from the "Great War" that had dragged on for more than four years and killed millions. The conflict scarred northern France with bloody trenches and ruined cities. It left Germany with ruinous debts and political chaos.

But postwar Europeans still held the optimistic thought that the nightmare would shock the world into sanity and enduring peace. A treaty had been struck with Germany. Its emperor had fled, the country would be disarmed, and a democratic state would be more easily dealt with by the Allied powers of Britain, France and the United States.

For Americans, Europe returned to its prewar status: beguiling and picturesque travel destination. France and Paris were again favorites. Allies during the war, the French regarded at least one American, Woodrow Wilson, as a heroic savior. Another inviting destination, for its landscapes and history—and for rather quaint, comic opera politics—was Italy.

Italy had joined Germany and Austria-Hungary as an ally in 1914, then had switched sides to fight with the Allies. Now, in the 1920s, the charismatic Benito Mussolini was striving for power with eloquent rhetoric and a pugnacious, scowling pose. Former editor of a socialist newspaper, he was a skilled talker and had a talent for making news of himself. His obedient minions were known as *fascisti,* for the Roman image of bundled wooden rods. They were a disciplined mob who would riot in the streets, murder opponents, and obey their leader without question. Mussolini's goal was the creation of a new man of action, answerable only to him, and to sweep away the ineffective and endless debating hobby known as democracy.

Reporters from the United States and elsewhere took notes. Benito Mussolini was certainly of interest to readers back home, at least those readers who found Europe and its issues interesting. Here was a new approach to leadership and governance. It begged for observation, cried out for explanation. Big events were happening.

Mussolini marched on Rome and seized power in 1922. Then came an attempted coup by his Austrian admirer, Adolf Hitler, in the Gerrman city of Munich in November, 1923. Hitler took his cue from the Italian, annoncing his plans for a new Germany and working up an image as a man of action and a fanatic patriot. His goal, too, was absolute power, and his promise retribution for the humiliation of disarmament and financial destruction by the Allies.

For some reporters, it wasn't complicated. They had been around the continent, and in these countries dictatorship was not really new. It was simply old-fashioned monarchy with a new script, and new wardrobe. Exhausted from its war, Europe was at last at peace, and if that peace brought some rude and violent politics, some social chaos, then this was only to be expected, especially in defeated nations such as Germany.

Other reporters scrambled to describe exactly what Hitler and Mussolini meant to their own countries and to Europe. For some, the effects were positive—the countries were run better, the mood of the people lifted, while the confusion of democracy was swept into history's dustbin.

Reporters appreciated novelty, and controversy in politics. The fascists gave them something new to write about, and a rich context for opinions. The charismatic dictators were drawing the masses to any open space they addressed: a city plaza, an open plain on the outskirts, a sports stadium. There were also the production values to delight the eye: the flags, uniforms, the pageantry of military parades and an entire population turning an adoring eye to the New Man standing on the balcony or the podium. Couching the fascists in good-or-evil terms would occur later, when an Allied coalition again ranged against Germany and Italy.

For now, they were simply interesting.

"In the 1920s and '30s, people really had to figure them out. They had this idea that Hitler would calm down and become a regular leader, that there was an impulse to moderation, or that the dictators would actually destroy each other…"

Karin Wulf, *Smithsonian*

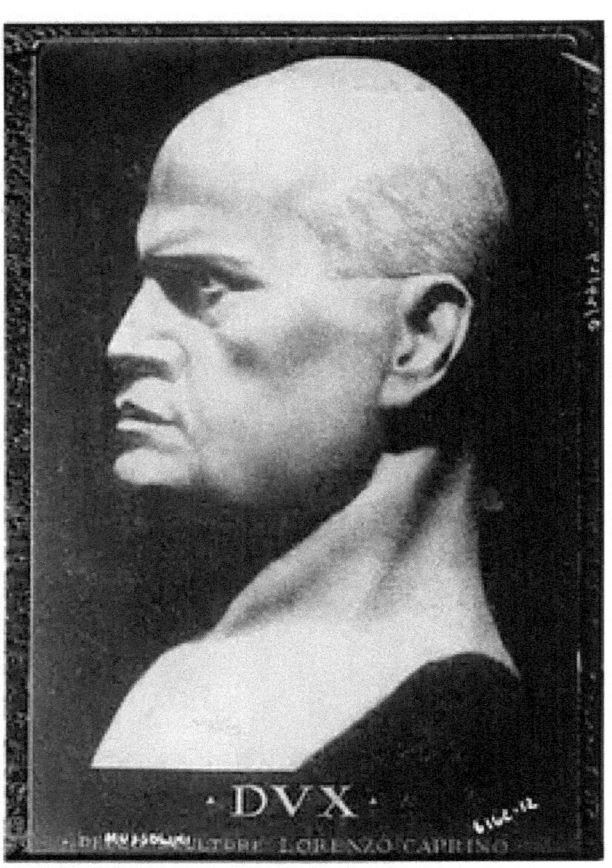

· DVX ·

DE MUSSOLINI SCULTORE LORENZO CAPRINO

Socialist Editor Acquitted
The Goltry News/April 17, 1914

Milan, April 15 — The Socialists of all Italy are rejoicing over the victory scored by *l'Avanti*, the official Socialist dally, when the Jury trying its editor in chief, Benito Mussolini, on charges cf having insulted the king and the army in articles on the massacre at Rocca Gorga, rendered a verdict of acquittal.

Strike in Italy Growing Serious
Nebraska State Journal/June 10, 1914

ROME, June 9. The general strike proclaimed yesterday as a protest against the repressive measures taken by the government in connection with demonstrations at Ancona Sunday, when several men were shot down, is gaining in intensity. The resentment of the workmen has been fanned by the killing of another striker at Florence today. The government views the movement with anxiety, as it is believed to be supported not only by the socialists but by the radical party, which is anxious to embarrass the Kalandra ministry. The premier was subjected to a strong criticism in the chamber today for prohibiting anti-militarist meetings on June 7. In reply he said there had been no trouble except at Ancona and that none regretted more than he the loss of life. He said that the policemen who fired the fatal shots would be prosecuted, but he pointed out that the police at the time of the shooting were surrounded by rioters and only fired when several of them had been struck down by bricks.

In Rome tonight a thousand strikers came into violent contact with the troops and police, who fired nine volleys in the air before the mob retreated. A large number of soldiers and strikers were injured. The strikers attempted to reorganize their shattered ranks and another fierce engagement with the police took place before they dispersed.

In cities where the strike was in force no newspapers were published. From many parts of Italy come reports of disorders. At Genoa the strikers compelled the storekeepers to close their places of business. At

Turin rioters seized two wagons loaded with tobacco belonging to the state and threw several cases of cigarettes through the window of a. cafe and burned the remainder before cavalry dispersed them.

At Venice several clashes occurred between strikers and police, one of the latter being seriously injured.

Pitched Battle at Turin

TURIN, Italy, June 9 A pitched battle occurred today between a column of strikers and the troops. One man was killed and two were mortally injured. A great number of others were injured, some seriously.

MILAN, Italy, June 9. A serious disorder has occurred here as a result of the general strike. All stores are closed and both newspapers and street cars have suspended. At the close of a meeting attended by 5,000 persons this evening strikers and their followers armed themselves with bricks and fell upon the police, who fled. A squadron of cavalry dispersed the rioters after a sharp fight. The strikers reformed their ranks and attacked a detachment of caribineers whom they scattered. They then captured a wagon loaded with cans of gasoline, to which they touched a match. A terrific explosion followed, causing a panic. Later the manifestants attacked tho police, and reinforcements came to the rescue, revolvers being emptied into tho mob. A large number of persons were wounded, including Signor Mussolini, editor of Avanti. More than a hundred arrests were made.

The railroad strike, which was to have been declared tomorrow, began tonight at various points, including Ancona and Turin. The night expresses were unable to leave Milan and Naples.

Strikers attacked the automobile of Prince von Buelow, the former Imperial German chancellor, and seriously damaged it. A barricade was raised in the Via Alessandria, near the coliseum. Troops drove the strikers away from the barricade and destroyed it.

Italian Arms Secret Revealed to Germany
Leavenworth Times/December 27, 1914

Rome, Dec. 2. According to the newspaper started by Mussolini, a Socialist leader who has broken away from the main body of Italian Socialists on account of his wish for Italy to go into the war against Germany, the Germans have acquired Italy's latest artillery secrets.

Some time ago the government ordered 2,000 automatic regulators for field batteries from the Monza works. They are patents and have a secret construction, which would render their fire most deadly.

Mussolini's paper accuses the Monza manager, a man with the German of Keller, of sending two of these regulators to Germany on Sept. 9 last, one by way of Barcelona, the other by Mulhausen. An employee of the Monza works, one Passerini Giuseppe, found this out and demanded an inquiry by an army officer and a senator. These two gave no verdict. Passerini then informed Mussolini of the fact.

Ex-Minister of War to Fight Socialist
Barre Daily Times/March 16, 1916

Rome, March 16. General Spingardi, ex-minister of war, has challenged Benito Mussolini, Italy's leading Socialist editor, to a duel. Mussolini was recently promoted to be a corporal because of unusual bravery at the front. He alleged that Spingardi was conspiring to become commander of the Turin army corps.

Benito Mussolini was editor of The Avanti when the war in Europe broke out, but owing to his stand on Italy's obligations broke away from that journal and started a newspaper of his own, the Popolo d'Italia, devoted to asserting the claims of the lost provinces. When Italy finally took a step against Austria Mussolini joined his regiment of Bersagheri and was promoted at the front.

Italian Editors to Fight Duel
Wisconsin State Journal/January 13, 1919

MILAN, Jan. 13.-- Benito Mussolini, editor of the *Popolo d'Italia*, has sent his seconds to Editor Pontremoli of the *Secolo*, it was learned today. The challenge is said to have resulted from an editorial in the *Secolo* in which Mussolini was called a "political adventurer."

The editorial was a discussion of former Minister Bissolati's undelivered speech regarding Italy's territorial ambitions.

One Killed, Eight Hurt in Italian Rioting
Journal and Tribune (Knoxville, TN)/November 15, 1919

Milan, Nov. 14.--One man was killed. eight persons were seriously wounded and many others less seriously injured in an election disturbance at Lodi today. The disturbance occurred when Prof. Benito Mussolini, editor of the Milan Popolo Italia; Signor Marinetti, the futurist leader, and another speaker tried to address the crowd at a meeting.

The Lodi advices state that they were attacked by socialists. Troops defended the speakers. Revolvers were fired by both sides during the affray.

64 Newspaper Men Candidates for Italian Parliament
Baltimore Sun/November 17, 1919

by Beatrice Baskerville

Rome, Nov. 16. Sixty-four newspaper men are candidates for the Italian Parliament, representing all parties, but the most prominent among them are Socialists and a few are avowedly Bolsheviks.

The best known, Leonidas Bissolati, a Socialist, is accused of having misinformed President Wilson regarding Italian aspirations in the Adriatic and on the Fiume question. He was an undersecretary in the Bozelli ministry and a bitter enemy of the Soviet party. His constituency is Cremona.

Giuseppe Sevione, a Liberal, has many friends in America, which he visited during the war.- He is running in the Turin district.

Benito Mussolini, a politician as well as a reporter, practically leads the combatant Socialist party and is on its Milan list. He, too, is a bitter foe of the Bolshevist party, which has newspaper men in its vanguard.

Bombacci, whose revolutionary speeches are causing anxiety, and three other reporters of the same paper, the Avanti, are on various lists. Glandio Treves, of Milan, millionaire, but an extreme Socialist with leanings toward Bolshevism, has refused to leave the Soviet party, although he openly deplores its violent methods. He writes for the Avanti. To him is due the credit for having upset the rank and file of the Italian Army during the war with the cry of "No more men in the trenches this winter." That cry was one of the causes of the Caporetto disaster.

The most astounding newspaper candidate of all is Pullipo Marinetti, a futurist apostle. His extravagances in verse and color are so fresh in the public mind that people refuse to take him seriously. He is a Socialist on the combatant list for Milan.

Ten days before general elections a large part of the Italian Catholics are uncertain whether they can or cannot vote for members of the Parliament of the Italian government with whom the Holy See is not on speaking terms. The question is a serious one for all Italian Catholics who still recognize the papal authority. They await an announcement from the Pope as to whether he approves of the large, well organized, powerful Catholic popular party, which is taking such an active part in the election campaign and forms the most important bulwark against Bolshevik propaganda in the cities and country alike. So far the Pope has not made any statement on this new phase of Catholic life, the appearance of prominent clergy and laymen in the political arena. Leo XIII forbade the Italian Catholics taking any active part in the politics of Italy's temporal government. Unless the Holy See speedily issues a declaration permitting the Catholics to vote, the Catholic party will lose many votes. The Catholic popular party itself is an anomaly, despite the fact that its leader, Don Sturzo, is a priest and some of its most active election canvassers also are priests. Moreover, it looks as if this political anomaly is going to be a great force in the coming Parliament. Therefore the attitude of the Holy See is greatly agitating friends and foes.

Socialist Leader Will Be on Trial
Calgary Herald/December 6, 1919

Charge of Raising Troops for Bringing About Revolution

PARIS, Dec. 6. A dispatch from Milan reports the coming trial of Prof. Benito Mussolini, the Socialist leader, and editor of the Milan *Popolo Italia,* on a charge of raising troops for the purpose of bringing about a revolution. Capt. Vecchi, president of the Arditl association,, and Dr. Marinetti, the futurist poet, are mentioned in connection with the case.

Italy is Not Poet-Crazy
Miami Daily Record-Herald (Miami, OK)/December 7, 1919

Populace Excited for a Time by D'Annunzio's Performance But Now Divided—Sane Element Deplores Encouragement of Army Insubordination—Rebel Spirit Abroad but Peasant and Business Men Still Carry On

SIENA, Italy. (By Mail.)—These are still agitating times in Italy. It is true that the great strike of last summer did not come off and that the people steadily hold their own but matters are not as they should be yet. There is a spirit abroad ever ready to stir up discord and to suggest mad attempts at improving the situation by the means of rebellion and a general overturning of all existing conditions

The belief of all thinking people is that there were the strongest of financial reasons, and those only, behind the obstinate and determined opposition of certain persons in power to the admission of Fiume and the Dalmatian cities into the kingdom of Italy. And this feeling has been erected during all these months in the minds and speech of the plainer folk who believe what they hear.

One of the men whose opinion I value is a certain pharmacist who lives not far away. He, too, is a most ardent patriot and how he worked for the propaganda during the war! He used to distribute it right and left and send it out into the country where it went round among the contadini. I asked him what he thought of D'Annunzio's expedition. As he is of a very enthusiastic nature I wondered if his head was upset by the present excitement. He said, however, as many quiet, sensible people do, that D'Annunzio had been imprudent, that he had not chosen the best moment, no matter what great motives lay underneath the action. And he added rather sadly as we parted, "I am afraid of the opportunity which this gives for the bad element, the camorra of the nation, to come to the top."

The case is just this, of course. Fiume has decided to become Italian and so have the Dalmatian cities, and Italian they ought to be. In time all ought to come right and the world be convinced of the justice of the question. But as there was already such a great amount of unrest, and there were so many people looking for changes and for opportunities to upset things, this action opened the door too wide. If the regular army had not been dragged into it, if the "soldier-poet" had taken with him only a company of volunteers, it would have seemed a more knightly adventure, and one more reasonable. The encouragement of insubordination in the army spoiled it.

Patience is Worn Out

Yet it is almost to be expected that something was bound to happen The patience of Italy was worn out; the slights put upon her in the conference even yet ever present in the popular mind.

The press has naturally been very active. The "Popolo d'Italia" of Milan edited by a famous Socialist, Benito Mussolini, is a paper that is very widely read just now, and is doing harm. Its editor is a wise man sometimes and has used his influence well, particularly at the time of the strikes; but he has gone wild over Fiume. Some of his editions of the last week have been full of invectives against the government, that is against those who were in power at Rome, though never against the House of Savoy The censorship has been applied again of late to the press and some of these things which the "Popolo d'Italia" has wanted to publish have been suppressed.

Fiume Boiling Pot

One of the principal objects of this paper during the last month has been the collecting of subscriptions for Fiume, and how the money has poured in! Besides money, volunteers have not been wanting. It is safe to say that almost every young man or boy—and some older ones: too, have been filled with longing to get to Fiume and throw in his lot there, in many cases without much Idea of the right or wrong of the enterprise The country has grown so tired of waiting and hearing the same story day after day that almost any action seemed welcome. But the great motto of the Italians--Pazienza—must be put into practice a little longer if there is to be peace in the country.

Shopkeepers are disgusted with the present condition of things, the strikes in one industry after another, and the consequent impossibility of keeping their little stocks supplied.

You find this "carry on" spirit also in the Italian business man and manufacturer. In this part of Tuscany or near here where the river flows through to the sea, the district is known as the Valdarno, the valley of the Arno. It is one of the most fertile and best cultivated parts of Italy and possesses besides many industrial enterprises. There has just formed an association called the Liberal Democratic Association of Valdarno, and the names of every man of any importance in towns and villages of this large district are on the list of members. The association proposes:

"To renew the Italian public life in harmony with the new aspirations of our people and the new needs of the nation.

"To sustain in the social field all the legislative reforms understood to insure the progress and rapid ascension of the working class endeavoring to elevate in it the grade of culture and of moral sentiment.

"In the economic field to promote and encourage every initiative which can in any way contribute to augment production and to reconstruct the national resources."

There are similar organizations elsewhere throughout the country and under their guidance industry and agriculture will be encouraged and prosperity increased.

Milan Editor in Revolt Plot
St. Joseph Gazette (St. Joseph MO)/December 7, 1919

Paris, Dec. 6.--A dispatch from Milan reports the coming trial of Prof. Benito Mussolini, the Socialist leader and editor of the Milan Popolo d'Italia, on a charge of raising troops for the purpose of bringing about a revolution. Captain Ferrucci Veochi, president of the Arditti association, and Dr. Marinett, the futurist poet, are mentioned in connection with the case.

Italian Socialists Want More Police;
"Fascisti" Fighters Driving Extremists from Streets in Cities
Brooklyn Daily Eagle/February 1, 1921

The farcical political situation in Italy is emphasized by a socialist motion, introduced in the Chamber, which virtually consists of an appeal for more police protection against the activities of the fascisti. It is amusing to see the socialists, who until lately were supposed to dominate the whole country and once asked for a reduction of the police strength, now finding it very useful to have even more police enrolled to protect them. Several recent episodes fully justify the request, for both the homes of Socialists and the Socialist organization's buildings lately were the objects of determined attacks by the fascisti.

The fascisti must not be confounded with the nationalists, for really they are a distinct organization, although many nationalists also belong to the fascisti. It can be said that while the nationalists are particularly interested in foreign policy, the fascisti are exclusively interested in internal policy. Originally only comrades of the great war were enrolled in the fascisti "combattimenti," or fighters' leagues, but gradually students, young clerks, professionals, even peasants and a few workers of conservative leaning were admitted.

They are calling a halt on the habit, which has become prevalent, of giving way to socialist insolence. In some provinces during the summer and autumn of last year the socialists had become drunk with success and assumed a bullying attitude. It is just in Bologna, Modena, Ferrara, Pisa and Florence, where the Socialists made themselves impossible, that the fascism has prospered. It was a product of irresistible reaction.

The fascisti, taking a leaf from the socialist book, began to descend into the street and at the slightest pretext coming to immediate blows with the socialists.

Their methods are not blameless, as they often use revolvers and hand grenades freely, but the curious fact is that the system has worked like magic in places which were particularly in the hands of a few extremists.

Now the socialists in the Chamber proclaim that the fascisti are leading to a civil war, which is an exaggeration. No doubt fascism is a transitory phenomenon, but up to now it has been effective in subduing the dictatory attitudes the extreme socialists had assumed. Now that the state is called upon to re-establish order by the same socialists, it is hoped the government will step in to avoid conflicts, which have been increasing in number. The socialists in the Chamber had opposed the government bill aiming at disarming all citizens, but perhaps now they will see the absurdity of such a stand, as no hope of avoiding battle royals among the socialists and fascisti can be entertained until both are deprived of their weapons.

Arrogant "Iron Division" Departure; Cold-Blooded Murder of Sightseers
Birmingham Post/March 20, 1920

Berlin, March 19.—The so-called "Iron Division" from the Baltic and the Naval Brigades left Berlin yesterday to return to Doeberitz. At 4:30 company after company went down the Unter den Linden and passed through Brandenburger Tor in spite of the rain. Crowds of onlookers were in the street, the majority being extreme Radical workers. The soldiers had drums beating and Prussian banners flying. They were armed with rifles and carried them in a most striking position, with their fingers on the trigger. They could not possibly have behaved in a more provocative maimer, and even to a neutral onlooker their conduct seemed unbearable.

The workers were boiling over with excitement. No one could understand how these rebel soldiers had been allowed to carry away their arms. No one believes they will keep their promise to disarm in Doeberitz. The workers entertain no doubt that the soldiers will presently return, bringing back conditions far worse than before.

Luttwitz's troops were disarmed in Spandau, and though it entailed fighting and blood the workers succeeded in their undertaking.

The Berlin workers are particularly furious with the new Commander-in-Chief, Von Seekt, whom they accuse of being not one whit better than Luttwitz.

Many of the soldiers, as they marched off yesterday, grinned threateningly at the crowd as if they would have said: "Wait a while, we shall return."

The spectators grew more and more excited. They shouted, whistled, and "cat-called" in an attempt to drown the regimental music. They howled at the soldiers and called them the worst of names: "Rotten scoundrels," "beasts," and "'swine." The soldiers responded with hateful smiles. They, too, were boiling with rage, and some of them threatened the crowd with hand grenades.

From the Adlon Hotel elegantly-dressed women waved their handkerchiefs to the soldiers, a proceeding which raised to white heat the temperature of the workers, who suddenly made an attempt to rush the hotel.

Some of them actually invaded the vestibule but were driven back by a strong detachment of Siewitz troops on guard over the Allied Missions.

Hardly had the last soldier passed the Brandenburger Tor when the rear turned and fired a round of lead as a farewell salute into the crowds that stood in the Unter den Linden.

We who were in the middle of the street had no recourse but to throw ourselves down in the roadway.

All down the Unter den Linden, Summerstrasse, and Budapesterstrasse men started to run. These were either killed or wounded by the shots, the firing lasting for half a minute.

Four killed and ten wounded had to be carried into a hotel. — Exchange.

The Parties of the Right
The Nation/June 20, 1920

FUNDAMENTALLY there is little difference between the two parties of the Right—the German National People's Party and the German People's Party. Both are intensely national, bitterly anti-Semitic, and strongly anti-Socialist, but the former lays primary emphasis upon the necessity to maintain the capitalist system against all attempts at socialization. At the last elections, both accepted the republic in principle, but their opponents insisted that their republicanism was insincere. The Nationalist Party now openly admits its monarchism; the German People's Party still insists upon its republicanism. The two parties are very strong in the army, especially among the officers; they do not compete with each other, and both are certain to register marked increases in the new elections.

Many of the local officials of the Nationalist Party were implicated in the Kapp coup d'etat; the national officers of the party took no open position either for or against the Kapp regime until after it had fallen; then they condemned it and insisted that they had had no share in it. Their opponents claim that the whole Kapp affair was engineered by workers of the German Nationalist Party.

The avowal of monarchism by the Nationalists is carefully worded. It calls for "the restoration of the German imperial monarchy (Kaisertum) established by the Hohenzollerns." It carefully refrains from calling for the restoration of the ex-Kaiser or even of a Hohenzollern. The party program protests against "rule by Jews" and against the influx of foreigners who profit by the low exchange to exploit the German people. It demands a "moral rebirth of the people by deepening its Christian consciousness," declares that "the purity of the family and the health of the state are dependent upon the vital absorption of Christian religious forces," and in general endorses the alliance of church and state. It demands government by experts rather than government by politicians, and advocates the formation of a second chamber in parliament in which the various professions and industrial groups shall be represented as such. Like the Communists, it proclaims the bankruptcy of democracy.

Throughout the campaign the two Right parties have given vent to the most virulent expressions of anti-Semitism. A Berlin branch of the German National Party issued the following statement:

"The Jews must get out of Germany. The property of the Jews must be seized. Jews should be kept out of German high schools and colleges. They should be deprived of electoral rights. Jewish banks and warehouses should be seized. Jews should be put out of the stock exchange. The guilds should be reestablished. Physical labor should be introduced for Jews. Germans should be forbidden to work for Jews and punished if they do so."

Karl Helfferich, the former director of the Deutsche Bank and wartime Finance Minister, and Count Posadowsky are the most conspicuous leaders of the Nationalist Party. Stresemann, the former National Liberal leader, and Count von Westarp, the former conservative leader, are active in the German People's Party. The latter party had an almost equally compromising position during the Kapp affair, and is only second to the Nationalists in its violent anti-Semitism. It has recently received reinforcements from the right wing of the Democratic and Centrum parties. Its position is today virtually that of the Nationalist Party at the January, 1919 elections. Both parties make vitriolic attacks upon the present regime. Their opponents claim that they favor a military dictatorship. The recent purchase of sixty-four newspapers by a syndicate headed by the Schwerindustrielle, Herr Stinnes, has probably aided the campaign of these parties."

The Plot for Reaction in Italy
The Nation/December 15, 1920

by Giuseppe Prezzolini

RUMORS of an impending counter-revolution are rife in the political circles of Rome. Serious talk is current of a change in the Government, even in the dynasty itself, quite apart from the general revolutionary chatter. The discussion is both too widespread and too much heard in high places not to be deeply significant. The press has seized on these rumors, embroidering them to suit the color of the particular paper— the Socialist organs to denounce reaction and promise resistance to the bitter end; the Nationalist papers to appeal for "order at any price"; the Giolittian dailies to smooth the public for the right way and say, "Don't worry. The 'old man' who got us out of the mess with the iron workers is still on the job."

No specific statements have been made as to the probable direction the contemplated coup is to take. Some people say that a greater show of firmness on the part of the Government would carry Italy past the crisis. Others openly appeal to those patriotic forces which saved the country after Caporetto, declare their lack of faith in the present parliamentary system, and insist that all the men hitherto associated with Italian politics be scrapped as so much worthless junk. Not to mince words, the jingo group is urging a military dictatorship, pure and simple.

What has happened, in the six weeks since the Government surrender to the iron workers, to bring the apparently effete Italian bourgeoisie to life? A number of political and economic factors are working to produce an entirely unprecedented brand of discontent. Minister Sforza has concluded a compromise agreement with the Yugoslavs on the basis of a concession of Dalmatia (with the exception of Zara) to Yugoslavia in exchange for a rectification of the Istrian and Giulian frontiers beyond the "Wilson Line." Such a compromise is distasteful to various small but influential groups: the Irredentists, the Nationalists, the Dante Alighieri Society, D'Annunzio and his friends. Then, thousands of military officers, including generals and colonels, are angry at demobilization.

They are losing not only their salaries but also their privileges, which include allowances for living expenses and mileage. Many military men, long in the public eye, find themselves obliged to seek civilian occupations. The task is not easy, as not a few have lost all aptitude for business and professional life.

The iron and steel manufacturers, too, notoriously close to the Nationalist movement, are enraged at workers' control in their factories. Iron and steel stocks have dropped heavily on exchange, and many plants, especially those not equipped to meet honest competition, face early closure.

Finally, shopkeepers, people living on unearned income, government employees, technicians, small business and professional men, teachers, have all been outraged by a series of protest strikes, interference with railway and streetcar service through frequent rioting, bomb explosions, in short, by the generally prevalent acute living conditions. Moreover, the laboring classes have been flaunting their high salaries and, on the basis of class solidarity, insulting, maltreating, and generally harassing other people who ask only to live in peace.

This state of general discontent furnishes the opportunity for a number of political groups which came into being during the war on patriotic platforms and thoroughly understand the advantage attaching to armed organized minorities intent on seizing power. Such groups are described in Italian as "fasci" (coalitions), though neither the "interventionist coalitions" which in 1915 organized democratic and moderate Socialist forces against Italian neutrality, nor the "parliamentary coalition" which after Caporetto organized all the elements hostile to Giolitti and a separate peace any longer exist.

These "coalitions" undoubtedly served a purpose during the war. But they have never understood that, once the war was won, the important issue was peace and reconstruction. The mass of the Italian people was weary of fighting, anxious to return home, take up its interrupted labors, and see realized the promises just and unjust, cautious and imprudent, which the Government had made in the stress of the world conflict. The "fasci" did not understand that a new psychology, a new kind of politics, a new kind of political leadership were necessary in Italy. On the contrary, they worked to keep the country in a state of perpetual excitement, saying that Italy had lost the war unless Fiume, Istria, and Dalmatia were annexed, conducting a propaganda of hate against Italy's former Allies, and especially threatening new wars for a country profoundly shattered and generally determined not to have another conflict. "Coalitionism" then took a peculiarly dangerous turn because of the political groups composed chiefly of demobilized officers and "arditti." To such malcontents was due the expedition of D'Annunzio in Fiume and numerous armed attacks against the Socialists in Milan, Trieste, Pola, Lodi, and other cities.

The "arditti" were one of the most characteristic Italian inventions of the war—a select body of adventurers presenting all the traits most loved of Italians. They were "shock" troops, but their love of individual glory and their lust for combat were skillfully disciplined by a military ordinance which left them much liberty during periods of rest, but demanded complete sacrifice in battle. These troops, made up of young men enlisted without much regard for moral character, were not only fired by love of country: in their eyes war was primarily a great adventure. Among such people, after demobilization, "coalitionism" found willing recruits alike for the Fiume expedition and for the hoodlum city gangs, who broke up Socialist demonstrations and burned the plants of Socialist newspapers, such as the Avanti and the Lavoratore.

Naturally these groups could be nothing but tools. They had to have "men" behind them for their movement to acquire political importance in Italy. The persons who have been most identified with the movement which, for convenience merely, I am calling "coalitionism"—it could just as well be called "reactionism"—are the following: the King's uncle, the Duke of Aosta; General Giardino, former Minister of War; Benito Mussolini, editor of the *Popolo d'Italia,* and Gabriele D'Annunzio, patron saint of Fiume.

General (Senator) Giardino is a professional soldier, a staff officer, and commanded the Fourth Army, the immortal corps that held Monte Grappa against the Austrian avalanche and covered the retreat of General Di Robiland from Cadore. For a brief term, also, he was Minister of War. He is a soldier of the old style with old-fashioned ideas of army discipline, stern and iron fisted. Before the war, indeed, he quarreled with the journalist Borelli, an advocate of discipline through persuasion rather than of obedience through terror.

Benito Mussolini is a native of Romagna, a man of thirty-five, and self-educated. During the "red week" of 1914 he was an ardent revolutionary. At one time he lived in political exile in Switzerland with the recent editor of the *Avanti*, Menotti-Serrati; later, with the martyr Cesare Battisti he edited the *Popolo* of Trent, then an Austrian city, and was driven out of that town. On his return to Italy he was drawn into the Socialist Party, and at the congress of Reggio [Emilia] in 1913 he secured the expulsion of Bissclati's faction from the party for its approval of the Turkish war. Thereupon he became editor of the *Avanti* and practically controlled the Socialist Party. At the beginning of the European War, however, he was so thoroughly convinced that Italy should fight Germany that he left the *Avanti* and the Socialist Party, founded the *Popolo d'ltalia* and gathered around him all the elements in the democratic parties of the Left who wanted war. He changed his name, enlisted as a private, became a corporal, and was wounded in the very first days by a gun explosion. On leaving the hospital he returned to the *Popolo d'ltalia* and wrote such nationalist and anti-socialist editorials that he fell under suspicion of acting for the iron and steel manufacturers and incurred the bitter hatred of his former Socialist friends, whom he insults and accuses in every possible way.

Gabriele D'Annunzio is too well known to need description. He is now in Fiume, infatuated with a literary dream in which he sees himself as a great figure of the Renaissance drawn by Machiavelli—unscrupulous and fearless, mystical and religious—a dream that advances the idea that he is himself the predestined savior of a world oppressed by capitalistic powers. Thus only can some of D'Annunzio's political extravagances be explained with their culminating declaration of war against the Italian Government.

Lately the warnings of a coup d'etat have grown more numerous. The Duke of Aosta, who is proclaimed as a substitute for the present King, has broken his silence and made a speech at Milan. His allusion to the present state of affairs and his exaltation of Christian ideals have lei people to believe that he was trying somehow to please the nationalist Left as well as the Catholics. Moreover, meetings of "coalitionists" are being held everywhere, and it ii reported that many manufacturers have formed and armed "white guards." The editorials in the nationalist "coalitionist" newspapers are more violent than ever.

There was a rumor that the movement would come to a head in Rome in November on the anniversary of the battle of Vittorio Veneto. It was said that the troops assembled from all parts of Italy for the great military review would not neglect the opportunity to arrest the principal ministers of state, seize the organs of national life, and proclaim E new military government. The ceremony, however, passed off without noteworthy disturbances. But talk of the reactionary plot is no less current. I can say with assurance only that the Government is quite aware of the movement and of the rumors that are openly circulating.. Giolitti is in a position to know whether they are serious or mere talk. At any rate the Government has begun to give signs of energetic acts and life. It has put Malatesta in jail and made moves to suppress anarchist agitation. It is probable that Giolitti will, with his usual astuteness, succeed in carrying Italy quietly also through this crisis by a show of force against extremists on the Left.

A Fascist Split; The Rise of Benito Mussolini
The Observer/June 5, 1921

The politician, like the general, must know how to seize a situation and turn it quickly to account, and so Signor Benito Mussolini, the newly elected journalist deputy for Milan—elected, by the way, with the record number of preference votes—has managed by means of one interview to set the whole country talking of him, and to bring about what looks like a crisis in the ranks of the fascisti. The moment was favorable. The Ministerial Press tried for as long as was possible to pretend that the elections had gone the way everyone expected them to go, but there were too many signs of unrest in the air. It was the moment for the political prophets and they have not failed to avail themselves of it. Conjecture of every kind regarding the future of the government and the grouping of the parties in the new Chamber has been running life. There has been no lack of variety and imagination in the work of the political prophets.

A Republican Gesture

Then Benito Mussolini threw his bomb by announcing that the fascists would absent themselves from the opening of the Chamber by King Victor, as they were "in tendency" republicans. Protest and threats of resignation followed from all over the country, as did also telegrams and letters supporting Mussolini. The result is that the fascists seem to be in some danger of splitting up into monarchists and republicans. The former promise to become a separate corps under the title of fasci d'ordine, or "fascists of order." A deputation has made arrangements to take D' Annunzio's opinion on the subject; he being considered a kind of spiritual sponsor of the movement. Further, a fascist congress is fixed to take place at Milan. Mussolini is apparently immovable in his determination to boycott the royal sitting of the Chamber, and it is clear he has some of the group with him.

Fascism, in any case, is obviously at a crisis in its brief but lively history. That the interests which have hitherto supported the movement and helped to provide the sinews for it have suffered some disillusion since the results of the elections have become known seems pretty clear. Moreover, I have heard it stated by people whose opinion has a right to be duly weighed that the surprising cases where the "red" leagues in Emilia are said to have gone over to the Fascisti must be explained in a different manner from that usually adopted. It is said that what has happened in these cases is that the syndicalist leagues have possessed themselves of the best elements of the local fascist organization and persuaded them to come to a kind of pact with them.

What eventual policy Signor Mussolini's move covers it would be rash to guess, but it may be that the phenomenon of amalgamation between syndicalist (not communist) leagues and fasci may at a later date take place on a larger scale than has hitherto happened.

The Man Of The Week

Meanwhile Mussolini has attracted a great amount of attention to himself, and has become, so to speak, the man of the week. This journalist deputy, editor of the "Popolo d'Italia" of Milan and a great friend of D'Annunzio, began his career as a socialist, and was once a writer on, if not the editor of, "Avanti." He is nominally a kind of socialist today, though of course anathema to the party. He was an interventionist, that is, advocated Italy's entry into the war. He has been associated with the fascist movement almost from the beginning, and up to the moment of his interview with the *Giornale d'Italia* was considered the inevitable leader of the fascist group in the new Chamber. As matters stand at present, it is hard to say how many of the group will follow him in his tentative and sudden republicanism. Here we see all the elements for a little crisis in the fascist movement.

Signor Mussolini is still a young man. He is a very combative character and writes in a vivid, not to say violent, style. He may be lacking in balance and far-seeingness, but he possesses those qualities which appeal to the crowd. He has the leader's gift of seizing the right moment and of staking or, perhaps more truly appearing to stake, everything on a bold stroke. He shaves his head after the fashion of D'Annunzio, has a striking face, and an arresting personality. He has come to the front this week; how long he will stay there remains to be seen.

Bolshevism is Answered in a Pugnacious Manner by the People of Italy
Dayton Daily News/June 19, 1921

New Fascism Movement, Now Rapidly Gaining Adherents, Is Fully Explained by Beatrice Baskerville.

Here is the first of a series of five articles on the political, social and industrial conditions in Italy. In this article Miss Baskerville treats of Fascism and Bolshevism, two factors which are causing more attention abroad than any other phase of Italian life today; bureaucracy, Italy's greatest problem, which is now suffering, as the writer styles it, from "elephantiasis;" Italy's budget and the strike of the state employees, and Bolshevism in the great industrial plants.

In this series I will not dwell long on Bolshevism and Fascism in Italy, the two factors which are attracting more attention abroad than any other phase of Italian life today. Both have been getting more than their fair share of attention at the hands of cable agencies. Enough to clear the ground by saying that Bolshevism is out of fashion in Italy and Fascism is not a political party.

Fascism is a movement; it might almost be called a national

movement. It is the outward and visible sign of the nation's reaction against Bolshevism and Lenin's too-zealous if well-paid efforts to extend the paradise of the Soviets to Italy. The Fascist program includes, to quote one of their leaders, Benito Mussolini, "the liquidation of Nitti and Giolitti and the beginning of a new era for Italy." It is national, patriotic and avowedly pugnacious. It is homemade and home nurtured, even to the extent, says the Socialists, of being supplied secretly with funds by the government to keep the Socialists in their places.

Bolshevism was an imported complaint, Asiatic of feature, destructive and violent. As Asiatic and destructive it was and is still at variance with the habits and traditions of the Italian people. Every Italian, be he ever so ignorant, has inbred in his very fiber a pride for his country's glorious past, the knowledge that Rome once ruled the world and did it so well that she gave longer periods of world-peace to humanity than any other government has been able to give since.

Bolshevism owes the small measure of success it ever enjoyed in Italy to the fact that it came wrapped round with bank notes and was surrounded by a halo of mystery, thanks to the distance and to stringent passport barriers built by non-Russian governments, who seemed to imagine that the Bolshevik microbe could be kept out of Europe that way. To the credit of ex-Premier Nitti it must be said that he was the first statesman to see that if Socialist leaders were allowed to visit Russia Bolshevism would lose most of its dangerous fascination for other countries.

Events have proved he was right. Some of those Italian Socialists who started for Russia filled with enthusiasm for Lenin were so shocked with what they saw there that they broke their vow of silence and warned the Italian people against adopting soviets; others, either because Lenin really fascinated them or because his generosity did, hotly denied Russia's plight but they refused to join the Third Internationale and have preached the impossibility of revolution here ever since. Only a few, whom the hot tempered Bombacci leads, are still faithful to Lenin, and they are a small minority.

The Italian people meanwhile, seeing that golden promises of wealth without labor and power without responsibility were barren, that the land refused to yield food unless it was tilled, that wine would not grow in neglected vineyards, that wages do not increase when factories cease to produce, turned their backs on the Russian mirage, took down Lenin s picture from their walls and left off wearing red carnations and waving the red flag.

The Fascisti gained enormously. Whole unions and leagues which were Bolshevik last May are Fascisti this. It is the natural swing of the pendulum, the very natural result of disappointment. But such violent changes in mob psychology can't take place in any country without broken heads and even loss of life. Least of all can Italy, with its quick-tempered, warm-blooded people and its plentiful wines, change internal political currents in order and silence. Hence the rioting and burning, the street fights and loss of life.

I think it is safe to say that these fights are nothing more serious than the expression of an impetuous and excitable people suffering from all the ills of after-war reconstruction and a Bolshevik scare to boot.

One of the most cheerful facts of Italy's situation today is the return of public confidence in national industries, and the funds. The exit of capital, a big feature in 1918 and 1919, has decreased. The enemies of ex-Premier Nitti are now blaming him for that exodus, saying he caused it by his public warning of national bankruptcy and set a bad example by sending his own money abroad, till the lire went down fast and foreign credit was not to be had.

During the last year, however, there has been a net increase of capital invested in private enterprises of 4,834 million lire, as compared with a net increment in 1917 of 1,288 million lire, of 2,949 million in 1918 and 2,778 in 1919. The new industries started this year were chiefly chemical and mechanical; textiles came next.

The state, too, has been able to register a larger increment, for 1920 was a heavy year for Italian taxpayers; probably no country in the world has been more heavily taxed than this. In 1914 direct taxation yielded 556 millions; now they yield three milliard and 806 million lire. In 1913-14 indirect taxation yield 657 million lire; now they yield one milliard and 700 million lire; monopolies in 1913-14 gave one milliard and 67 millions; they now guarantee four milliards and 90 millions, according to Minister of Finance Facta.

There are taxes on every commodity, on nearly everything needful for even humble people's daily life, and the poorest subject of the realm who eats hot food but on feast days pays his full share. There are taxes on matches and salt and sugar; on vinegar, tobacco and coffee; on all foodstuffs brought into the cities and on every article that the widest stretch of imagination can call a luxury, from umbrellas and gloves to soap and theater tickets. From the time he gets up in the morning to the moment he goes home at night the Italian and the stranger within the gates must pay his dole for every article he consumes. And he is doing it without a murmur.

The fruits of this widespread and probing system of taxation are already beginning to appear and anxiously does the taxpayer watch for them. Premier Giolitti was able to state not long ago that the deficit on this year's estimate has been reduced from 14 milliards to four milliard lire, or, at the current rate of the American dollar, from $70,000,000 to $20,000,000. The country still bears the burden of a paper currency of three milliard, 350,000,000 lire, or, in today's American money, of $167,500,000.

The cost of living is higher yet in Italy than in France, Belgium, Great Britain or even New York. Only wine and oil have shown any tendency to drop since the new year. Other foodstuffs, especially meat, milk, sugar, bread, macaroni, potatoes have gone up. It is therefore doubtful whether the country can stand more taxation than now pays, so there is great talk of reducing four million of the deficit by economies in public expenditures.

Unhappily this looks like mere talk, for while some state employees, including railway men and post and telegraph employees, have obtained salaries equal to their needs, the employees in other public offices and all state departments have gone on strike this week for higher pay at once. Government has assured them they will get an extra high-cost-of-living allowance when the chamber meets, but they want it now, by decree, like the railwaymen and postmen had theirs last year.

The state of its bureaucracy is one of Italy's most burning questions today, for unless its expensive machinery is very much reduced the four-milliard deficit will grow again. Everybody admits that there are far more state employees than the country needs. Ever since her independence and union Italy has been absorbing civil servants and swelling the ranks of bureaucracy. For nothing is so popular here as a soft job in a public office, with short hours, little to do, a pension and a quiet life. It offers irresistible temptations to a nation which has not yet had time to produce a strong, enterprising middle class and where before the war living was so cheap that state salaries sufficed.

Of course such a big bureaucracy in a poor country like Italy is badly paid. Before the war it did not matter, for living was cheap, but now, when a secretary in a public office only gets from 6400 to 8500 lire a year he can't make both ends meet. For, though this meant from $1200 to $1700 before the war, it only means from $320 to $425 now; and no family man in Italy can live on that.

The employees claim an extra allowance of 200 lire a month which means $10. The commission of inquiry, which has been examining the state of bureaucracy for some time, suggests half, but even supposing that the men will be contented with 100 lire for H. C. L., that means another 300 millions added to the deficit right away, and if, as is supposed, the men insist by continuing their strike on the 200, they will cost the country another 88 million lire a year. The natural result will be more paper money, a higher foreign exchange and dearer food.

Even the employees themselves agree that the only way to settle the question is to dismiss the many needless and idle clerks and raise the pay of the capable ones. But will the government have the courage to perform this painful operation in a country where bureaucracy is looked upon as the resource of all who like soft jobs?

The industrial situation in the north is still turbulent. Here the results of Bolshevik propaganda are more visible and seem to be more enduring than in the south or in the country districts among the landless peasants. Though the factories in Lombardy, with Milan as their center, have to a great extent recovered from the bad effects of the seizure of them by the men last September, those of Turin, Genoa and the littoral are still upset.

Here the great Fiat metallurgical works are the center of unrest; here still flourishes a system of imported Bolshevik organization with factory councils, corresponding to those factory soviets which were a feature of early Bolshevik rule in Russia, but which Lenin has stamped out long ago.

The issue now being fought out by men and employers in the Fiat works, which I mention because they are the center of unrest, is whether the men shall rule the factory, or the employers shall. The factory councils have gained the upper hand to such an extent that the employers can no longer dismiss a hand without the council's consent; and these, entirely made up of workmen, always side with their comrades against the "masters."

Not only that, but the councils down tools and meet during working hours for the most trivial disputes between hands and overseers so that the nominal working day of eight hours is generally reduced to five and even less. Moreover, the Fiat men have been found making bombs instead of automobiles and other goods manufactured by the firm; and as if this were not enough, they meet in the cellars during working hours for gun practice. Needless to add that they demand and have been getting full wages for time spent in meetings, in making bombs and in drilling for fights against the Fascisti.

Not unreasonably the owners grew tired of this sort of thing which has been going on since last September, and a few weeks ago decided to lock out the men in those departments of the works where indiscipline was most serious. Negotiations are now going on for reopening the works. The owners lay down one condition, that they shall have the men's written agreement to abide by the factory rules.

Fascism: Its Rise And Decline
The Observer (London)/September 18, 1921

Italy's Revulsion Against Communism

Medieval Scenes

The Emblem Of The Hatchet

Future Of The Movement

The first thing I heard on my return to Florence was the story of how young Berta, guilty only of being a fascists, was trapped by the Communists as he crossed the Arno, beaten senseless as he clung to the piers of the bridge, to fall back into the river without one friendly hand held out to save him at the last. It has passed into the popular literature of Florence:

Giovinezza, Giovinezza,
Primavera di Bellezza.
Il Fascism la salvezza
Della nostra Liberta.

This fascists chorus, together with the song of Berta, sung even by the children in their perambulators, symbolizes in the minds of the people their deliverance from a nightmare which oppressed Italy from the summer of 1919 to the spring of 1921, when the Tricolour seemed banished for ever to make room for the red flag of the Communists.

A Florentine cobbler was sitting inside his shop giving vent in provocative song as he hammered away, to his scorn of young Berta and of all that he stood for, when Count Foscari, a Venetian legionary from Fiume, passed by with some fascisti friends and ordered him to stop his song. That quarter of the town was soon in an uproar. The cobbler and his allies were severely knocked about; Foscari was mortally wounded. His funeral was made a national expression of mourning. Representatives of the fascisti came with their banners from every part of Italy. The steel helmet of D'Annunzio's legionary gleamed among the flowers on the hearse: a wounded companion followed close; ex-soldiers, workmen, communal dignitaries and eminent professors fallowed with many hundreds of university students and other youths, their long hair brushed loosely back and waved in the new fashion among "young bloods"; there were those splendid looking dare-devils too, from Montevarchi, wearing red shirts "alla Garibaldi" and red caps with long blue tassels. Fascisti leaders, holding heavy hunting crops with jaunty aggressiveness, walked at intervals on the outside of the procession; soldiers guarded the city. Would the Communists shoot at the pall-bearers as they had done before? Had they not even thrown bombs at a patriotic procession in which children had taken part? But that had happened early in the year, and now this silent army of young fascists walking through silent streets past Communist strongholds proved that the enemy was cowed.

"We have saved Italy," the fascisti declare with pride. And one wonders how far a fresh appeal to violence has really helped to solve the social problem.

As the party which brought Italy into the war belonged to the bourgeois class and fascism is the legitimate offspring, a very vociferous one of "interventismo." The new movement is often described as the rising of the middle classes against the proletariat. This gives a false idea of what, in the beginning, was a patriotic rush to defend both the Italian flag and the liberty of the Italian people during a severe crisis of their history. Although composed of the best elements of all classes and political creeds (the Catholic party holding aloof), fascism has its roots in nationalism. It was the exuberant expression of that new national consciousness which Caporetto gave to Italians and which developed with such notable rapidity after Vittorio Veneto.

Directly after the armistice, the "Fasci dei Giovani Combattenti" were formed, and a vigorous propaganda was engineered by a violent military party, aided by a portion of the press and D'Aununzio against the Allies. Everything was done to poison public opinion and to picture Italy as the Cinderella of Europe at the mercy of sly, grasping ministers at Versailles. The Fiume episode was used to force the hands of the latter, and the failure to deal with the situation added fuel to the fire and endangered peace. Because it was made a question of "Italianista," Fiume became a rallying platform which united nearly all parties, and brought the country to the brink of fresh disasters. The exchange flew up to an alarming extent. The neutralists now enjoyed themselves. They could say: " I told you so," and ask where was the paradise promised by the "Interventisti," which Italians deserved after losing half a million dead. The victories of the Piave which had given Italy back her self-respect and self confidence were on one side overrated, and on the other undervalued. Communism became triumphant.

The fires of advanced socialism set alight before the war now burst into a blaze which even reached the Tuscan and Umbrian peasant who, quietly prosperous with his ancient system of co-operative land tenure, had always been regarded as safe from revolution. The pictures painted by agitators of Soviet rule made many feel that Russia had solved the economic problem. Hymns to the Madonna and to Lenin, as dispensers of all good things, intermingled strangely in the countryside. They waited for those promised shiploads of corn to arrive. How the Communists followed in the footsteps of the Bolshevists, trampling on the national flag, seizing land, occupying factories, looting, shooting at trains, and throwing bombs at innocent people, is still fresh in our minds. Then, just as Communism thought to hold Italy in a vice, it bumped up against fascism.

Mussolini, ex-socialist, founder of the "Popolo d' Italia," and an ardent pro-war champion, is the acknowledged father and leader of fascism, which, he tells us, started in a small way in Milan on March 23, 1919 and very soon numbered over two million adherents. As an organization this can be celebrated as its birthday, but the spirit rose out of the events which followed the Armistice, and fascism is a spirit, not a party, we are always told. Within five weeks of the Armistice Italy had a volunteer army of over a million young men, prepared to do anything for the glory of Italy and the Tricolour, known as "I Giovani Combattenti."

The first task they set themselves was to rouse Italian pride in their victory, "la valorizziene della vittoria." The second labor was to clean out the Augean stables of Communism. The fascists chose for their badge the emblem of the emperors of Rome, and the hatchet was a symbol of prompt action. Their policy was an eye for an eye, a tooth for a tooth. For every crime against the flag or liberty a Communist leader was killed, or else the Camera del Lavoro or their newspaper offices in an offending town were set on fire. Not a night passed but shots rang out in most towns and villages in Italy. Syndics judged to be disloyal citizens were peremptorily ordered to resign. Elections on the side of the government "Blocco" were controlled to a considerable extent, and sham warfare was waged against profiteers. There were happy spells, all too brief, when prices went down under the iron hand of fascisti.

The "punitive expedition," led by ex-soldiers, became a feature of their methods of campaign. Racing through the country in motor-lorries to hunt out Communist centers proved an alluring sport for the younger generation who, without having experienced the hardships of war, suffered from its exciting influences. Many disreputable characters had joined up, and violence was made an end in itself. Citizens watched from their walls, children ran home screaming, and women bolted their doors when the cry went round, "The Fascisti are coming." It was galling for a venerable syndic to be harangued by these youths, some barely seventeen, armed with revolvers and "mazze ferrate," and told that they had come to set things in order for him. In June and July of this year, when the fascisti were at the height of their power and the lowest ebb of their fame, it was immaterial whether one read the daily papers, so as to keep in touch with events, or the medieval chronicles of Guelphs and Ghibellines.

The punitive expedition of Monzone, in the Carrara mountains, of which the tragic events of Sarzana were the inevitable consequences, proved how low the movement had fallen. Quiet had reigned for some time in the district, and the fascisti only found a picnic party, one man wearing a red carnation, which hardly justified a military raid, promiscuous shooting, and the robbing of the till of the co-operative stores. Later, the captain—a legionary from Fiume—was taken prisoner with another ex-officer by Communists, and three hundred fascisti marched on Sarzana to deliver them. Before they could enter the city gates they were dispersed by carabineers, on whom they had fired. Many wandered about the countryside and were found by their enemies, who fell upon them like wild beasts. Old scores were settled between profiteers of the Sarzana and Spezia markets and the fascisti. Among the tortured victims was a boy of sixteen.

When fascism as a whole refused to obey the terms of peace with the extreme Socialist party, it showed its feet of clay, and Mussolini resigned his leadership. Deploring the events of June and July, he disowned it for, as he said, "it was no longer a liberation, but a tyranny; no longer a safeguard for the nation, but a defense of private interests of the worst kind." As there are signs of drastic reforms taking place, a re-kindled fascism promises to arise. It is more than likely that it will be formed into a political party with a definite programme, and their new task will be to tilt against the P.P. I., or Catholic Party, which looms alarmingly big in the horizon.

Italians, in reviewing past events, bitterly regret the seeds of class hatred sown, and the return to medievalism and violence, but they do not put all the blame on the Fascisti. What about the government's consistent policy of neutrality through every crisis of social unrest; and was it quite fair to use the fascisti as government scavengers?

Italian Editor Slashed in Duel With Fascisti Chief
New York Tribune/October 28, 1921

Report Is Sword Combat Is To Be Followed
by Fight With Pistols Today

LEGHORN, Italy, Oct. 27. Ettore Ciccotti, editor of "Il Paese," was wounded seriously to-day in a duel with Professor Benito Mussolini, leader of the Fascisti. Swords were used. The duel was due to references to Mussolini made by Ciccotti in "Il Paese." The combat lasted an hour and a quarter. It ended in the fourteenth bout, when the surgeons pronounced Ciccotti to be in a serious condition and unable to continue the encounter.

LONDON, Oct. 27. A dispatch to "The Times" from Milan says it is believed there the duel between Signor Ciccotti and Signor Mussolini will be resumed tomorrow with pistols. The dispatch adds that the combat to-day was suspended because Ciccotti was so fatigued that his heart nearly collapsed.

Fascists Triumph in Italy
The Guardian (London)/October 30, 1922

Signor Benito Mussolini Belongs to the New School
Which Knows Better than the People what the People Want

Signor Mussolini, the Italian Fascist leader, has been invited to form a Government. If an English political leader of any party organized armed followers throughout the country and on the occasion of a Cabinet crisis ordered a "general mobilization" and seized Government offices in the important towns, so that Lancashire, Yorkshire, and the Midlands were under his control, and if under threat of war the King were to invite him to form a Government of his own, we might congratulate ourselves, as they appear to be doing in Italy, that this military occupation had been achieved "without disorder," and we might call the "solution of the crisis" by any names we chose, but we should in reality have submitted to revolution.

The Fascists, our Rome correspondent says, declare that their action is "only intended to enforce a swift solution of the crisis in harmony with their aims." They could not very well say more. Signor Mussolini belongs to the new school which knows better than the people what the people wants, and proposes not only to give it to them but to see that they accept it, if need be, at the point of the bayonet and the machine-gun. That is the school in which Lenin and Trotsky sit in the front row and de Valera is an industrious pupil.

Mussolini's aims are his own, but the principle is the same; he will no more allow the Italian people to pronounce freely on his repressive anti-Socialist programme at home and his nationalist policy abroad than he would the workmen who seized the factories two years ago submit to constitutional delay.

So, with the threat of war to help him, he is called to form a Government. And if the day comes when the Communists also can effectually threaten war, what then?

Italian Home, Politics
The Guardian (London)/August 25, 1922

The Problem Of Fascism

The recent disorders have renewed, in Italy and abroad, the sense of the seriousness of the problem of Fascism. Because, if these disorders have been impressive on account of conflicts and bloodshed and the partial stoppage of public life, they have been even more impressive as showing that within the State there has grown up a gigantic force capable of menacing the State itself.

Since 1919, when Fascism began, much has been written on the subject, but the romantic beginnings of Fascism, its picturesque characteristics, the black shirts and the flags, are much better known than the political substance, which is generally confused with that of a more violent and combative nationalism. To understand this political substance we must turn to the figure of the founder of Fascism, the Hon. Benito Mussolini, Romagnolan, now 38 years old, ex-Syndicalist, and until

1914 editor of the Socialist official organ the "Avanti." Mussolini left the management of the ' Avanti " and the Socialist party on account of his Interventionalist tendencies. He founded, in November, 1914, the *Popolo d'ltalia*, Syndicalist-Interventionalist. He took part in the war as a plain soldier. After the war the ex-soldiers organized themselves into various associations. Some sent men to the Fiume undertaking. Mussolini did not oppose this enterprise; but his interest was different, all concentrated on internal politics.

The Birth of Fascism

In 1918-1919 Italy was suffering to the full from war-weariness, disillusions of the peace, and unemployment, and these caused violent reactions in advanced Socialism. There was the sacking of shops in the summer of 1919, and the elections of November of the same year were a triumph for Socialism. This triumph culminated in the occupation of the factories in September, 1920. It was then that Fascism was born. It came into being as a patriotic counter-stroke to the excesses of the Socialist Communists; and Mussolini gathered about him numbers of ex-combatants drawn from the young middle-class intellectuals and ex-Socialist Syndicalists, and from other elements without political prepossessions who were moved only by romantic dueling and the spirit of adventure. To these were added people who had acquired a taste for the business of bearing arms and did not wish to be demobilized, many of the unemployed, and some desperate characters who were out for gain. And the Fascist reaction had, at the start, a useful effect. The Communists had been overbearing, because they imagined that all spirit of resistance was dead in the middle classes. As soon as this spirit of resistance made itself felt they lowered their heads. Unfortunately, the adherents of Fascism soon began a campaign of violence not only against the anarchic elements but against the poor peasants of the rural organizations.

At the beginning of the war the middle classes had already lost almost all the communes. Now, through Fascism, they sought to regain them and to demolish the agrarian organizations in the districts, like Emilia, where the big properties require a united workpeople. The middle classes gave financial assistance to Fascism, and gave it a reactionary character. Fascism sought in every way to break the agrarian organization; and in Emilia even tried to break up the big estates (latifundia) and form small properties out of them. If it has, where necessary, re-established the liberty of workmen, it has damaged the Red agrarian organizations without putting anything efficient in their place. It depends on violence and the money of the agricultural owners, and has done nothing to create a new regime of production.

The city workers who, protected by troops and police, are less exposed to the pressure of brute force, have resisted better. It can be seen, in fact, that whilst a strike can really stop public services in the cities, the so-called mobilizations of the Fascists do not disturb these services; that is to say that they do not withdraw important bodies from the city populations. Fascism tends now most of all to control communal administrations directed by Socialists. During the recent general strike the Socialists in many communes fled; in others they were obliged to resign.

Why does the State appear to be powerless before these facts? It is because 400,000 young men, well organized and armed, owning motor-lorries, used to war, ready for anything, would call for considerable force to put them down, and that would mean putting the whole of Italy under martial law for an indefinite period. A Socialist reaction would bring complete civil war, unless the Socialists were strong enough to enforce sufficient respect to paralyze Fascism; but today they are infinitely far from being so. The fact is that the State has allowed itself to be led by the hand by Fascism. The Conservatives and Liberals thought that Mussolini worked for them; even Giolitti, in 1921, was imprudent enough to hold the political elections quite frankly on the Fascism basis. Everyone was mistaken. If it was possible to think a year ago that Mussolini would be satisfied with a position of complete reaction, it is clear today that these were illusions. Mussolini has always aimed at the republican tendency of Fascism. He has never denied its Syndicalist origin. He knows that Fascism can never develop if it does not get into touch with the working-class masses and if it does not create economic organizations.

Future Amalgamation with the Left?

Mussolini has often affirmed that an understanding with the extreme Left in the field of proletarian action would be possible; and it would be nothing to marvel at if Fascism ended by amalgamating with its adversary, transforming it and being transformed. It is undoubted that the

Socialist masses are becoming more and more detached from their weary official representatives, who limit themselves to Parliamentary action, and are ready to collaborate with a Government which is powerless in face of Fascism. Mussolini has discussed openly in Parliament the question whether Fascism will remain within legal bounds or accept illegal action, and has evidently chosen the second alternative; and the 30 Fascist deputies are ready to leave Parliament rather than give up this action, which certainly has great effect on the masses. The day that Mussolini, showing that he knows how to realize their aspirations, shall have attracted within the Fascist orbit strong working-class organizations he will, perhaps, jump the ditch, kicking over the agrarian middle classes and the Conservative banks. At Ancona in the last few days the metalworkers have passed over to the Fascist organizations. Something of the same sort is happening at Genoa with the harbor workers. A gradual saturation of this kind would probably be the means of introducing a political and economic force into Fascism, and of making it a real power in the country and its government.

Mussolini
The Observer (London)/October 29, 1922

Career Of The Fascist Leader

Conversion Of A Socialist.

His Army Of 400,000 "Black Shirts"

An Editor At Work

Mussolini, on whom every eye in Italy is now turned, was born in 1883 near Forli, in Romagna, a province which breeds sons of fire and of "a melancholy cruelty." His father was an unlettered blacksmith and an ardent apostle of Socialism, who preached internationalism to the discontented people of Piseaza with so much success that he ended in prison. Mussolini grew up restless and passionate. "I often came home with a broken head, but I knew how to take revenge," he tells us in a laconic diary quoted by "Arros." Sometimes he was allowed to blow the great bellows in his father's forge, but most of his early childhood was spent scouring the woods and fields in search of birds. "My love of birds was very great, especially of owls, and I was an audacious little country thief," he tells us. His peculiar love was shown by stealing call-birds from a fowler, which reminds me of an English boy who told me that he was so devoted to animals that he longed to be apprenticed to a butcher.

The Socialist blacksmith opposed his son's education, but his mother and grandmother insisted upon sending him to school and taking him to church. The long services unsettled him, and he tried to escape them. "The rosy lights of the candles, the penetrating smell of incense, the color of the sacred vestments, the droning cantalena of the faithful and the tones of the organ moved me profoundly."

Schooldays

At nine years old his father finally consented to his going to college with the Salesian Missionary Fathers, whose schools were then very famous; and he even drove him there himself in the family donkey-cart. The donkey fell before they had gone any distance. "A bad omen," groaned the father. "A high-spirited boy," half-groaned the Rector, when he met Mussolini's fearless dark eyes and saw the bandaged hand, the result of a last "round" with another truculent spirit before leaving home. The little wild lover of the fields had been sadder to leave his caged canary than his brothers, but now as the heavy door closed behind him, upon his father and the familiar donkey, he burst into passionate tears.

A pen-knifing incident with an obnoxious companion led to his expulsion from college, and was followed by a further trial of college life at Forlimpopoli, which at this moment is the center of strife and bloodshed between Socialists and Fascists. At the age of twenty, after a brief period of sonnet-writing and an attempt to write for the Socialist organ Avanti, he obtained a post as schoolmaster at the communal school at Gualtieri Emilia on the River Po. His salary for teaching forty little boys, whom he soon learned to love, was fifty-six lire a month; forty lire went in board and lodging. No wonder that when the long vacation came he sought his fortunes in Switzerland. It is characteristic that while on the tramp he heard of his father's imprisonment and hesitated whether he should return; he went on. Full of faith, enthusiasm and ideals, the young Mussolini gained a following and became editor of a violent revolutionary paper, spreading Marxist doctrines, and was soon expelled as an undesirable alien.

The Gypsy Journalist

Hungry, irate with God and with himself but undaunted, Mussolini is again upon the road. He begs for bread—no, I should say, he demands bread in resolute, defiant tones, as he bursts into a family supper-party in a courtyard just off the road. He steps back into the darkness of his silent pilgrimage, drives his teeth into the bread with rage, closing his eyes, vainly striving to shut out the picture of that family circle, the wondering eyes of the startled children, and of that friendly hand holding the white bread out to him under the lamp-light.

He worked as a laborer for two and a half lire a day, he suffered imprisonment for sleeping vagabond style in an empty wooden box, but it was a period more of spiritual than of material suffering. One day, while wandering towards a city where fame glanced at him, he met a Russian, a fair young man with mild blue eyes and a smile of humble resignation. He carried a parcel of books under his arm, an alarm clock in his hand. There was a dignified exchange of civilities between the pilgrims, the clock being delicately set down on the roadside while the Russian showed his visiting card—"Student in Philosophy, doctor in Medicine, doctor in Law, professor in Fine Arts." They shook hands, and the Apostle of Tolstoi and the Apostle of Karl Marx tramped the road together. But there is one thing that Mussolini has always objected to: the sharp "trin trin" of a telephone bell drives him distracted. He looks with suspicion at the alarm clock.

"Why do you carry that clock?" he finally asked.

"I do not know where to put it."

"They will take you for a thief and imprison us both."

Then came an ultimatum--the company of Mussolini or the possession of an alarm clock? The Russian knew his clock; he did not know Mussolini.

"Good-bye," he said, firmly clasping the clock and his books.

"Good-bye," said Mussolini, "and, by the way, what time is it?"

Socialism and Journalism

Mussolini did not mean to remain in vagabond obscurity; he felt his powers, and people soon flocked round him. His gifts of leading and organizing masses of people, and his incisive pen were welcomed, and as quite a young man he became an acknowledged leader of the Italian Socialist Party, and was even made editor of their chief organ the Avanti. The war came as a shock to Mussolini; it showed him that Socialism led to a precipice, and his acute political instinct made him realize the necessity for intervention if Italy were to remain a nation. He resigned his posts, left the ranks of the Socialists, and founded a daily newspaper, the Popolo d'Italia; he then volunteered for the front. He was wounded, and returned to Milan to continue another kind of warfare in the columns of his newspaper, which was getting an immense circulation among the rising generation of young patriots whose mentality Mussolini thoroughly understood.

No one will understand this strangely interesting man if they do not realize his newspaper and his passion for it. The Popolo d'Italia is his own child, born of his spirit; Fascism, born of the spirit of the war, is his carefully trained foster-child. His imposing head office at Milan is both fortress and home to him. Ho has gathered there a varied company of writers, chosen more for explosive talent than for culture. No spectacled academicians, no musty tomes of reference for Mussolini's electric journalism. He seems to think that life-enhancing qualities will enable them to jump the pitfalls of their profession. Thus the Popolo d'Italia is growing up like a precocious, bold, and rather insolent child, somewhat unkempt but brimful of verve and personality. The articles on foreign affairs have a fascinating originality, as if written by perennial youth teaching us about the future, careless to learn the lessons of the past.

It was a shock to the Socialists when such a patriotic paper was founded during the war, and they immediately said that it was financed by France. The accusation was disproved by a jure d'honneur who studied the balance-sheets. During those early days of struggle there was sometimes only enough money to pay the compositors and porters, but the staff never minded rough times. They had Mussolini, and what did anything else matter? they said. He is the life of the place; he darts in and out with that quiet rapidity which keeps his people on the qui vive. When Mussolini shuts himself up in his lair to write one of his impassioned articles, seated under the black flag of the Arditti, skull and dagger its device, with revolvers resting among his papers, a hunting knife glistening upon a volume of Carducci, the bravest of his staff dare not approach him.

What People Think He Is Like

I have seen and spoken to Mussolini several times; but who can know him? He has a part to play. He struck me as a taciturn man with a gift of speech; one who loved no man and all men; who would be kind and generous to friends but crush an enemy without a pang. His penetrating eyes watch one, and he avoids being the first to speak. I had the sensation of being in the presence of a volcano at rest but by no means extinct. In the apparent simplicity of his character lies its complexity. Like Napoleon he would rule the word "impossible" out of the dictionary, and orders must be carried out at once, if not sooner. A hard worker, morally and physically courageous, with amazing driving power, he commands respect. But he rules successfully more because he inspires fear and admiration than love. E tremendo, say his followers.

The alarming thing about Fascism is that all the Fascists long to look like Mussolini. His "army" now consists of 400,000 well-disciplined "Black Shirts," who would follow him anywhere without questioning. He is called "Il Duce," and they think that he could fill any position on earth or in heaven better than any other mortal. He has the great quality of being able to delegate work and authority. There is the "fighting Fascio," and the "Syndicalist Fascio," which include the 400,000 youths on active service and 700,000 workmen, each with its own organization. At the same time they all know that Mussolini is the mainspring of the whole movement, and when there are difficulties he alone has the grip of the situation and can command obedience.

Dangers

With Fascism at the crest of the wave it is impossible to exaggerate the political power of Mussolini and the far-reaching influence he at present exercises in the Italian home. Everyone will realize what rocks lie ahead for a leader who governs by force. Je m'en fiche for his motto—who allows no other ideals but his own, and teaches a particular brand of patriotism which exhilarates national vanity. Italia dev' essere fascists, says the Chief. Italy is to be molded afresh, and the new mold is Mussolini's patent.

Fascisti Form a New Cabinet
Daily Telegraph/October 31, 1922

Mussolini In Rome

Interview With the King

Signor Mussolini, the Fascisti leader, arrived in Rome yesterday morning from Milan, and had a great welcome. He at once paid a visit to the King at the Quirinal, and later in the day the composition of his Cabinet was announced. It comprises, besides General Diaz and Admiral Thaon de Revel, who are officers not identified with any party, five Fascists, five Nationalists, one Democrat, and one member of the Popular (Catholic) party. Reuters wires the full list, as follows:

Prime Minister, Minster of Interior, and Minister of Foreign Affairs —Signor Mussolini.

War—General Diaz.

Marine — Admiral Thaon de Revel.

Treasury — Signor Inaudi (Nationalist)

Industry — Signor Theophile Rossi (Nationalist).

Finance — Signor de Stefani (Fascist)

Colonies — Signor Federzoni (Nationalist).

Liberated Regions — Signor Giuriati (Fascist)

Justice — Signor Oviglio (Fascist)

Education — Signor Gentilo (Demorat).

Agriculture — Signor de Capitani (Fascist)

Public Works — Signor Carnazza (Nationalist)

Posts and Telegraphs — Signor Colonna di Cesarn (Nationalist)

Social Welfare— Signor Cavazzoli (Popular Party)

Under-Secretaries:

Prime Minister's Department—Signor Acerbo (Fascist)

Interior — Signor Finzi.

Foreign Affairs — Signor Pasqualino Vassalle (Democrat)

War — Signor de Belo (Fascist)

Marine — Signor Giano (Fascist)

Pensions— Signor de Vecchi (Fascist) — Reuters

It will be observed that Signor Mussolini himself has taken the portfolios of the Interior and Foreign Affairs. It is, however, not expected that this will be a permanent arrangement. There is reason to believe that the new Foreign Minister will be Signor de Martino, who has been Ambassador to the Court of St. James since November, 1920.

It is understood that the Chamber will be dissolved as soon as possible and new elections held. The Fascisti are credited with the intention of issuing a Royal Decree changing the system of voting from the form of proportional representation now existing to a simpler and more direct arrangement. The effect of this alteration, they believe, would be to eliminate many of the present groups and give the new Cabinet a working majority.

Loyalty To Allies

Rome Monday (5:45 p.m.) Signor Mussolini called on the Presidents of the Chamber and Senate at 4:30 this afternoon. In an interview with journalists, the Fascisti leader said the new Government's foreign policy would be firm without being sensational and would be based on loyalty and friendship towards Italy's Allies.—Reuters.

King And Mussolini

Welcome To Capital

From Our Own Correspondent

The Fascist revolution is triumphant today over Italy. The Fascisti this morning, when marching into Rome, were acclaimed by tens of thousands of people, and Signor Mussolini, called by special telegram from the King, has come to undertake the task of forming a new Government. Italy is thus on the threshold of a new period in its history which, it is hoped, will lead her on to greater destinies. Mussolini, the man of iron nerve, of dauntless courage, of striking initiative and patriotic ardor, has imposed his will and personality on the entire nation. Hundreds of thousands obey his beck and call. His army of Fascisti, with their black shirts and strict military discipline, recall the red shirts of the days of Garibaldi, and Mussolini himself is like a second edition of the great hero of Italy's "Risorgimento." When I interviewed him two months ago he told me confidently: "We shall get to Rome" and today he has kept his word. The following is the telegraphic message sent to him by General Cittadini yesterday by the King's order:

His Majesty the King begs you to come to Rome as soon as possible, as he desires to entrust you with formation of the Ministry. Best regards.

The telegram was sent at one o'clock yesterday afternoon and published in an extra edition of Mussolini's paper, the Popolo d'Italia, and the news spread like wildfire. Milan was swept by a wave of enthusiasm. A cortege of thousands of Fascisti marched to the Piazza del Duomo. The whole city was beflagged, and Deputy Finzi made a speech at the foot of the monument to Victor Emmanuel. Tens of thousands of Fascisti had marched into Milan during the day from all parts of Lombardy. They occupied the postal and telegraph offices and chased away the censors stupidly appointed by the outgoing Ministry. Next they appeared before the newspaper offices and forbade the publication of the Socialist papers Avanti and Giustizia, which were issued nevertheless, and intimated the same order to the *Corriere della Sera,* which did not appear. At 8:30 a huge crowd saw Mussolini off at the station as he was leaving in the train for Rome. Before leaving for Rome Mussolini had a telephone conversation with D'Annunzio at Gardone, and it is supposed that some understanding was reached by which an important portfolio was offered to the poet.

Rome, meanwhile, was preparing a triumphant reception for the Fascist leader. All the Fascisti forces, some 60,000 strong encamped near Rome were to march into the city, and they are already pouring in from every gate as I write. They march through the streets gaily acclaimed by the entire population, and the whole city is decorated with flags. Mussolini was timed to arrive at nine o'clock, and at that hour the square in front of the station and the Piazza Venezia, the Piazza Colonna, and every open space in the center of the town were teeming with Fascisti and crowds of spectators. The trams have been stopped, and it is impossible to find any vehicle. All Rome is out on foot. The Fascisti have received orders to concentrate in the park round the Villa Borghese, where they will encamp. The headquarters of Mussolini will be at the Hotel Bristol, and the Piazza Barberini in front of it has been occupied since yesterday by an imposing force of Fascisti awaiting their leader.

The "Big Four"

A quadrumvirate of all the Fascisti forces in Italy has been established at Perugia, which, by the orders of Mussolini, hereafter takes the supreme military and political command of all the Fascisti forces in Italy. General de Bono, Signor Michele Bianchi, General Balbo, and a fourth whose name is not yet known constitute this quadrumvirate. They have issued the following proclamation:

Fascisti of Italy, the hour of decisive battle has come. Four years ago the national army undertook in those days its victorious offensive. Today our army of black shirts reaffirms this triumph, and marching resolutely on Rome will lead in glory to the Capitol. Today all are mobilized. The martial law of the Fascisti enters into vigor. Upon the orders of our Duke the military, political, and administrative powers are assumed by our quadrumvirate of secret action and with dictatorial mandate. We are not marching against the agents of public force nor against the nation, but against the class of inept politicians who for four years have defrauded our nation of the fruits of victory. The upper classes will find a return to discipline and the encouragement of the forces of national expansion, and the laboring classes will have all their rights loyally protected. God and the spirits of our 500,000 dead soldiers will inspire us, and we have only one aim, the safety and greatness of our country.

The Fascisti Command in Rome has issued another proclamation to the Fascisti in the capital strictly forbidding any individual action or excess, which will be severely punished. The Fascisti army has been most orderly and marvelously disciplined. There were some incidents in Rome yesterday. Copies of some newspapers, including the *Paese* and the *Epoca*, were burnt, and they were prevented from appearing. In the Trastevere quarter some Communists fired at a group of Fascisti; this was followed by immediate reprisals, and one workman, supposed to be a Communist, was killed. One of the Carabinieri was stabbed to death by Communists in the same quarter. Some conflicts occurred in places outside Rome between Communists and Fascisti, and four or five deaths occurred, three at Palestrina, one at Mentana, and one at Genazzano. Otherwise the Fascisti mobilization has been remarkably quiet and undisturbed.

Castor Oil For Communists.

The Party Disbanded.

The Communist leaders at San Remo, Pigna, and Alessio were arrested by Fascisti. It is declared that the Fascisti made them swallow a strong dose of castor oil and then let them go.

The *Azione*, which has now resumed publication, has announced that the Communist party has formally disbanded, and all its members are freed from the party's discipline. It is understood that the Communist deputies will resign simultaneously. The General Confederation of Labor has issued a manifesto to Italian workmen requesting them to maintain order — Exchange Telegraph Company.

The offices of the newspaper Secolo have been raided and sacked by a force of Nationalists about 100 strong. The invaders destroyed the machines — Reuters.

People And Monarch

The King received Signor Mussolini at 11.15 a.m. When he went to the Quirinal the Fascisti immediately organized a gigantic concentration outside the building.

After Signor Mussolini's departure from the Quirinal, the King suddenly appeared on a balcony of the Palace and was loudly cheered by the enthusiastic crowd. The King, who was visibly affected, withdrew after thanking the crowd for their greeting, but was compelled by renewed demonstrations to step on to the balcony again. Perfect order prevailed throughout the proceedings.

The newspapers published telegrams exchanged between Signori Mussolini and D'Annunzio. Signor Mussolini declares that he will exercise discretion and will not abuse his victory, to which Signor D'Annunzio replies that what they must do is to muster their forces and direct the path of Italy towards her great destinies.

A Bordighera message states that Queen Margherita, mother of the present King, received the local Fascisti at San Remo, and that her Majesty conversed in friendly fashion with the Fascisti, who paid their respects and presented flowers.—Reuters.

Fascism

Durham Morning Herald/November 8, 1922

Fascism, the world is advised by the *Messaggero*, Rome is "an affirmation of life and a revival, and foreigners must recognize this elementary truth if they wish to judge Italy rightly." Foreigners will probably find it difficult to appreciate the fine qualities of a revival that begins business by making a mockery of the constitutional safe-guards that have been erected to secure the translation of the public will into government by the orderly means of election.

To imagine an American counterpart of what has just transpired in Italy, one would have to conceive of a coalition of the Ku Klux Klan and the American Legion, united in a nationalist league of youth, descending upon Washington in force and compelling President Harding, under threat of a national uprising, to discharge his Cabinet and reassign the portfolios to men pledged to a new set of foreign and domestic policies. This has happened in Italy and the world is invited to applaud it as an "affirmation of life and a revival." It may mean that in Italy, but in nearly every other western nation it would means the affirmation of mob rule and the beginning of the decadence of constitutional government.

But the Italians, including, it seems king, people and press, appear much inspired by the event and it is not for the world outside to criticize the form or content of a sovereign nation's political pleasures. If fascism—a new word is being born—will bring to Italy the domestic content that Giolittism, Nittism and Factism have so far failed to achieve for her, the evil manner of its entry into power will be forgotten in the general rejoicing. It begins with a show of genius, but its wearing qualities cannot be determined until it begins to put into practice the program to which it is pledged. Here will come the crucial test and there is no reason today for believing that fascism will be more skillful in meeting it than the governmental genius of the ministries that have tackled the job and fallen by the way.—*Virginia Pilot.*

Class War Won By Bourgeoisie

Capitol Hill Beacon/November 9, 1922

The recent abortive attempt at a general strike in Italy has resulted in what now appears to be a colossal disaster for the Italian socialist government, writes Louis D. Kornfield from Rome to the New York Times. Proletariat organizations which had been dragged into the strike against their will, for no other object than to assist a political maneuver which the socialist deputies in the chamber endeavored, without success, to effect, are now suffering for their indiscretion in the dismissal and suspension from employment of thousands of their members.

Distrustful of the leadership which provoked this calamity, they are withdrawing from the Italian Labor alliance and are passing into new syndicalist combinations which the Socialist party, for the purpose of future proletariat action, will find difficult to control. The situation points clearly to a dissolution of the Italian socialist structure and a movement toward new foundations.

Even more important than the actual fact of the socialist rout is the manner in which it was brought about. A resort to armed force by the bourgeoisie produced the debacle; not the armed force of the government, but the force which the bourgeoisie created of itself and for itself in the fascisti. In short, "armed bourgeoisie," a phenomenon novel to modern democracy, is Italy's most recent and special contribution to the science of class war. It is a method of action which cannot fail to stop strikes and crush any move of the proletariat toward Bolshevism.

An armed bourgeoisie takes Marxian socialism at its word, accepts class war as a reality and at every opportune moment actually takes the offensive. It rushes in where the hesitant angels of democracy fear to tread, and by swift organized strokes drives the enemy to cover—or into the hospitals—and thus restores order, discipline and industry.

An armed bourgeoisie presupposes, of course, complete neutrality and noninterference on the part of the government, that is to say, unlimited freedom of action during the period of the crisis. In fact, it temporarily supplants government. In Italy the government, conveniently took a vacation until the classes in opposition had settled their dispute.

For disinterested observers, the Italian experiment of August 1 to August 5 could not fail to produce the conviction that, given a force of its own, independent of government authority, such as the Italian middle and upper classes have developed in the fascisti, the bourgeoisie of any country need never fear the success of general strikes or Bolshevist agitations. By reason of superior intelligence, superior leadership, superior freedom of action and resources, an armed bourgeoisie can always win.

Consider, to begin with, the fascist movement: A fascist leader thus defined it to the writer: "The fascist movement is the awakening of Italy to a full sense of its own greatness and destiny as a nation. Its appeal is essentially and always to the patriotism of the Italian people as an Italian people and it proposes at any cost, even at the cost of democratic conventions, to crush any tendency that may threaten to drag the Italian people into the morass of socialism, Bolshevism and internationalism."

Except for the fact that it specifically names socialism in its indictment, this program is as old as Italy itself. One naturally marvels that so old an idea could have aroused so great a reclame in a people so recently emerged from the sophisticating flames of a European war.

The answer is to be found in the new generation of Italian youth; the youth that had just missed the war and yet had sniffed the fumes; the youth that found itself upon the declaration of peace hunting for an organizing, animating ideal, such as wars or revolutions produce; such as youth always hungers for; something for which to shout, fight and die, if necessary.

But the cause of proletariat revolution in Italy had not then and has not yet developed a spokesman sufficiently eloquent and dramatic to capture the imagination of the Italian youth. Upon its vision at Flume four years ago there did burst a skyrocket of great brilliancy, but it pointed in another direction: Gabriele D'Annunzio! D'Annunzio had no new ideal to offer. He had an old ideal—Viva Italia! —which he made seem new through the force of his own imagination, fervor and magnetism. And the youth of Italy responded. This fresh outburst of patriotism found an objective in Bolshevism, and from the contact of the two hostile forces, bourgeois nationalism and proletariat internationalism, fascism was born.

Fascism in every stage of its development naturally encountered the bitter opposition of the socialists. This opposition reached a critical stage in July last when the liberal democratic elements joined forces with the socialists in demanding suppressive measures against fascism, on the ground that fascism, however patriotic in its intentions, had adopted a program of action openly defiant of law, productive of internal disorder, and in direct contradiction to all the principles and ideals of democratic government.

Not to compromise itself in either direction, the first Facta government there did nothing but utter feeble admonitions against subversions of law and make vague, incoherent threats of disciplining offenders whoever they might be. But by no such safe middle course, however, could the government solve the "problem of pacification."

The government announced late in July a deficit in the national budget of six billion lire. It was desperately trying to draw the attention of the chamber to a financial program that was to be based largely on faith, hope and charity when a band of irresponsible youngsters, wearing black shirts and calling themselves fascisti, amused themselves in Cremona one afternoon by setting fire to the homes of two socialist deputies.

An uproar ensued in the chamber, led by socialists and supported by the democratic factions in the center. The burning of the abodes of the two socialist deputies was a veritable outrage. What was the government going to do about it? The government decided the time had come to act. It therefore announced that it would investigate the Cremona scandal and punish the culprits as soon as they could be apprehended. Then the popular party, from the center of the chamber, unexpectedly and without warning, out of whim purely political in motive and totally unrelated to the issue of the hour, swept to the support of the socialists on an order of the day and left the Facta ministry without a majority in the chamber. The ministry collapsed automatically.

For about nine days Italy had to get along without a ministry. It got along surprisingly well. The king called upon Orlando to form a new cabinet. He failed.

De Nava and Bonomi and Meda in succession endeavored to procure a more or less similar solution, but they in turn had no better success than Orlando.

The bankruptcy of Italian statesmanship assumed the character of a national scandal. The king recalled Orlando and again he failed.

The king finally called into consultation, for an exchange of views, the socialist leader, Turati. The conference of July 29 was acclaimed by the Italian press as "historic." It lasted forty minutes. Turati, however, merely utilized his interview with the king as an exceptionally dramatic moment in which to hurl the socialist ultimatum. Either immediate steps should be taken to form a government that would crush fascism or the socialists would call the general strike. The king declined to budge.

On the following day, August 1, the labor alliance at Genoa issued the call to a general strike. In the face of this national danger, the parliamentary factions were frightened into consolidation; the popular party deserted the socialists and Facta was recalled to power. Before the day was over Facta had formed a second ministry, with a few changes in personnel, but with no change whatever in political complexion. It was the same government that had been overthrown with the same "puntarella" to the right. Turati had played his trump card and had lost.

The scene of conflict now passed from parliament to the country. Fascism received the order to march. The marvelous potency of an armed bourgeoisie revealed itself at once. Fascisti armed, organized and led, encamped in the squares and principal streets of the big cities.

For such an organized demonstration of hostility the Italian proletariat was utterly unprepared. The call to strike itself had taken the proletariat by surprise. The response of the working classes on the first day was sporadic, disorganized and lacking in leadership.

Without losing time the fascisti launched at offensive with three specific objectives. The first was to keep the railroads and other instruments of public service in operation, by taking up with elements of their own the work abandoned by strikers; the second was to crush the proletariat press, the socialist municipal administrations wherever they existed, the co-operative unions and other working-class organizations from which the strike might derive moral or material energy; the third was to terrify the strikers into submission by the application of armed force and execution of drastic reprisals against any attempt to revolt.

The centers of strike activity were Genoa, Milan, Parma, Livorno, Ancona and Ravenna.

Forty-eight hours after the strike was called Turati realized he was licked. To save as much as he could from the ruins, Turati rushed to Facta and offered to call the strike off if Facta would promise that the government would take the strikers back.

Facta gave the socialists the required assurance. On the following day—August 3—the labor federation called upon the strikers to return to their posts, announcing that the proletariat had achieved its object. But if the socialists were through the fascists were not. They had a definite program to complete, and they proceeded to complete it. In Milan they drove the socialist administration out of power and took possession of the Palazzo Marino. On the following day they attacked the Avanti, the leading socialist newspaper in Italy, put the editors to flight and set fire to the plant.

In Genoa they suppressed the publication of the Lavoro and marched in force upon the Palace of San Giorgio, where the socialist consortium of the port was located. The fascisti demanded the surrender of the consortium, and when surrender was refused they seized it by force.

In Ravenna they seized and suppressed the elaborate co-operative organization which had served as a model of socialist co-operative development for students from all parts of the world. In Ancona they destroyed the printing plant of the socialist organ *La Difesa* and set fire to the headquarters of all the principal labor organizations, including the Federation of Railway Workers, the Society of Soviets and the Chamber of Labor. They marched into Parma 6,000 strong and took possession of the city. They destroyed the printing plant of the Piccolo and disrupted the co-operative unions.

Considering the violent nature of the reprisals that occurred against the working classes, there was surprisingly little blood shed during the course of the strike.

On August 5, when it was all over, the government came to life and confided to military control the cities of Genoa, Milan, Ancona, Parma and Livorno.

In the special terms by which the fascisti and the socialists subsequently defined "victory" the claims of both were justified by the facts. Whether the victory of either faction meant victory for the Italian people and for the nation as a whole was a question which seemed to concern neither of the opposing forces. When indeed Facta, in his second inaugural, declared that Italy could be ruined by such a "victory" Lupi, the fascisti leader in the chamber, responded with a challenge which clearly indicated that although civil war was not yet an actual fact in Italy, it could any day become one.

Mussolini
Chicago Tribune/November 18, 1922

By Tribune wireless. De Santo of the Tribune Foreign News
Service in Italy presented a vivid picture of what may be one of the great
historic scenes of our time—the first address of Benito Mussolini to the
Italian parliament. What is to come no man can prophesy, but there is
that in Fascism and in the personality of its leader that promises, at least,
noteworthy, perhaps epoch-making events.

Premier Mussolini's utterance was remarkable in tone and
substance. Sig. de Santo notes that he addressed the members not in
the usual form as "honorable colleagues," but in the briefest term,
"gentlemen"; and there was a hint implied in the following sentence: "My
coming before yon today is an act of deference for which I do not ask any
particular thanks"—which was not lost on the assembly nor will be on the
Italian public.

Mussolini was not speaking as a representative of parliament.
He offered no resemblance to the modern politician balancing on the
difficult footing of parliamentary strategy. The resemblance is rather to
Cromwell, though the Italian leader warned rather than rebuked, and when
the implications of the address were stern enough he exhibited a restraint
which promises well. Unquestionably he has the power to expel the Italian
parliament as Cromwell did the long parliament; but he has offered the
assembly a chance to save itself by service.

Fascism, despite its militant action against the Reds and its refusal
to be checked by forms, has shown a disposition to preserve the political
structure of the state so far as that seems compatible with what the
Fascisti think essential to the salvation of Italy. The backbone of Fascism
is youth, and youth is violent, but we have no respect for the fuss made
over Fascist violence directed against a body of revolutionists which had
not hesitated to use violence in their own cause. It is easy for American
ideologues and parlor pinks to condemn the Fascisti for the use of illegal
force, but Fascism confronted conditions, not theories. The machinery of
government was in the hands of weaklings and was not functioning. It had
become an empty form, and Italy was almost without government. In such
a situation unlawful and subversive force was loose, and it was the task

of Fascism to defend Italy from it, not by futile protests or appeals to a legal government which had demonstrated its inability to enforce laws or protect rights. The Fascisti used force, moral and physical, because force alone counted; but their total of violence is a Sunday school performance compared to the conduct of the Reds wherever and whenever they have had power or opportunity.

During the period of violence Fascism did not get very intelligent observation or report from some of the American correspondents. That was because the official sources of news are easy to get at and the expression of the official view or coloration is comfortable. This is a serious defect in foreign correspondence, which is seldom independent and too often reflects official color. Admiral Chester's tribute to the accuracy of Tribune reports from the Near East emphasizes an evil by no means confined to that region. Report colored by foreign partisanisms or official influence perverts American judgment in matters as to which straight thinking is of increasing importance to us all. The Tribune takes satisfaction in its reports on the Fascist movement, which from the first have shown grasp of its real nature and of the conditions with which it was dealing.

Up to its present stage, we believe, Fascism has been more than justified, not in every act of every member, for the Fascisti are human, but in the main course of its conduct. Italy was slipping into the Red morass. The Fascisti have stopped that descent. They have restored the essential of ordered society, discipline. They have laid the foundations of restoration, and we think they deserve and have the cordial sympathy of America, to which they have appealed.

The danger to Italy under the Fascist regime is obvious. Premier Mussolini told parliament that "the foreign policy is the most important subject for the moment." and this may be true, though we in America are inclined to think that foreign ambitions, disguised or idealized as rights, are more important for the harm they do than the benefits they are likely to achieve. At any rate, we are sure that unless the Fascist regime avoids inordinate nationalist ambitions and exercises a very sound judgment in its foreign relations it will ruin itself and Italy, too.

What Italy needs is peace, government retrenchment, relief from the burden of bureaucracy, economy, and hard work. New territory may easily cost far more than it ever can be worth to the Italian people.

Friendly relations with neighbors, profitable treaties, and commerce are better worth the having than dubious victories and unmanageable colonies.

We hope Premier Mussolini proves to be a great constructive statesman. If he is he will keep the peace, contrive wise compromises, and turn the genius of the Italian people to the task of financial and economic restoration. That way lies a revived and truly victorious Italy.

Mussolini Assured of Success Before He Seized Power in Italy

New York Tribune/November 19, 1922

King Wavered, Then Gave Over Power to "Black Shirt" Chief

by Wilbur Forrest

ITALY, sliding along past the car window on either side looks as peaceful as any semi-tropical landscape—smiling fields and hills dotted with dark green olive trees all bathed in a yellow sun. Towns and villages through which this train has passed since it left Rome appear as normal and quiescent as usual, restful to the nerves by their lack of commotion and agreeable to the eye in their architectural yellows and reddish browns.

A few days ago it was another story. Throughout much of the length and breadth of Italy there was a something in the air, at first difficult to see, but easy to feel—waves of revolt converging on Rome.

Italy was passing through a revolution such as has seldom been equaled in history. The rebels were not comparatively small bands of men gathered secretly for simultaneous surprise attacks on federal strongholds. They were tens of thousands, mostly in their teens, answering a sort of holy order to mobilize by any means of transportation available, from railway trains to cars, carrying whatever weapons came to hand, at the several gates of Rome to there await the orders of the high chief, one Benito Mussolini.

Sixty thousand of Mussolini's young blackshirts were converging on the capital as early as Saturday, October 28, and twelve hours earlier the news of their coming had given the king and the government the choice between resistance and submission. The government decided on maintenance of order by force, and hastily prepared a decree declaring Italy in a state of siege. King Emmanuel was not agreeable to a measure which would have prepared all the elements of civil war and possibly a political upheaval of such abrupt nature as to shake the throne. He refused to sign the siege order and made overtures to the Fascisti chieftain at Milan, offering him liberal part in the formation of a new government.

King Surrenders to Power Which Mussolini Possessed

But Mussolini, up north there in Milan, held the big cards and knew it. His men were at the moment on all spokes of the wheel moving toward the hub—mobilizing on the capital. The King, too, knew that Mussolini held the cards and made his bid for peace. His second telegram to Milan gave Mussolini unconditional control of a new government, with the Fascist chief as Prime Minister.

Mussolini hurried from Milan to Lago Garda, the seat of Gabriel D'Annunzio, his friend and counselor. Then he accepted the King's invitation.

Whether ex-Premier Facta and his colleagues knew it or not, Benito Mussolini and King Victor Emmanuel saw that the country was virtually behind this unique mobilization of black-shirted army then "bumming" its way toward Rome. Mussolini and his followers must have known that chances were strong for only passive resistance from all but a small percentage of the regular Italian army. A few loyal units in Rome would have obeyed orders to bar the gates against the besieging forces, but the bulk of the country's established military organization would doubtless have risen in sullen protest against bloodshed.

From sources which obviously cannot be given here I am informed that Mussolini had examined all aspects of his radical means against the Facta government. He knew that his men—who look upon his person as that of a demi-god—were with him, come what may. He knew also that Italy was sympathetic, and that success, either by force or intimidation, was certain.

The mobilization of this Fascist army was as unique as it was impressive. I was able to witness an important section of it, but without knowledge at the time that Mussolini's experiment was to pass off as it did, and was also fortunate enough to slip into Rome by the only gate remaining open to the military on Sunday, October 29. All trains at that time had ceased to leave or enter the capital.

It was in Turin the previous day that the something which was in the air began to be felt. Wild rumors were afloat, all telegraphic communication with the outside was forbidden and black-shirted men, mostly young men, began to board railway trains headed south. They carried shotguns, rifles of various calibers, blackjacks, hand grenades, and loaded clubs. They offered no tickets as fare and a heavy guard of troops in charge of the Turin station did not molest them, but looked on with what seemed a certain approbation.

Troops Offered No Bar as Fascists Board Trains

The train in which I traveled south was liberally sprinkled with these young legionnaires. We picked up more of them at Genoa and proceeded on south, boarded at every station by small groups. At Pisa another contingent mingled with the regular troops in the station and came aboard. The force grew throughout the night and the morning. At Civita Vecchia the train was crowded to the guards with these young bloods, carrying their mixed assortment of arms and wearing raiment as nondescript as the weapons, except the blackshirt badge of the Fascisti. Many wore the small black fez-like cap, but many were hatless. Some had the crude insignia of their local branches embroidered on their caps or shirts, and many had affected the skull and cross bones designed, undoubtedly as a warning of death to all categories of radicals, communists, socialists and others—the sworn enemies of Fascism.

Civita Vecchia, the ancient fortress city on the blue Mediterranean, is less than two hours by train from Rome. In this town more than 5,000 Fascisti had massed by Sunday noon, fed into it by the railway line from the north within twenty-four hours after the general mobilization order had been flashed to all parts of Italy.

Here were all the elements of a bloody battle. Five thousand troops were also on hand, 6,000 government troops and 6,000 Fascisti, opposed to the government and bent on its overthrow. Troops held the railway station but allowed incoming Blackshirts to leave their trains and join their comrades in the town. The railroad from Civitavecchia to Rome was broken in spots and controlled by 10,000 Fascisti further on. Trains could only turn back north.

Armed Fascisti faced armed troops in the streets and a quarrel, a stray shot, a small riot would have started serious bloodshed.

Troops had formed barriers across the wide avenue paralleling the sea. Fascist groups made no attempt to force their way through these barriers, but calmly maneuvered their way over walls through residential gardens around them. The troops made no effort to stop them. It looked like trouble. Every man was carrying a man-killing weapon. A quick succession of shots sounded from a side street. A squad of troops leisurely detached from one of the barrier positions and led by a young officer marched in the direction to investigate. There was no sequel. A Fascist youth of sixteen had been trying out his small automatic pistol on an alley rat and he was located and told to be quiet. He good-naturedly accepted the advice and sauntered off. Had he fired into a group of soldiers it would have been different.

I afterwards learned that the scene in Civita Vecchia was typical of that in many towns which marked the breaking points of rail communication with Rome. If such a situation could arise in the United States, armed irregulars advancing on all sides toward Washington, it would take little imagination to develop the scene.

My trip from Civita Vecchia to Rome in a motor truck requisitioned by an Italian general was strictly reminiscent of the big war. Civita Vecchia, which incidentally is a name hard to say but which means "Old Citadel", though a moderate sized town on the sea, was a good side-line seat in the big show that appeared ready to begin, but Rome was the extra special reserved seat, and Rome therefore appeared the normal place to "get."

Someone was once credited with that ancient platitude "All roads lead to Rome," but it wasn't true on this particular occasion. For the individual anxious to get to Rome there remained one road, and it was a roundabout route at that. All others led into the camps of the Fascisti, who had a great deal to say about ingress and egress for that matter.

The problem was only solved after locating the Italian general commanding the local garrison. This officer was found to have a genuine admiration for Americans in general and John J. Pershing in particular.

He sympathized with my desire to get to Rome, but notwithstanding his great regard for Americans in general he was forced to explain that the pestiferous Fascisti had requisitioned every private motor car in Civita Vecchla and the garrison itself was without transportation not urgently needed in the present crisis. He kindly offered a military pass in case I might locate a vehicle, and even suggested the pass might operate on a walking tour, but the shortest route to Rome via Marinello was cluttered up by 10,000 Fascisti, and they might not honor the pass. To go by this route in an automobile anyway would risk the confiscation of the car.

It was here that it became necessary to invoke the name of John J. Pershing, America's military leader, signed with his own hand in May, 1918, a military pass on which was attached my picture and general description; likewise thereon permission to circulate freely in the zones of the American army. Together with other pieces of identification, the Pershing pass was presented to the Italian general. This officer spoke excellent French, but read no English. But he could read the firm handwriting of Pershing and recognize the attached photo, not yet sufficiently worn and faded to obscure the United States insignia.

Name of Pershing Brings Assistance in Nick of Time

The situation changed immediately. The general promised to do all possible, and within thirty minutes a privately owned motor truck and civilian chauffeur and military passes were ready, and, with several others permitted to take advantage of the transportation, the Tribune representative was en route to Rome with orders scrupulously to dodge the road via Marinello, with its stronghold of 10,000 Fascisti.

The road taken, therefore, was the only one remaining in the hands of the military. We passed through many barriers of wire entanglements, hastily constructed, and through cavalry, infantry and artillery prepared for business. It was a unique view of Italy's revolution and sufficient in itself to show that the governmental turnover was not the result of a bit of "horseplay," as the heavy censorship of Rome sought to make it appear. The road over which we "motor-trucked" through fifty miles of campagna, via Lago de Bracciano, to Rome, was conspicuous for its lack of Blackshirts, but notwithstanding this extraordinary situation, their cordon around the Eternal City was practically complete.

This was on Sunday. Only on Monday was Rome absolutely sure that the Fascisti had won their bloodless revolution and that Mussolini was to arrive personally to set up his new government.

Sunday Rome was virtually cut off from the outside world.

Monday Mussolini arrived, and Monday night groups of his men from the camps on the outside began to enter the city. Tuesday Rome saw with its own eyes enough to show that King Victor Emmanuel's haste to turn the government over to Mussolini had been a wise precaution. All previous attempts at news censorship, by manifesto or otherwise, to cover up the real situation could not curtain the more serious side of the political turnover when some thirty thousand Fascisti, in scrupulously correct military formation, filed through the streets.

The discipline of these men was admirable. They were but half the number that had gathered at Rome's gates. The others turned around and retraced their steps homeward without a glimpse of the capital which they had come to take. But those who were allowed to march in Rome were a fair sample of what Rome might have seen under different auspices if the King had seen fit to support the Facta ministry in its decision to resist.

Pieces of Artillery Mark Line of Black Shirt Marchers

It required about five and a half hours for the black-shirted demonstration to pass a given point on the Corso Umberto. Wicked little machine guns mounted on motor cars spoke silent volumes about what might have been. Contingents appeared here and there in line equipped with regulation arms and with a bearing which told of no mean knowledge of military matters. There were even some pieces of artillery. There were war veterans, their chests laden with medals. But the majority were youngsters, cloaking adventure with patriotism—handsome faces and wicked faces mingled together. What would have happened in Rome if this Fascist "division" had been turned loose upon it, out of control? Romans asked themselves, and the answer demanded no great stretch of imagination. As it stood, they were under admirable restraint, directed by a discipline which told of many months of secret preparation in all parts of Italy for the day Fascism would become the government. The parade over, they marched to the railway stations and were taken home to demobilize.

Italy today is a Fascist nation. The country's national hymn may well be said to be "Giovinezza," the catchy air which has played a significant part in the growth of the movement. It means literally "Youth," and restaurants and theaters played it constantly during the brief black-shirt occupation. One orchestra leader discovered to his sorrow that he had left the song out of his repertoire. He was directed by a handful of playful Fascisti to go out and buy it and until he returned one Rome theater was without music other than a many-throated "Giovinezza" from the audience.

While a few serious riots occurred with some loss of life Rome took the invading force with placid tolerance. A few Communists who dared to remain and talk were roughly handled. Some found their heads forcibly shaved and the pates decorated with stripes of red, white and green, the Italian national colors. But others fled to the country well in advance of the arrival of the anti-red hosts.

Dramatic Gesture Was No Surprise in Trend of Events

Benito Mussolini, who has guided the semi-secret organization which Italy has now watched walk entirely into the open, is, in the opinion of many observers of Italian politics, the vital force of character that Italy needs. An American who has spent, much time in Italy and who is in a position to observe the "inside" of Italian politics from a "reserved seat" told me:

"Mussolini's dramatic gesture came with no surprise to those who have been watching him closely for the last few months. He is a man of resolution and force, and if he has not yet proved statesmanship his chances are good for success. I have observed political crises before in Rome, but I have never seen such general optimism with coming of a new government as now. Usually the Italians are as pessimistic after a ministerial shake-up as they were previously. The Cabinet which he has chosen I would call not only good but excellent."

To those who have talked to the new Italian Chief of State there can be no doubt as to his force of character. I called at the Savoia Hotel the day before Mussolini announced his ministry, which was the same day he arrived from Milan. He had just been to see the King. It required little argument with his entourage to convince them that Mussolini should say something at once for publication in New York. Ten minutes later I was ushered through the heavy fascist guard which barred the hotel stairway and was standing in the small anteroom of the leader's suite, where he and Deputy Finzi, his constant companion, were about to sit down to lunch.

The first impression was that Mussolini was a poseur. He stood there very erect—almost scowling. After the handshake he wanted to know what was wanted and gave the impression that time was worthwhile. He did not offer a chair or take one himself. Information required was shot back something like a good tennis player handles a fast serve.

Mussolini answers his questions firmly and clean cut. This is only normal, because any student of character would expect nothing else from him.

The new Italian Premier has not a benevolent face. He would not make a good minister or missionary or Y. M. C. A. secretary or male nurse. This is due mainly to his chin, which is that of a fighter. His eyes show a trifle more of the white than with the ordinary mortal, and his nose is aquiline and his lower jaw is wide. Determination is written all over the face of Mussolini. His comment was on all points brief. He named his "coup d'etat" a "successful, nationalist, legal, bloodless revolution"; his foreign policy, "one of peace and dignity, expansion, equilibrium friendly to all countries friendly to us"; his future internal policy "strict government economy, work and order."

With such a program, which could not be more beneficial or safe in any country, and with Mussolini's jaw there is optimism in Italy. He has the country with him. It has seen what he can do in revolution. They are willing watch him in statecraft.

Members of the ex-government are silently respectful of the new leader. Many have sought his friendship.

Carlos Schanzer, ex-Foreign Minister, possibly known better than most Italian politicians in the United States because of his part in the Washington conference, and who lost his job through Mussolini, told The Tribune he felt that it would be very inappropriate to comment on the political situation "at this time." It is rumored that he hoped for a new portfolio. Ex-Premier Facta is known to hold ill feeling toward Mussolini, who placed a Fascist guard of honor at his Rome hotel. Giolitti, the grand old man of Italian politics, expressed favor for the new order. Others less prominent have either swung into line or declined to be hostile. With the elections several months hence, Mussolini may expect clear sailing and Italy is with him.

All Europe Feels Grip of Mysterious Fascism
New York Tribune/November 19, 1922

Move to Force Governments into Activity Appeals to Untold Thousands

Preservation of Outlines of the Present Economic Order is Urged

With the Fascisti now firmly seated in power in Italy, developments of the last ten days abroad make it clear that their movement, which its adherents outside of Italy prefer to call Activism rather than Fascism, is not merely a local phase of Italian politics, but is fundamentally part of a continent-wide revulsion of feeling against the ultra-liberal economic tendencies and the governmental ineptitudes that have plagued Europe ever since the close of the war.

Followers of the daily news cannot but have been struck recently by the number of foreign dispatches telling of the birth of Fascist organizations outside of Italy. Particularly has this fact been to the forefront of the news from Germany during the last week. It has also been mentioned in connection with Poland, Romania and Hungary.

Reliable information indicates that there is something more behind this than coincidence or mere imitation. It has just been learned that Activist leaders from all over Europe were in communication in September, before the Fascisti staged the successful coup d'etat that gave the movement the name by which it is generally known and the prestige which it now carries. At that time tentative plans were laid for the formation of an Activist internationale, to borrow the term made famous by Activism's antithetical movement, Socialism, and a definite agreement was reached to hold an international conference in March, 1923. Modes of action were also discussed, and the process by which the Fascisti later gained their objective was explained in advance to the Activist leaders of other countries for their guidance and use when the time should be ripe.

Events Show Studied Course for Fascist Movement

Consequently it is evident that in sporadic reports that have been appearing lately of scattered Fascist activity can, in all likelihood, be strung upon a common string, and that history will fit together into a perfect mosaic the current bits of evidence that to observers both here and in Europe seem unrelated and merely analogous.

Practically every European country, including both England and Ireland, is reported to contain embryo organizations which, if time and circumstance be favorable, will germinate into full-fledged Activist bodies. These organizations are diverse in political make-up, diverse in religious creed, diverse in temperament and nationality and diverse in leadership, but they are all said to be firmly united in one object—the injection of vigor into governmental activities, and particularly in the preservation of the broad outlines of the present economic order.

In Ireland, the movement has an anti-Sinn Fein color and is composed of both Roman Catholic and Protestant Ulsterite elements, united by a desire for the restoration of law and order, plus a more forthright handling of the whole Irish situation. In England its strength, as might be expected, is mainly among the members of the Conservative party, some of the most prominent of the Conservative secretaries of state in the new Bonar Law Cabinet being said to have declared themselves thoroughly in sympathy with Activism. In this connection it seems logical to expect that the movement will receive fresh impetus from the victory which the Conservatives have won at the polls, as its followers predict.

Church and Former Soldiers Back Campaign in France

French Activism draws its main strength from the Ligue des Combatants—the French "American Legion"—and from certain powerful Roman Catholic organizations traditionally opposed to anything that smacks of socialism or sovietism, and strongly critical of anything that looks like an official attempt at a rapprochement with Bolshevist Russia. In Belgium the same elements exactly are thought to be imbued with Activism. The German movement is largely monarchist, principally, it seems, because German republicanism has been so closely identified with socialism. Curiously enough, however, not even the French Activists believe that this monarchical character indicates that German Activism is either anti-Ally or anti-French.

The Fascisti in Italy have made their position quite clear. The movement is strong in Hungary; in Austria clashes between its representatives, the newly formed Heimwehr, and workmen's bodies have been reported during the last week. The Activist current in Poland, Romania and Jugo-Slavia is clearly discernible, being formed in each of these Little Entente countries of the elements of the population who fear and hate their near neighbor, Soviet Russia. There are signs of it in Switzerland, too.

Scanning this list of countries in which the principles and methods of the Fascisti find large groups of admirers, and in which it seems possible that a repetition of Fascist actions may become a political problem, it is interesting to note that what Activists say when they declare the movement is not concerned with forms of government, but rather with the form of the economic order, is probably true, for in the roster are included monarchies and republics of every shade of democratic control.

No Revolutionary Tactics Used Bring About Results

Any arbitrary characterization of the movement as either reactionary or revolutionary, moreover, is certainly mistaken. Nowhere is it revolutionary surely, although without doubt a section of public opinion in this country believes that to be the case because of the manner in which the Fascisti grasped the reins of government in Italy. Nor when the newly revealed evidence as to the conscious connection between Fascism and Activism is considered can Activism be deemed reactionary, at least at present. Fascism is headed by an ex-Socialist and manned by workingmen; it seems hard to believe that it could be in any sense reactionary. If there is any truth in the hypothesis here set forth, therefore, that Activism is both modeled upon and connected with Fascism and is pursuing the same aims, it follows that there is no taint of reaction attaching to the former.

Activism seems to have two main foundations, as indicated before. One of them, the desire to preserve the broad outline of the current economic order, needs no detailed discussion. The other moving cause seems to be, as it was in Italy, a phenomenon clearly visible to students of politics even before the war. It is a general pessimism, amounting almost to distrust, about the efficacy of parliamentary government and about the capacity and willingness of a body of politicians who have to trim their sails to the varying desires of a mixed constituency to take decisive action when such action is necessary.

Activism does not demand or suggest, in its present form, the abolition of parliamentary government, but it does demand that government shall take a firmer grip upon the affairs of state. Here again it follows Fascism. Here, too, in passing, is another evidence of the fact that it is not reactionary, for no reactionary wants to see a government controlled by the masses of the electorate more firmly entrenched in the life of the state or more drastically active in regulating affairs. "Reactionary," of course, is a relative term; to the Socialist doctrinaire the democrat is a little reactionary. But in the broader sense of the term, that of wishing to see popular government curbed or destroyed, activism cannot be tagged with the reactionary label, because what it demands essentially, apparently, in view of the moving cause just explained, is not the overthrow of popular government, but its greater responsiveness to the will of the bulk of the people.

The movement's exact attitude toward the governmental structure is probably best described by the word "anti-politician." Once again Activism coincides with Fascism. The Activist leaders who met two months ago, it is said, after roundly condemning the leading politicians of their respective countries for "wishy-washiness" in their efforts to tranquilize Europe, resolved to disregard politicians and parliaments in the struggle for reforms and to create instead strong, militant organizations to smash dangerous conditions wherever they might be found.

When it is remembered that this resolution preceded Mussolini's seizure of the Italian government, and that events in Italy have actually transpired along the lines indicated by this expression of theory, it will be seen that the connection between the two movements is close, whether or not it can be proved to be formal or not.

Activism's possibilities are obviously boundless. If its followers all over Europe can sink their nationalistic and religious difference in favor of their common ideals—a thing which it is said they have not yet fully done—they will furnish a leaven in Europe's political dough that will work great things in quickening the spirit of government. It may well purge parliamentary government of its dross for a time at least, and most certainly if it is successful on a large scale it will furnish a new and valuable basis for a most desirable kind of international solidarity.

Political Dynamite Lurks in Widespread Movement

On the other hand, it is equally plain that the movement is charged with political dynamite. It cannot be concealed that it has this avowed purpose: to influence the regularly constituted organisms of government by extra-legal methods. All such movements hold a threat of tyranny that is but lightly veiled, and if the seeds of European Activism, already more firmly planted, seemingly, than men realize, should bear continent-wide fruit, then the peoples of Europe may well pray that Activism keep untarnished its ideals of justice and democratic control of government as well as its ideal of vigor in administration.

Whatever be the outcome, in many ways this Activist movement that is taking shape before our eyes is a most remarkable historical event. Its partisans in Europe are already comparing it with the process whereby the Protestant Reformation sprang into being four centuries ago, and while it is much too soon to subscribe to this opinion, or to predict that Activism can possibly compare in importance with the Reformation, the analogy is by no means so far fetched as it may seem at the first blush; many striking points of similarity lend strength to the comparison.

Like the Reformation, Activism is neither revolutionary nor reactionary like the Reformation, which dealt with religious issues, than paramount in the minds of the people, Activism is chiefly concerned with the economic order, which is today, at bottom, the question closest to the people. Like the Reformation, which was an expression of discontent with the Church's policy and with the Church's dignitaries, Activism reveals, as a collateral issue, the dissatisfaction of the masses with the steps which their governments have taken to safeguard the present economic order.

Again, both the old religious and the new politico-economic movements are primarily international in character and recent events indicate that the younger of the two will imitate its predecessor in becoming international in action. Finally, both movements are clearly the return swing of the pendulum of human affairs from a period when existing institutions have been vitally challenged, the one by a liberality verging on paganism, the other by a liberality verging on Bolshevism.

New Popular Idol Rises in Bavaria
New York Times/November 21, 1922

*Hitler Credited With Extraordinary Powers of
Swaying Crowds to His Will*

Forms Gray-Shirted Army

*Armed With Blackjacks and Revolvers and Well Disciplined,
They Obey Orders Implicitly*

Leader a Reactionary

by Cyril Brown

MUNICH, Nov. 20 — Next to the high cost of living and the dollar, "Der Hitler" and his "Hakenkreuzlers" are the popular topic of talk in Munich and other Bavarian towns. This reactionary Nationalistic anti-Semitic movement has now reached a point where it is considered potentially dangerous, though not for the immediate future.

Hitler today is taken seriously among all classes of Bavarians. He is feared by some, enthusiastically hailed as a prophet and political economic savior by others, and watched with increasing sympathetic interest by the bulk who, apparently, are merely biding the psychological moment to mount Hitler's bandwagon. Undoubtedly the spectacular success of Mussolini and the Fascisti brought Hitler's movement to the fore and gained popular interest and sympathy for it. Another condition favorable to the outburst of the movement is the widespread discontent with the existing state of affairs among all classes in the towns and cities under the increasing economic pressure.

Hitler's "Hakenkreuz" movement is essentially urban in character. It has not yet caught a foothold among the hardy Bavarian peasantry and highlanders, which would make it really dangerous. As a highly placed personage put it:

"Hitler organized a small insignificant group of National Socialists two years ago, since when the movement has been smoldering beneath the surface. Now it has eaten its way through, and a conflagration of course is not only possible but certain if this now free flame of fanatical patriotism finds sufficient popular combustible material to feed on."

Hitler has been called the Bavarian Mussolini, and his followers the Bavarian Fascisti. There is nothing socialistic about the National Socialism he preaches. He has 30,000 organized followers in Munich alone. His total following throughout Bavaria is uncertain, since the movement is in a state of rapid flux. He is wasting no time working out political programs, but devotes his whole energy to recruiting fresh forces and perfecting his organization.

Blackjacks Silence Opposition

"Herr Hitler regrets he is unable to meet you as he is leaving town on important business for several days," was the answer received by The New York Times correspondent. His important business was going to Regensburg with three special trainloads of Munich admirers for the purpose of holding a series of reactionary inflammatory meetings and incidentally to beat up protesting Socialists and Communists with blackjacks if any dare protest, which is becoming increasingly rarer.

His simple method is, first, propaganda, and secondly, efficient organization. He personally conducts patriotic revival meetings for this purpose, often descending from his stronghold, Munich, on other Bavarian towns with special trainloads of followers. He has the rare oratorical gift, at present unique in Germany, of spellbinding whole audiences regardless of politics or creed. The new converts made at these rallies, those who absolutely and unconditionally pledge themselves to Hitler and the cause, are carefully sifted through and the pick of them who pass standard military muster are organized into "storm troops" with gray shirts, brassards in the old imperial colors, black and an anti-Semitic Swastika cross in a white circular field on red; armed also with blackjacks and, it is popularly whispered, revolvers.

According to a reliable specialist informant, there are probably 400,000 military rifles and 150 cannon still concealed in Bavaria. So that some fine day Hitler's legionaries might well make their debut with rifles.

Hitler's strength is in the combination of his undeniable great gifts as an orator and organizer. He exerts an uncanny control over audiences, possessing the remarkable ability to not only rouse his hearers to a fighting pitch of fury, but at will to turn right around and reduce the same audience to docile calmness and good order. A typical instance is related by the informant mentioned:

"At the height of the recent Bavarian Government crisis Hitler was holding a mass meeting in Munich and had worked up the big audience when a rumor spread through the hall that he had planned a coup and that he would overthrow and seize the Government that night and was about to give the signal at this rally. His followers burst into an enthusiastic uproar, drew and brandished blackjacks and revolvers, and with shouts of 'Heil, Heil, Heil,' prepared to follow Hitler and storm anything.

"With a few electric words he worked a magic change in the audience. Their duty, on which the success of the cause depended, he said, was iron discipline and implicit obedience to orders when orders were given. The time for action had not come yet. And the riot was nipped in the bud."

A Different Show of Power

A different exhibition of Hitler power: during a mass meeting in Nuremberg, a stronghold of Bavarian socialism, the radical elements undertook a counter-demonstration outside the meeting hall and sang the "Internationale." The strains of the hated tune heard in the hall enraged Hitler's followers. At his word of command shock troops of gray shirts with fine discipline marched from the hall, pulled their blackjacks, and charged and dispersed the crowd with many a broken head.

Hitler is credited with having a rapidly increasing following among the workers disgruntled by the high cost of living. It is also said many have flocked to his reactionary banner. He is beginning to draw support from the politically sluggish middle classes, which in Bavaria, however, are not so sluggish as in Berlin. Even more significant there is some active, more passive support and to a still greater extent more sympathetic interest for the Hitler movement among the Bavarian loyalists, among monarchists and militarists and in government and political circles, apparently coupled with the idea that the movement would prove a useful tool if it could be controlled by their special interests. But there is also the latent fear that the movement might wax beyond control.

70

Hitler, in addition to his oratorical and organizing abilities, has another positive asset—he is a man of the "common people" and hence has the makings of a "popular hero," appealing to all classes. It is reported that he was a worker before becoming leader of the Bavarian Social Nationalists. He served during the war as a common soldier and won the Iron Cross of the First and Second Classes, which for a common soldier is distinctive evidence of exceptional bravery and daring. To Bavarian mentality he talks rough, shaggy, sound horse sense, and according to present Bavarian public opinion a strong, active leader equipped with horse sense is the need of the hour.

Chief Points of His Program

Hitler's program is of less interest than his person and movement. His program consists chiefly of half a dozen negative ideas clothed in generalities. He is "against the Jews, Communists, Bolshevism, Marxian socialism, Separatists, the high cost of living, existing conditions, the weak Berlin Government and the Versailles Treaty." Positively he stands only for "a strong united Germany under a strong Government."

He is credibly credited with being accentuated by lofty, unselfish patriotism. He probably does not know himself just what he wants to accomplish. The keynote of his propaganda in speaking and writing is violent anti-Semitism. His followers are popularly nicknamed "the Hakenkreuzler." So violent are Hitler's fulminations against the Jews that a number of prominent Jewish citizens are reported to have sought safe asylums in the Bavarian highlands, easily reached by fast motor cars, whence they could hurry their women and children when forewarned of an anti-Semitic St. Bartholomew's night.

But several reliable, well-informed sources confirmed the idea that Hitler's anti-Semitism was not so genuine or violent as it sounded, and he was using anti-Semitic propaganda as a bait to catch messes of followers and keep them aroused, enthusiastic and in line for the time when his organization is perfected and sufficiently powerful to be employed effectively for political purposes.

A sophisticated politician credited Hitler with peculiar political cleverness for laying emphasis and over-emphasis on anti-Semitism, saying: "You can't expect the masses to understand or appreciate your finer real aims. You must feed the masses with cruder morsels and ideas like anti-Semitism. It would be politically all wrong to tell them the truth about where you are leading them."

The Hitler movement is not of mere local or picturesque interest. It is bound to bring Bavaria into a renewed clash with the Berlin Government as long as the German Republic goes even through the motions of trying to live up to the Versailles Treaty. For it is certain the Allies will take umbrage at the Hitler organization as a violation of the military clauses of the treaty and demand disbandment, even as in the case of its predecessor, the Orgesch.

How Fascisti of Italy Put Down Bolshevism
The Spokesman-Review/November 26, 1922

American Member of Organization
Describes Inner Workings and Experiences

When I arrived in Rome last March my intention was to stay awhile in the Eternal City and see as many of the sights that I could. To see them all is practically impossible, as there is hardly a stone in the ancient town which has not some historical interest or other. After a week or two there, my plans were to go to Spain and spend the rest of the winter there. Florence had not entered into my calculations at all.

One day, however, I met a friend who was going there, and he staked me to come along. I agreed, but intending to stay two weeks at the most. We left Rome that afternoon, arrived in Florence in the evening, and I stayed five long months.

One of my friends in Florence, a Count di Lucca. was a director of the local organization of fascism there. We talked politics several times, and one day he asked me if I should like to join the fascists.

I answered that it would give me a great deal of pleasure, as I sympathized with the movement, but wondered if, being an American citizen, the affair could be arranged. Lucca said it didn't make any difference what nationality I was, as long as I was not German or Russian.

So one evening in April Lucca and another director and I walked down several narrow streets and stopped finally before a small door with a grated peep-hole in it. After we had knocked and been inspected by the doorman we entered a large, bare room with a stone floor, benches and a few maps hung on the walls.

This room was filled with men smoking and talking rapid Italian. One of them got up to meet us, and led us into an inner chamber, furnished with a rolltop desk, two or three chairs, and more maps. Lucca introduced me to the treasurer in Italian and I was given blanks to fill out.

When I had done this I paid an initiation fee of 44 lire for the year, received a fascisti pin and was enrolled among the members of the organization. So much for joining, which was simple enough. It was very interesting, however, and I am proud of being, so far as I know, the only American fascists.

Joins Peasant To Noble

What I noticed about the crowd gathered at the headquarters of the organization was its heterogeneous quality. There were peasants from the country, small shopkeepers of the city, and members of the well-to-do bourgeois, all mingling together and all very friendly and companionable.

This is, of course, the strength of the movement; it is all-embracing. Fascism has filled in the gap between the peasant and the noble; it has united both to the middle class.

And what is fascism? It is organized and militant resistance to the ideas and practices of Bolshevism and communism. The fascisti are for law and order, and therefore against the bolshevists.

After the war, Italy was in a pretty chaotic state. The communists got possession of many of the factories, and succeeded fairly well in further disrupting the government. It was at this time, when it looked as though Italy would follow in Russia's footsteps, that the idea of fascism was born.

All patriotic Italians joined the organization, and with their sticks and axes started to make things hot for the bolshevists. Even now there are still occasional encounters between the communists and the fascisti; while I was in Rome there were two or three street fights, with four or five casualties. But compared with the state of affairs of a year or so ago, absolute peace reigns.

In Florence, at the time of the greatest trouble, there was a pitched battle on the bridge of Sta. Trinita, in which machine guns and hand grenades were used. In fact, it was quite a usual thing two years ago to see a fascists in his black shirt, khaki trousers and green sash, with a grenade in each hand, rushing down a narrow street to help his comrades hold a barricade.

My Mild Experiences

My own experiences as a member of the fascisti were mild enough, due to the fact that the communists had been pretty well cowed, and most of the fighting was over. There were 1500 fascisti in Florence in uniforms, not counting older men who had no special costumes.

Once a week there was a march into the country with flags and a band, which created great enthusiasm among the people, and was an impressive sight to see. When the king came to Florence all the fascisti turned out to meet him, and marched in procession to the station. I formed part of this parade, and had a very interesting time.

There was music and flags, the streets were lined with troops and people, and every time we passed the spot where a fascists had been killed by a communist all hats came off and the flags were lowered.

I fancy I must have created a rather strange appearance. I did not have a uniform, so walked along in a blue tweed suit, with cane and a gray fedora hat. The Florentines probably thought I was wearing the uniform of the American fascisti.

Split into Five Parties

To anyone living in this country, where we have a strong central government, the situation in Italy, where the king and cabinet allow movements such as fascism to exist and prosper, must appear inconceivable. You forget, however, that the Italian government as its stands today under the fascisti numbers five parties, not counting representatives of the army and navy who sympathize with them.

There are five members of the fascisti party, two Catholics, two democrats, one nationalist and one liberal.

This gives control to the fascisti, who I hope will agree with each other; the prospects of the rest of the cabinet being d'accord is small indeed.

In America we have two strong parties, with issues pretty definitely cut; in Italy public opinion is, or was, divided into five parts, and the stability of the government correspondingly precarious. The king was never sure of the cooperation of his ministers, and, consequently, always felt hampered in action.

Now, however, it looks as if the fascisti had public opinion pretty much their own way, and could give Italy the stable government she needs. I hope so, for she's a great country.

Black Shirts, Italian Style

Like Bloodhounds on Trail of Bolshevism

Clayton S. Cooper of New York tells interesting details of the fascisti movement in an interview in the Tribune as follows:

ANYONE who chanced to be in Italy in August, especially in the neighborhood of Milan and Genoa, would have concluded that young Italy's wish for an active ministry was being fulfilled with a vengeance. The socialists and communists called a strike on railways, street car lines and in a number of industries. The fascisti promptly informed Roma that unless the government intervened to break the strike at once or in 24 hours they, the fascisti, would run the cars and break it.

The government, as in the industrial strike of 1920, when the workers seized the factories in north Italy and tried to run them, did nothing, remained passive or neutral, and the fascisti kept their promise. They sent out a nationwide mobilization order for their 400,000 or more active adherents, and in a week they had not only broken the labor strike, but also virtually routed and largely destroyed the socialistic and communistic power in Italy.

They Run Cars

On the morning of August 21 I was awakened in my hotel at Milan about 6 o'clock by the voices and cheering of hundreds of people gathered in the great square before Milan cathedral. I looked out to see a half dozen trolley cars swinging into the plaza loaded with black-shirted fascisti, the cars with their sides draped with tri-color and fascisti emblems, with fascisti at the motors and fascisti as conductors, even some of the more enthusiastic youths of the order riding on the roofs of the cars, crying "Viva fascisti!" and leading in the singing of their national songs.

The square was filled with citizens seemingly of all classes, many of the applauders being of the employer class evidently, and there was no doubt as to what public opinion generally thought about the matter. I wondered at the lack of resistance to the strikebreakers on the part of the socialists. Perhaps the vigor with which the fascisti went to the attack overawed them, or they may have read the signs of the times during the preceding months when the Mussolinian legions were enrolling by the hundreds daily fresh recruits with which to fight radicalism and all forms of Bolshevism in Italy.

Like Bloodhounds

To be sure, there were some fatalities and some broken heads, for the "black shirts" were like bloodhounds on the trail of any communist or radical who showed himself in public. While I was in Genoa the fascisti stormed the socialist headquarters, and the streets for a day or two were swept clear of pedestrians, while armored cars and machine guns and bands of fierce looking youths with clubs and wearing their deaths-head belts filled the main thoroughfares. It was clearly a case of clan war, with the radicals on the defensive. The fascisti had accepted the challenge of Marxian socialism, driving it to cover by the use of its own rough and violent method, and doing it first.

It is not easy for an American to understand bow such a bloodless revolution could come about as that which marked Italy the last days of October, when over the ruins of a ministry forced out by threats of violent seizure a large composite army, representing peasants, industrial workers, sons of wealth and culture, farmers and nobility—an army even more picturesque than Garibaldi's famous "thousand"—entered the gates of the historic Roman city, borne along on the applause of the multitudes like legions of some Caesar returning from their wars.

It seemed less incongruous to the Italians, evidently, for the king himself, keeping his head and saving the day, received the new Garibaldi with embraces and extended to him the premiership, saying: "I am persuaded that with the best energy, enthusiasm and faith of the country enlisted all will go well."

Against the Socialists

As a matter of fact one must understand something of the genesis of this movement of fascism in Italy in order to judge the present situation. The fascisti did not originally anticipate any such national power and prestige as force of circumstances has now thrust upon them. The movement began as a more or less loosely organized band of ex-soldiers, students and shock troops, who were determined that the wars suffering and tragedies would not go for naught. Fascism first represented a justified reaction against the excesses of the socialists. With many other Italians these early fascisti also felt that Italy had not received just treatment at the Versailles conference and they were particularly desirous that the country for which they had fought should secure its rightful place in the sun. At first, when the bolshevist influences appeared among the Italian workmen the fascisti assumed some of the characteristics of the Ku Klux Klan and their methods could hardly be justified in anything like a law-abiding democracy.

In Florence, for example, the fascisti were frequently reported to have captured socialist and communist leaders and under threat of violence and even death at times ordered them to induce their men to go back to work. The engineer of a large power house in Florence was seized by the representatives of this self-appointed police and notified that if the lights of the city were not restored in an hour's time both he and his family would suffer the consequences .

It is needless to say that such pressure brought to bear by armed men usually had the effect of producing prompt action. In certain instances the work of the fascisti in its earlier days was decidedly for the benefit of the community, as in the case of the strike of the peasant laborers at Ferrara at the moment when the harvest was being gathered. The fascisti appeared upon the scene, gathered the crops, then nailed a notice on the church door warning the strikers that the fascisti been there and that any reprisals against the landlords would be met with instant death.

In accordance with the Italian love for the dramatic and the picturesque, the fascisti methods were both vivid and unexpected. The massing of large numbers of fascisti in the midst of communist or socialist uprisings was a common method of impressing the enemy. Last summer, when trouble arose in the vicinity of Florence, the fascisti organized a parade, calling in their adherents from the surrounding country, and marched 80,000 armed men through the streets of the Florentine city.

Fascism Makes Rapid Strides
Charlotte Observer/December 25, 1922

The Fascisti Movement is Growing in Mexico, Says Report

Preparations Are in Progress for National Convention in Mexico City

The fascisti movement which at its inception in Jalapa several months ago was ridiculed as of no importance has made such rapid strides during the post few weeks that high government officials are now recognizing it as a political factor to be reckoned with in the near future.

Reports from various cities of clashes in which the fascisti have taken part against the radicals indicate that the movement is gaining impetus. Thus far these clashes have not been of a sanguinary character. President Obregon said recently there could be no fascism in Mexico because it was a movement against Bolshevism and Bolshevism did not exist in Mexico.

Senor De La Huerta, minister of the treasury, speaking to the newspapermen Saturday, admitted the presence of fascisti organizations in Mexico; but he described fascism as a "mere exotic plant" and as "the conservatives' war cry against the Mexican people." The minister added that fascism flourished In other countries "by accident, and under circumstances which do not obtain in Mexico."

Senor De La Huerta expressed it as his belief that the proletariat would reject the idea of fascism and not "commit suicide."

Fascisti headquarters here report that the movement is receiving hundreds of new adherents daily and that preparations are in progress for a national convention which is to be held in Mexico City during the second week of January. Every state in the republic is to be represented by several hundred delegates.

Following the appointment of a temporary board of directors the fascisti have issued a manifesto to the nation in which the aims and ideals of the organization are explained. The regional federation of labor from its headquarters in Mexico is active in its propaganda against the fascisti.

German Fascism
The Post-Crescent/December 28, 1922

Berlin—Writing in the BERLINER VOLKSZEITUNG Hermann Schutzinger gives warning of the dangers of Bavarian Fascism. He says:

"Under the ruins of the fallen Empire lurk the same spirit of violence and brutality in home and foreign politics as existed under the old rule. The ancient land of Germany is again in effervescence ever since the exploits of Mussolini beyond the Alps, and we see unscrupulous firebrands preparing secret fires here and there whence Germany fascism will be engendered.

"The great flame which at the proper moment is to set light to Germany can only come from a part where public power has only blunted arms to fight fascism, that is to say, from Bavaria.

"The German Mussolini, Hitler, proclaims in public: 'With five hundred courageous Germans, we shall gain the day! The time for action will soon be here.' His adjutant, Esser, is traveling through the Rhine countries, through Central and North Germany to rally the partisans of revolution, to raise their enthusiasm for the day of the great upheaval. The HEIMATLAND, the organ of the former Bavarian civil guard, seems to think that the hour has come. It announces the 'triumph of fascism' and advocates, under the protecting cloak of the Bavarian police, storming the parliaments, the houses of syndicates and newspaper-offices.

"Bavarian fascism is a product of the Kahr government. It has been favored by the Bavarian police, financed by the federation of Bavarian industrialists and protected by the ancient civil guards.

"The leader of the Bavarian fascisti, Hitler, is only the instrument of forces in higher positions; he is no imbecile, he is a very clever

79

demagogue. The man behind him is Ludendorff. The aims of the Bavarian fascisti are very high. They abandon the collaboration of the Bavarian Landtag. They aim at nothing less than the establishment of a national dictatorship in German-speaking territory. They have connivance with the Germans of Austria, Hungary, Northern Italy and even Poland. Their propaganda has very cleverly made use of the state of mind of the middle classes following the war. Their object has been clearly expressed: the constitution of a thoroughly disciplined army of three hundred thousand men, divided first into secret regimental associations.

"It goes without saying that the Bavarian fascisti have the moral and material support of the whole Bavarian reactions: the peasants of Upper Bavaria, the Munich officers of the 'bourgeoisie', the Bavarian newspapermen all cheer when Hitler's battalions march past . . . . Mussolini has electrified all the world in Bavaria; the peasant association, the leagues of ex-soldiers, the editors of national papers and the national-socialists.

"It is true an immediate revolt would meet with obstacles on its way. The Bavarian clergy cannot follow fascism on all its points . . . . Escherich also makes difficulties. He thinks it would be imprudent to start too quickly. On the other hand the extremists, consisting of money-lenders, etc., are impatient. . . The question is who will carry the day.

"Everybody who has seen Hitler's well organized battalions marching in Munich to the music of the Reich's troops camouflaged as civilians, with the flag, ornamented with a hooked cross (antisemitic), the cudgel and the pistol at the waist, have realized the danger which threatens us. . ."

Dictatorship, With Hitler As Dictator, Is Dream of Bavarian Radicals, Spurred On by the Success of Mussolini in Italy

St. Louis Post-Dispatch/January 4, 1923

National Socialist Peril is Growing Along With the Distresses of the German People, Count Hugo Lerchenfeld Writes

Anti-Semitic Nationalism Feeds Passions of the Masses but Their Leader Denies He Plans to Use Violence to Attain Goal

Premier Bonar Law declares that the German republic is about to collapse, financially and otherwise. Count Hugo Lerchenfeld, the author of this article, is ex-Premier of Bavaria. He married an American woman, Miss Ethel Louise Wyman, admits that Germany is undergoing a process of intense unrest and fermentation, that the old imperialistic order has passed and that the new order struggling to assert itself in the German Empire, from Bavaria as a center, is firing Germans with a new enthusiasm and a new hope.

Kemal Pasha in Turkey, Benito Mussolini in Italy and now Otto Hitler in Bavaria! What is the mysterious force in these leaders which commands unquestioning fidelity?

The ancients believed in the existence of demons, powerful spirits between the gods and men.

Goethe defines the inexplicable, incomprehensible in nature and humanity as demonic.

Not in the leader's art of oratory nor in the mere words he uses, for he often takes refuge in platitudes. A mysterious driving force communicates itself to his audience and inspire them to action.

In such a leader the hopes and aspirations of thousands crystallize. A group of blindly faithful adherents gathers round him and forms the backbone of the new movement.

Hitler calls this bodyguard his "storm troops," as the small detachments of picked men in every regiment were called, to whom specially daring missions were intrusted. Official National Socialist headquarters organizes the party system, the registered members provide the funds, but when courage and reckless determination are necessary.

Hitler calls out his storm troops. They maintain order in the great mass meetings, break up the meetings of political opponents, lead sensational recruiting raids into the provinces with brass bands and red flags bearing the anti-Semitic emblem.

Funds Must Be Plentiful

Funds must be plentiful, for special trains, extravagant posters, and mass meetings with admission free are costly luxuries! Radicalism of every kind appeals above all to youth, and Hitler's storm troops and active workers are all young. They have been called the Bolsheviks of the Right, and since they aim at the destruction of constitutional government and the dissolution of, the existing order of things that a free and powerful Germany may rise from the ruins, a certain similarity of method cannot be denied.

Communism on a nationalistic and anti-Semitic basis! National Socialism plays with fire and upon the passions of the masses. This movement has already become a political factor which no statesman can afford to ignore, and may possibly develop into a great danger. It refuses to subordinate itself, to follow any beaten track. Hitler himself has probably only vague ideas of what he would do if he came into power tomorrow. He despises Cabinets and Parliaments, and looks upon all political parties as limited by petty party interests and incapable of preparing the way for a better future.

A dictatorship, with Hitler as dictator and savior of the country, the elimination of Cabinets and Diets—this sums up in a few words the ideals of the National Socialists. The storm troops are supposed to keep the Socialists in order, while the army and police force look on in benevolent passivity!

Denies Planning Violence

Will Hitler attempt to attain these ends by means of violence? He himself denies this, declares that no rash coup, but only the unanimous will of the people can vest him with the dictatorial powers necessary to carry out his ideas of reform. It remains to be seen whether he can really restrain his excitable followers in the critical months to come.

The extreme Nationalists in Munich, enraged by the compromise of the Cabinet with the Central Government in Berlin over the defense of the republic act, planned to over throw the Bavarian Government the end of August. Hitler used all his authority to prevent it.

The former Prime Minister von Kahr and especially Poehner, former President of the Police, encouraged the National Socialist movement and considered Hitler an ally against the Socialists. whom they bitterly opposed. The Lerchenfeld Cabinet held itself aloof from all nationalistic influences and realized that the Bolsheviks of the Right were hardly less dangerous than the Communists, the Bolsheviks of the Left.

It is my firm conviction that it is useless to try to fight Socialism with violence or artificial means. I hold that it is wiser to give the Socialists responsibility and to raise the political education of the people to a plane of ideals beyond the Socialist level. This, however, is too slow a process for the National Socialists, who have fought me from the very beginning.

The Danger Grows

Their lawless methods must bring them into conflict with every moderate Government, and my successor von Knilling, in his first speech in the Bavarian Diet, has declared his determination to uphold. State authority at any cost.

I repeat with emphasis my former statement: The danger of the National Socialist movement grows with the increasing hopelessness of the German people, and will diminish in exact proportion as practical help, a loan, a moratorium makes it seem probable that the worst is over and that the path begins to lead upward toward the light again.

As Mussolini's success in Italy has been a great spur to Hitler and his followers, and since many people believe that he will shortly make an effort to follow Mussolini's brilliant example, a comparison between Fascism and National Socialism is not without interest. Both leaders have traits in common. Both appeal to the patriotic youth, both plan great reforms at any price, both despise constitutional governments, but here the similarity ends.

Italy is a free country with a monarchy and an army. Germany is completely disarmed, weakened by dissension and discontent. The foreign occupation of the proud provinces on the Rhine is a thorn in festering flesh. Italy is master of its fate, Germany is not.

Public Always Loser

The origin of both movements, in Italy as in Bavaria, lay in the weakness of the Government and of state authority generally.

Ever since the close of the war, one parliamentary Cabinet in Italy has followed the other without achieving either improvement at home or success in foreign policy. Things simply drifted. In the conflict between employers and employed all over the country, terror and syndicalism triumphed and the Government, inert and neutral, did not dare to intervene. There was no personal contact between the Government and the army or the former soldiers. The army was no longer a reliable instrument in the hands of the Cabinet, and the King, partly owing to his personality and partly to his peculiar constitutional position, was forced to stand aloof.

In Germany the very feeble authority of the state is due to the revolution and to the impotence imposed upon the Government by the Treaty of Versailles. Many German citizens detest the republic. Under the united pressure of the allies, no Government so far has brought back from the numerous conferences in Spa, London, Genoa and elsewhere, anything even remotely resembling concession or success which might have won the respect of the German public. They are always on the losing side and this, of course, does not tend to make them popular.

Italy's Dreams Revised

But there is another fundamental difference between the two nations. Italy is a united and centralized country and from the Alps to Sicily, Italian youth arose as one man in response to Mussolini's call. Germany, in spite of the centralizing tendencies of Socialism and of the Constitution of Weimar in 1919, is a union of distinct Federal states, and the forces at work to prevent the formation of a centralized Government are preponderant. Hitler is essentially South German in type and his National Socialist party was localized here in Bavaria until Within the last few months.

Mussolini has awakened the spirit of Italy. Caporetto was a crushing defeat for the Italian army, and it only retrieve itself in Vittorio Veneto, thanks to the demoralization of the Austrians. This little detail however, it is more comforting to ignore. Victory is intoxicating, and

84

the triumph of the Italian troops in the Veneto was wind in the sails of Mussolini's cause. He has revived Italy's dreams of the grandeur of ancient Rome, and restored to his people their pride in their beautiful country. Even the Italian working man is ashamed of having coquetted with Moscow and reproaches the indifferent Cabinets of the last four years with having failed to pluck the fruits of Vittorio Veneto.

Greater Than He Is Needed

The basis of National Socialism is much narrower and less positive in comparison to Fascism. Germany can nourish no illusions comparable to Vittorio Veneto, no Fata Morgana such as the domination of the Mediterranean. The German people is divided in its judgment upon the war and upon the possibilities of escape from present difficulties. Thousands seek salvation in Socialism and turn with loathing from every reminder of imperial greatness. Others lose themselves in the mazes of a nebulous pacifism and the reactionaries see no hope except in a complete restoration of the fallen empire.

Only a comparatively small number see conditions as they really are and their arguments in favor of moderation, consolidation and common sense, rendered futile by the merciless policy of our late enemies, fall for the most part on deaf ears.

It needs a greater man than Hitler to wild the conflicting convictions of a defeated people into national unity.

In spite of his deficient education Mussolini is a true child of Italy, and as such part heir to that classic culture which permeates Italian soil and Italian character to a degree impossible elsewhere. With an unheard-of gesture he has swung himself to the summit of power.

Becomes Constitutional

He has scourged the weakness of Cabinets, the insufficiency of Parliaments and has belittled political party creeds. Now, with the same gesture of supreme superiority, he calls a halt and becomes constitutional. He will, perhaps, find it difficult to convince his impassioned followers that the Rubicon is crossed, the Fascist revolution ended. The attitude of the King has greatly facilitated matters for him. Mussolini must now humbly await his messages as the Roman Senate awaited the messages of Octavianus Augustus backed by the power of the Roman Legions!

The most difficult part of his task lies before him; to build up instead of pulling down, work and responsibility in the place of irresponsible criticism. Mussolini's first speech was dazzling, but it contained very few practical propositions. I can only advise those Germans who burn to follow Mussolini's example to have a little patience until they see what the next few weeks of his domination bring forth.

Heaven grant that Germany be spared any such experiment! According to my views, her only salvation lies in Christian idealism, in prosaic hard work and renunciation, in national consolidation and common sense. Only these qualities will gain for us the esteem of the rest of the world, but we have the right to address one demand to all civilized nations:

Take us off the operating table on which we have been stretched out ever since Versailles!

Spare us these, amputations, interesting for the surgeons but deadly for the patient!

Spare us all these painful examinations to decide how much life's blood, how many vital organs can be tourniqueted without resulting in death! We are tired of it!

Mussolini, Europe's Prize Bluffer
Toronto Daily Star/January 27, 1923

Ernest Hemingway

Mussolini is the biggest bluff in Europe. If Mussolini would have me taken out and shot tomorrow morning I would still regard him as a bluff. The shooting would be a bluff. Get hold a good photo of Signor Mussolini sometime and study it. You still see the weakness in his mouth which forces him to scowl the famous Mussolini scowl that is imitated by every 19-year-old Fascist in Italy. Study his past record. Study the coalition that Fascism is between capital and labor and consider the history of past coalitions. Study his genius for clothing small ideas in big words. Study his propensity for dueling. Really brave men do not have to fight duels, and many cowards duel constantly to make themselves believe they are brave. And then look at his black shirt and white spats. There is something wrong, even histrionically, with a man who wears white spats with a black shirt.

There is not space here to go into the question of Mussolini as a bluff or as a great and lasting force. Mussolini may last fifteen years or he may be overthrown next spring by Gabriele D'Annunzio, who hates him. But let me give two true pictures of Mussolini at Lausanne.

The Fascist dictator had announced he would receive the press. Everybody came. We all crowded into the room. Mussolini sat at his desk reading a book. His face was contorted into the famous frown. He was registering Dictator. Being an ex-newspaperman himself he knew how many readers would be reached by the accounts the men in the room would write of the interview he was about to give. And he remained absorbed in his book. Mentally he was already reading the lines of the two thousand papers served by the two hundred correspondents. "As we entered the room the Black Shirt Dictator did not look up from the book he was reading, so intense was his concentration, etc."

I tiptoed over behind him to see what the book was he was reading with such avid interest. It was a French-English dictionary–held upside down.

The other picture of Mussolini as Dictator was on the same day when a group of Italian women living in Lausanne came to the suite of rooms at the Beau Rivage Hotel to present him with a bouquet of roses. There were six women of the peasant class, wives of workmen living in Lausanne, and they stood outside the door waiting to do honor to Italy's new national hero who was their hero. Mussolini came out of the door in his frock coat, his gray trousers and his white spats. One of the women stepped forward and commenced her speech. Mussolini scowled at her, sneered, let his big-whited African eyes roll over the other five women and went back into the room. The unattractive peasant women in their Sunday clothes were left holding their roses. Mussolini had registered Dictator.

Half an hour later he met Clare Sheridan, who has smiled her way into many interviews, and had time for half an hour's talk with her.

Of course the newspaper correspondents of Napoleon's time may have seen the same things in Napoleon, and the men who worked on the

Giornale d'Italia in Caesar's day may have found the same discrepancies in Julius, but after an intimate study of the subject there seems to be a good deal more of Bottomley, an enormous, warlike, duel-fighting, successful Italian Horatio Bottomley, in Mussolini than there does of Napoleon.

It isn't really Bottomley though. Bottomley was a great fool. Mussolini isn't a fool and he is a great organizer. But it is a very dangerous thing to organize the patriotism of a nation if you are not sincere, especially when you work its patriotism to such a pitch that it offers to loan money to the government without interest. Once the Latin has sunk his money in a business he wants results and he is going to show Signor Mussolini that it is much easier to be the opposition to a government than to run the government yourself.

A new opposition will rise, it is forming already, and it will be led by that bold, bald-headed, perhaps a little insane but thoroughly sincere, divinely brave swashbuckler, Gabriele D'Annunzio.

Fascism In Germany Threatens New Crisis
Daily News (New York)/January 28, 1923

European Developments Yesterday

The Ruhr was completely cut off from the remainder of Germany at daybreak today (Sunday).

Fascism sweeping Bavaria may force French to take further military action. Foreigners attacked and insulted.

German women and children reported attacked by French soldiers with sabers. Many wounded.

More French troops moved to newly occupied area to strengthen the customs barrier.

The German Government urges economy in coal, as present supply will last only forty days.

German Fascisti Again Threaten Government

Further French Military Action Feared; Bavarians Attack Foreigners

Fascism, sweeping over Germany, particularly Bavaria, may force the French to take further military action.

Persecution and attacks on foreigners, especially the French, including members of the Interallied Mission at Munich, threaten to develop into bloodshed and assassinations. The French are preparing measures to cope with such an eventuality.

Vivid reports of Bavarian insolence and outrages on foreigners—Americans and British, as well as French—in Munich, reached Paris tonight, recounting how armed parties forced their entry into hotels and warned foreigners to leave within forty-eight hours.

Americans Warned Out

Persons heard speaking in other languages than German were mobbed, spat on and driven out of restaurants in Munich. Additional cars have been requested to carry out foreigners seeking to escape from the menaces and threats.

American authorities in Munich are warning citizens to quit Bavaria, and visas of passports are not granted unless demanded by urgent business.

Any military operations necessary to enforce respect for foreigners' lives in Bavaria would require a considerable force and probably entail the usage of the Little Entente, as the Czecho-Slovaks are within the quickest reach of the scene.

Situation in Hand

Gen. Weygand today reported that the situation in the Ruhr was satisfactory at the cabinet meeting at which Marshal Foch was present. Gen. Weygand said Gen. Degoutte had the situation well in hand and complimented the French for their restraints under insults and the temptation to commit reprisals Thursday in Essen and Dusseldorf.

The cabinet decided today not to attempt to operate the Ruhr mines and factories if the strike ties them up, but merely to preserve order and hold the area.

Gen. Degoutte is concentrating much motor transport in the Ruhr to insure maintenance of communications and supplies for his forces.

French Saber Women In Outbreak at Trier

A number of German women and children were wounded at Trier today when French troops used sabers in dispersing a demonstration, according to reports reaching Berlin.

Many cities of the Ruhr were under virtual martial law today, and the situation, after a fortnight's occupation by the French, still was tense with possibility of trouble.

"Excitement in the Ruhr Valley is increasing rapidly, and an explosion is possible at any moment," Fritz Thyssen, Ruhr coal baron, said in an interview today.

German Fascism Threatens War; Grows By Leaps
The Leader-Post/February 5, 1923

Communists Desert to Join Forces With "Revolt Against Machine"

Germany's "Fascisti" movement has received strong impetus from the French advance in the Ruhr district. Recent dispatches showed that in Bavaria the organization came into the open with its own flag and a demand for the overthrow of the present republic. The following article by the New York World's Central Europe correspondent reveals the extent and the high importance of this movement, as well as its spirit:

Revolt against industrialism has come to Germany in its most fateful hour. It is a revolt against the machine of industry, against mass production, against the time clock, against the factory whistle.

It calls itself National Socialism, it is the German form of Fascism: it is at the same time similar to the anti-factory movement in India, China and Japan. It is part of the worldwide expression of individualism that is in "deaf revolt" against excessive government in any form. It is against the old German paternalism and is equally against Communism and the ideal of a factory state.

May Bring New War

Being a "mouvement sourd," as the French express it, it is an unknown factor in politics and may end by doing a lot of unexpected things. If it does not tear the world apart, it may prove to be its regeneration. Coming simultaneously with the nationalistic reaction which is following Bolshevism, it is more likely to send Europe into another period of warfare.

Adolf Hitler, an ex-Austrian army officer, is the first German Fascist leader to take advantage of the revolt, and the success he is having in Bavaria should make anyone realize it is a movement to be reckoned with, perhaps as important as the Marxian Socialism which culminated in the Russian Bolshevik revolution.

National Socialism is growing throughout Germany by leaps and bounds, and one of the possibilities to be reckoned with is a Fascist movement that would change everything. A Fascist revolt would jar the present Republican Government into something else; it would knock the Treaty of Versailles into a cocked hat; it would start out to construct a brand new map of Europe. These things it would do, and other things besides.

The new Fascist flag was solemnly raised in the Munich Field of Mars while 3,000 National Socialists saluted and swore to support it and then listened to their leader, Hitler, denounce the Republicans as traitors.

As the red banner with its black swastika in a white field and the inscription "Germany Awake," floated from the flagstaff which was surmounted with the old Imperial eagle, Hitler cried:

"Germany has had no flag since 1918, when the time honored flag was furled. Germany will only be master of both sides of the Rhine when she marches under the new swastika banner to victory."

The leader told the delegates, who had come from all parts of the country, to go home and get recruits for the party on the platform: "Down with the Versailles Treaty; death to traitors and profiteers."

91

It is significant that several factory organizations which were once Communist have turned National Socialist and had representatives at Munich. Communist leaders worried by this disaffection declared a fight to the finish against the Fascisti.

The Rote Fahne, organ of the Communists, says delay will mean that the National Socialists will overwhelm them.

Many of the Munich Fascisti at the flag raising wore steel helmets and carried revolvers. The Overland Corps, the most militant of German organizations, attended.

Although officially opposed, German monarchists are delighted with the success of the Fascisti. Reactionary papers print enthusiastic accounts of their activities in Munich. The Deutsche Zeitung declares Hitler has his followers well disciplined and "it was a notable occasion when National Socialists cried defiance to the French."

At the same time efforts are being made in Hamburg to get German officers, ex-soldiers and engineers to enter the Deutsches Bund. In Kiel Count Westap has demanded a German Dictator; in Luebeck. Gen. von Morgen called for a national uprising. All are signs of the beginning of a new reactionary movement.

At Work in Bewildered Land

It took Marxian Socialism seventy-five years, constant propaganda and the development of several generations of Socialists to reach a culminating point, but it was working against a powerfully organized world. National Socialism, as it is called, or the Revolt Against Industrialism, as it should be called, is at work in a broken world, one filled with violent and contradictory tendencies, in which the social and political currents are confused.

It is at work in a Germany which has not the slightest idea where it is going either socially or politically. Industrial life has become here an unbearable drudgery and the victim of the industrial machine has not even the hope of better things that comes of breaking away from the machine. It is excellent ground upon which to develop revolt of any kind, and this happens to be a spiritual, hence the most hardy of revolts.

Italian Fascism was a nationalistic movement that came out of the war. A year or so ago it was chiefly conspicuous among ex-soldiers and the young sons of ordinary bourgeois families. It was spurred to greater activity by the Communists, who threatened to seize Italian industry. It fed on its own strength, grew stronger yet with the taste of power, had a brainstorm and made of Mussolini dictator of Italy.

If this happened in comparatively happy Italy, there is no telling what such a movement could not do in a desperate Germany.

Grows in Rural Germany

But there is one practical consideration. The Italian Fascists had their greatest strength in the factory centers, Milan, Turin, Bologna. They hold the centers of Italy. The south of Italy, where there is no organized industry, played no role in Fascism.

In Germany, Fascism is growing for the present in the non-factory, the non-Socialist regions. It is strongest in Bavaria, Silesia, Mecklenberg, East Prussia. As a political movement it is checked by the existence of Marxian Socialism.

All industrial Germany is politically organized by the Socialists, and they have been able to defeat the inroads of National Socialism by labeling it a monarchist movement. Politically they have held it in check, but it is fundamentally a spiritual movement; that is the basis on which it is growing. As a spiritual movement it has for a long time existed in the midst of Socialism. It would not be so difficult as the Socialist leaders think to change the German Socialist workmen into National Socialists. The Italian Fascists did a similar thing in Italy. The German Fascists have misery and the French invasion of the Ruhr to help them.

National Socialism will not do things until it is just as strong in the industrial regions as it is in Bavaria. Every night these days the National Socialists are holding enormous meetings in Munich. The day they hold similar successful meetings in the great industrial centers—in Halle, for example—they will be masters of Germany. And this day may come sooner than anyone, including the Socialists, may think.

Romance of Benito Mussolini, Locksmith's Son, Who Rose to Dictatorship of Italy

El Paso Times/February 11, 1923

Correspondent Tells Remarkable Story of Young Man Who Governs Italy by Might

Premier a Man of Few Words, Who Is Tremendously Conscious of His Own Importance

One day last October the king of Italy, in his palace in ancient Rome, ordered his aide-de-camp to communicate with a certain young man in Milan.

The young man was neither a prince nor an eminent statesman. He happened to be the son of a locksmith. Moreover, he had been strangely named after the executioner of an emperor. He was dressed in a black shirt and carried a revolver. He had been a revolutionary, a tramp, a convict, an exile. He was then running a small newspaper. A peculiar young man for a king to seek out. But 100,000 other young men, also wearing black shirts, were at the gates of Rome. Never in its immemorial past of sieges and invasions had Rome seen such an army. The king was in a hurry. The shadows of the Romanoffs and the Hapsburgs and the Hohenzollerns, perhaps, haunted him.

King Calls Mussolini to Rome

The young man in Milan was at the telephone listening. His majesty invited him to come to Rome immediately. The aide-de-camp pressed for an answer. But the son of the locksmith shrugged his shoulders. He would not move upon a telephone request, even though it came from the king. Did the king need him in Rome? Very well, he could extend his invitation in writing.

It was Sunday. The king didn't wish to do any business on Sunday. But the long shadow of the impetuous army of black shirts hourly grew darker over the capital. Their commanders, Devecchi and Grandi, went to implore the king's aide-de-camp to dispatch a telegram to the obdurate son of the locksmith. There was no time to be lost.

The king finally realized that this Sunday was unlike any other Sunday in his life.

He dictated a telegram to Mussolini, the editor in the black shirt. Half an hour later, with unprecedented rapidity for Italy, it reached its destination.

It is 2 o'clock p. m. Sunday, October 20. The young man in the black shirt, his piercingly black eyes radiating a smile of triumph, turns to his brother at the desk.

Invitation Comes on His Birthday

"Arnaldo, we must issue an extra. The king has entrusted me with the task of forming a new government." And passing between rows of desks, he smilingly walks out into the street.

It is a striking coincidence that it was also on a Sunday, at 2 o'clock p. m., and on the 29th of the month, 39 years ago, that a son was born in the humble hut of one Alexander Mussolini, a locksmith notorious throughout the province of Romagna as a violent internationalist.

The locksmith admired revolutionary heroes. He christened his son Benito, after Benito Juarez, a Mexican revolutionary leader and president, who executed Maximilian, the Austrian emperor of Mexico.

Today the son of the locksmith, Benito Mussolini, is the dictator of Italy. Some of his followers believe he is Europe's man of destiny, the Napoleon of the 20th century, who will set the pace of the coming generations.

In three years he forged and welded together the most aggressive party in the world outside of Russia, the *fascisti* organization, an order of young and rash crusaders.

Two weeks after the king summoned him to "govern" Italy he declared in the venerable Italian chamber of deputies:

"With 300,000 boys armed to the teeth, ready for anything and almost mystically at my orders ... I can turn this dull and lazy chamber into an army camp."

Soon after this Napoleonic arrogance he demonstratively made Poincare and Lord Curzon, the prime minister of France and the foreign minister of Great Britain, who were awaiting him for a conference, journey to meet him at his stopping place instead of him going to theirs.

Benito Mussolini has let loose an old formula in a new disguise, the decadent Old World has rapidly taken up the catch-word, and the virus of fascism is now spreading like wildfire everywhere.

"All power to the young!" is Mussolini's popular cry, but its meaning, as ancient as human nature, has been expressed long ago by Louis XV: "The state, it is I."

Fascism has been described as Black Bolshevism. It has been glorified for its extreme nationalism and patriotism and its hostility to socialist and radical trade union organizations in the country.

Its agrarian character attracted small and large property owners and monarchists, and this brought to its ranks the officers of the regular army.

Its agrarian character made it a farmers' movement and its support by certain banks gave it the character of capitalistic conspiracy.

The presence in its ranks of Giolitti "defeatists" and pro-Germans, of adherents of the Vatican, alongside of the masses of war veterans, has bewildered many observers.

Some have analyzed fascism as an expression of Italy's overpopulation due to the immigration barriers in America which used to absorb the energy of hundreds of thousands of young Italians.

When all this is said about fascism, one asks more puzzled than ever, "What, then, is fascism?"

The answer is that fascism is Mussolini—a personality, not a new kind of government.

Who, then, is Mussolini? Born in poverty, son of a locksmith, he became a thief and ragamuffin in his childhood, an elementary school teacher in his youth, a hod-carrier, a revolutionary, a militant pacifist, a violent agitator, a convict in chains, an exile, a deportee as undesirable from two countries, a leader of the socialist party, a journalist and editor, and then a soldier, a patriot, a conspirator, a terrorist crusader, a commander of an army and a triumphant conqueror of Rome and now dictator of his country.

He can run the ship of state as boldly as he can drive an automobile, pilot an airplane, ride a motorcycle, or wield a gun. He can command a national assembly as effectively as he can hypnotize a mob or handle a gang of armed youths. His admirers point to the fact that he is the youngest prime minister in Europe.

An Actor Who Knows His Value

Mussolini made the impression upon me of an actor, of a man who knows his value. His rugged head is set on a frame of medium size. His very high forehead forms a strange contrast to his powerful jaws and fanatical eyes, which lend his face the appearance of a person not altogether normal. He likes to display his small, restless hands, which suggest a fidgety disposition.

I found a certain kinship between Mussolini and Trotsky. Both are tremendously conscious of their importance. Both have swift and eccentric eyes and imperious manners.

Mussolini is a man of few words. He is reserved and often surly. He is affectionate with no one. He has no confidants, no intimate friends. He can concentrate anywhere and write an article in a cafe, amidst a group of uproarious friends, on a street car, or in the theater between acts, surrounded by his wife and three children.

Mussolini is primarily a man of action. He is an admirer of Napoleon and everything Napoleonic in history. Willpower is one of his divinities. He derides the socialists because they lack will. The true followers of Marx, he holds, have no efficiency. History is made, he says, by men of action.

Mussolini hates professors, diplomas, commissions, or conferences. He never asks for proofs of identity or letters of recommendation from the members of his staff. He has one test for them: "Do it!" They are judged by their ability to act and obey and conform to his ideas.

Life-Story Reads Like Romance

His life-story reads like a romance from the age of adventure. In the following autobiographical record he described, in his abrupt style, his childhood:

"I was born July 29, 1883, in Varano de Costa, an old hamlet in central Italy not far from Bologna. I was born on a Sunday at 2 p. m., on the day of the patron of Camminate, the ancient leaning tower from which the last Apennines buttresses dominate the plain of Forli. The sun had been eight days in the constellation of the Lion.

"My father was called Alexander, He had never gone to school. When he was scarcely 10 years of age he was sent to a village Dovadola, as apprentice to a locksmith. From Dovadola he moved to Maldola, where he received internationalist ideas current in the years 1875-1880.

"Having mastered his trade be opened a shop in Dovia. This village did not enjoy a good reputation. The inhabitants were of a brawling disposition. My father worked and at the same time began to spread the idea of the internationale. He founded a society of followers, which was later broken up and dispersed by the police.

"Between the ages of four and five I mastered the primer and in a short time I was able to read correctly.

"The story of my life begins with the age of six. I went to the elementary school between six and nine, being taught first by my mother, then by Silvio Marani and later by the headmaster of Predappio. I was a turbulent and aggressive urchin. I loved only my grandmother. More than once I came home with my head gashed by a stone. But I knew how to take care of myself.

A Most Reckless Country Thief.

"I was a most reckless country thief. During vacation I would arm myself with a small shovel and together with my brother Arnaldo spend my time toiling in the bed of the stream. Once I stole from a bird-trap the birds which were put there as bait. Chased by the owner, I ran frantically down the hill, forded the stream, but did not abandon my loot.

"I would sometimes go to my father's forge. He made me blow the bellows. I had an extraordinary love for birds and particularly for the screech-owl.

"I observed the religious customs together with my mother, who was a believer, and my grandmother, but I could not remain long in church, especially during tedious services. The rosy light of the burning candles, the penetrating odor of incense, the colors of the sacred draperies, the drawling chant of the praying and the sound of the organ disturbed me profoundly."

Mussolini's mother wanted to give her son a higher education at a religious school, and suggested sending Benito to the academy of the Salasian Order.

"My father was at first resolutely against it," Mussolini continued, "but ended up by giving in. In the weeks preceding my departure I was more mischievous than usual. I felt within me a vague unrest. I had a confused presentiment that school and prison were nearly synonymous. I wanted to enjoy the last days of my liberty, to revel in the streets, in the fields, in the ditches in the vineyards among the ripe grapes.

"Finally, everything was ready; clothes, equipment, money. I was not grieved at leaving my brother and sister. Edvige was already three years old, Arnaldo seven. But it hurt me profoundly to abandon a canary which I kept under my window in a cage.

The Donkey Falls—An Ill Omen

At the parting I wept. My father and I seated ourselves in the cart drawn by a donkey. We placed the luggage under our seats and drove off. We had not gone 200 meters when the donkey stumbled and fell.

" 'An ill omen!' said my father, but he helped the donkey rise and we moved on. During the journey I did not utter a word. I kept looking at the landscape, which was beginning to lose its green in the autumn. I followed the flight of the swallows, the course of the stream. We crossed Forli. The city made a deep impression on me.

"I knew only that I had gotten lost there once and that they found me after several hours seated tranquilly near the bench of a shoemaker who had generously given me, a child hardly four years old, the stub of a Tuscan cigar to smoke.

"The strongest impression when we entered Faenza was made upon me by the iron bridge, thrown across the Lamone, which unites the town with the suburbs. It was about 2 o'clock in the afternoon when we knocked at the door of the academy of the Saleslani. The door was opened.

"I was presented to the examiner, who inspected me and said: 'He must be a lively boy.' Then my father embraced and kissed me. He was very moved. When I heard the big gate turn on its hinges I burst into tears."

His career at the academy was short lived. Benito liked a brawl. He attacked his comrades and was severely punished more than once. Finally he was expelled from the academy. His parents placed him in a school nearer home. Although of incorrigible conduct, he was tolerated for his intelligence and abilities. The headmaster, a brother of the famous poet Carducci, made a singular prophecy to the locksmith about his wild son:

"He is a boy of such intelligence that at 30 he will be a minister of state."

During his years at school the young Mussolini was guilty of many an escapade. Once there was a concert in honor of the composer Verdi, given in the municipal theater, which he wanted to attend. But a permit from the school authorities was not to be thought of.

He made a rope out of his bed clothes and with the aid of his comrades descended into the street. In the same way he climbed into the building after the performance and returned to bed.

At the age of 15 he graduated and qualified as an elementary school teacher. To that period belongs his first literary efforts, a controversial article and two sonnets. After long exertion he succeeded in finding a post in a village school. He was 19.

"Gualtieri Emilia," writes Mussolini in his autobiographical sketch, "is a village situated on the bank of the Po. The village is about a kilometer distant from the river and is protected against floods by powerful moles which are used as highways. I arrived there on a gloomy, foggy, afternoon.

"The same day I met the leading citizens of the village, the socialists and officials, and obtained board and lodging for 40 lire ($8) a month.

"My salary as teacher was 56 lire monthly. It was nothing to boast of. The following morning I opened school at once. I had about 40 boys of rather gentle disposition. I grew to love them. At 1 o'clock school was over, and I could dispose of my afternoons and evenings at my pleasure.

"Every Sunday there was dancing in which I also took part. In the meantime the months flew by and the summer vacation was upon us. I conceived the plan of emigrating to Switzerland and trying my fortune there. I telegraphed my mother for money and she sent me 40 lire.

"I arrived in Chiasso, on the border, in the evening of July 9. While waiting for the train which was to take me to Switzerland I bought a Seola (a Milan newspaper) and was more than stupefied and grieved to find in it a correspondence reporting the arrest of my father.

"In Bredappio the voters of the socialist and populist parties had smashed the ballot-boxes to prevent the victory of the clericals. The judiciary authorities had issued several warrants of arrest and one of these hit my father. I found myself at the crossroads as a result of the news.

"To proceed or to return? I decided to continue my journey, and on the morning of July 10 I got off the train at the station of Yverdon with 2 lire and 10 centimes in my pocket."

From Yverdon the young Mussolini walked all day and evening to the nearest city. He was hungry, but he walked on. He passed a house where a prosperous family was at supper around a table loaded with food. He wanted to resist temptation and continue his journey, but hunger drew hirn to the open window of the tantalizing dining room. He stuck his head into the window, his fierce eyes alarming the comfortable folk.

"Have you bread?" he asked rudely. No answer. "Let me have some!" No one spoke, but a hand took a loaf of bread from the table and gave it to the vagabond.

"Thanks, good night!" Not a word in reply. In the dark of the night Mussolini, filled with bitterness, was ready to fling the bread into the nearest ditch, but stopped at the last moment. Hunger conquered.

For a while he earned his living as a manual laborer. He worked as a hod-carrier. But he soon started out on the road again. Once he overtook a Russian tramping in the same direction and carrying a bundle of books in one hand and an alarm clock in the other. Mussolini became interested.

"What is your name?" he asked. The Russian pulled out his card. Under his name was doctor of philosophy, doctor of letters, and professor of something else.

Danger in an Alarm Clock

"Why do you carry your alarm clock like that?" asked Mussolini. "I don't know what to do with it," the Russian replied.

"But you will be taken for a thief." The Russian was not disturbed. When the two reached the nearby city, Mussolini addressed his companion:

"You haven't a penny, and neither have I. You don't know where to go, and neither do I. However, I have nothing in my hands, but you have an alarm clock. This rubbish, my friend, may bring both of us to prison. A police officer could not see the logic of two gentlemen such as we owning an alarm clock but lacking the means to provide ourselves with a bed.

"Therefore, either throw that clock into the first ditch or we shall part. It is better to avoid being awakened tomorrow in jail facing a charge of robbery."

"Goodbye," said the Russian, who preferred to keep his clock. "Goodbye," replied Mussolini, "What time is it?"

"A quarter of nine," was the reply.

"Thanks, let us hops at least that it is correct." And Mussolini walked off. He went through the illuminated center of the town, enviously peering into the bright restaurants, and stopped at a bridge. He descended to the stream and found it dried up.

Sitting under the bridge, his back against the wall, he fell asleep. In the middle of the night he woke up, finding his bed uncomfortable, and moved to a neighboring barn. There he was awakened in the morning by a policeman,

"What are you doing here?" asked the officer of the law.

"I? Why, I am about to get up," replied the youthful tramp.

"You better hustle then."

"Walt a moment. I'll call the servant, if you please, to bring me my clothes."

Helped to the Police Station

"Get up quickly, or I will make you get up," retorted the officer and helped the future prime minister to the police station.

It was Mussolini's first arrest. As an extreme socialist he was yet to know prison and exile.

When he if turned to Italy he became the socialist candidate in a local election. His opponent, who was wealthy, won. Infuriated, Mussolini, after the example of his father, smashed the ballot-box.

He was tried and condemned to prison, but fled to Switzerland. Now his real struggle began. As a political exile Mussolini came in touch with the Italian intellectuals in Switzerland. He worked and studied. While he attended the University of Lausanne, where he took a degree as professor of French, he earned his bread as a common laborer at odd jobs.

But his views and character were not to the liking of the Swiss authorities, and he was expelled as an undesirable. He moved on to Austria, but there, too, he soon attracted the attention of the police by his radical propaganda.

He edited a socialist paper in the Trentino and contributed to various provincial papers. It was not lone before the Austrian government, following the example of the Swiss, deported him as an undesirable.

Expelled from Austria, Mussolini returned to his native district in 1908. He was 25 years old, an intransigent socialist, already a dominating personality. He founded a newspaper, the Class Struggle, and began to rise rapidly as a leader of the revolutionary elements in Italy.

His cutting oratory, his acid pen, his fierce and intrepid nature, his practical approach to things, his abhorrence of phraseology and his preference for action, his dramatization of everything he did and uttered, made him a nature leader.

When he founded his paper, the socialist party in Italy was nothing but vast body without energy or life. confined itself to parliamentary opposition to the government. Mussolini was its revolutionary inspirer.

Swept Away Democratic Traditions

Mussolini swept away its democratic traditions and preached direct action revolution. He taught it the tactics violence, of sabotage, of general strikes, of militant anti-patriotism, of active pacifism, of aggressive republicanism, in a word, all that which has made Italian socialism almost synonymous with Bolshevism.

And when Mussolini later turned his own party and crucified his child, when he formed the fascisti, who set fire to his former paper, who murdered his former comrades and followers, who sacked the labor unions he created, he was still true to himself, his buccaneering nature, to his love of adventure and violence, to his predilection for a fight.

"If I did not know that surrounding me was a quagmire of loves and hatreds, that life was a battle, I would not tolerate it," he said epitomizing his philosophy of life.

Mussolini's first attempt at revolution ended disgracefully. There was a strike in his town. Day and night there followed speeches, shouts, arguments, but no action. Mussolini watched the movement until he lost all patience. He addressed the leaders of the strike:

"It's time to stop this nonsense. Either go back to work or make a revolution. Are you willing? All right, let everybody come to the public gardens at 4 in the afternoon and there will be revolution."

At 4 the public, gardens overflowed with strikers. For the first time in his life Mussolini dominated a mob. There was applause after every sentence. He concluded:

"Enough babble! Enough parading Yours is the strength of brawny arms. You lack a head. I will give you mine Revolution! Here and now!" Tremendous cheers. "I will lead you! To the railroad! To the railroad!"

Mussolini Alone Faces Enemy

A pause of silence. The mob is undecided. Suddenly the clatter of distant hoofbeats is heard. A confused murmur runs through the crowd.

"To the railroad!" Mussolini thunders above the mob.

"Cavalry! Cavalry is coming!" yelled in answer. The cry is caught up. A panic ensues, a mass of terror-stricken, fleeing humanity. In a minute the square is emptied. Mussolini alone remains to face the enemy. A moment later a peasant on horseback turns into the square and trots tranquilly past. The deserted leader steps down from the platform and returns home, having learned his first lesson in the art of revolutioneering.

In 1911, during the Italian war in northern Africa, which ended with Italy's annexation of Tripoli and Libya, Mussolini was a firebrand pacifist. He condemned the war as an adventure, agitated against the monarchy, and preached resistance to the government. He was arrested for sedition, tried and sent to prison. He spent seven months in chains as a convict. When he came out his prestige among the socialists throughout the country had grown enormously.

The following year Mussolini emerged as the outstanding figure at the national socialist congress held in Reggio Emilia. Although only 29, he swayed the congress at will, compelling the expulsion from the party of the conservative majority which supported the government's war in Tripoli and committing the party to his radical program of direct action. He was elected editor of the Avanti, the great socialist organ published in Milan.

In the spring of 1914, Mussolini made a second attempt at a revolution. The so-called Red Week in the central provinces of Italy, which was accompanied by the establishment of a "republic" in the region of Romagna, by the seizure of government and municipal institutions, the arrest of army officers, and by incendiary outbreaks, was all planned and initiated by Mussolini, whose desire was to augment the small mutiny into a national uprising.

Colleagues Repudiate Insurrection

But his colleagues on the executive committee of the socialist party disagreed with him and repudiated the insurrection. This repudiation caused the first deep split between Mussolini and his comrades. He considered it a betrayal of the masses by their leaders. He was bitter because his attempt to engineer a revolution was frustrated as an adventure by his own organization.

The outbreak of the world war widened the breach between Mussolini and the majority of the socialist leaders. Italy in August 1914, was the ally of the central powers. The socialist party favored neutrality. Mussolini was for joining the war on the side of the entente. In November, 1914, he was expelled from the party. He warned his judges in an impassioned speech:

"I tell you that from now on I will have no mercy, no forbearance for all those who in this tragic hour do not speak out for fear of being jeered at or shouted down."

He founded a new paper in Milan and carried on in its columns a relentless campaign for Italy's entering the war on the side of the allies. His nationalism now was as intense as his internationalism some months previously.

"The betrayal of the German socialists compelled those of the other countries," he declared, "to return to the camp of nationalism and national defense. It has been justly said that the internationale is like love.

"It takes two to make love, otherwise it is sterile. . . We must act, move, fight and if necessary die. Neutrals have never yet dominated events, they always bow to them. It is blood which sets in motion the sonorous wheel of history."

Aided D'Annunzio in Call to War

Italy's entry into the war in the spring of 1915 was due principally to the fiery eloquence of D'Annunzio, but the much younger and little-known Mussolini greatly aided the world-famous poet.

Giolitti, then prime minister, was opposed to entering the war. On the eve of the defeat of the Giolitti ministry Mussolini addressed a gathering of his followers crowded into a small room:

"Enough talk, boys. Tomorrow I will have at my command 200 men, brave fellows and ready for anything. Now let us divide this force into four squads. The first squad will attack the armory tomorrow night, imprison those who offer resistance and seize all that is needed to dominate the city militarily. The second squad will occupy the station. No train must leave.

"The third will take the municipal building. There will be little resistance there, I think. The fourth must capture an artillery depot. This is the plan. No more discussion! Those in favor raise their hands!"

Completely surprised by the suddenness of the conspiracy, hypnotized by Mussolini's imperious look, all hands but one went up. The objector was a lawyer.

"I must warn you that the day after tomorrow I have an important case in court, and I don't think I will be able to show up tomorrow.,"

"And what about arms?" asked another voice. No one had thought of that item. It seemed easy to make a revolution with bare hands while Mussolini spoke.

"I will take care of that." replied the chief after a moment of reflection. The following day he appeared in the office carrying a sack full of revolvers and cartridges. The staff was taken aback when he proceeded to load the guns and distribute them to all present. "Shoot and set up a republic when I give the order," he muttered rudely and locked himself up in his den.

A couple of hours later he came out and looked about There was a picture of Giolitti, the leader of those who favored neutrality. He pulled out his pistol and aimed it at the picture, warning those nearby to step aside. He fired. The picture began to smoke and burn. The neighbors were alarmed. Women and children stuck their heads out of the windows. Finally two policemen arrived.

"What has happened?" they asked.

"Nothing." answered a member of the staff, "the editor was writing his editorial for tomorrow."

"By Jove, we should like to read that article in the morning." they said departing. It bore the inflammatory title, "War or a Republic!" and was one of Mussolini's famous manifestos. Thus ended Mussolini's third attempt at revolution.

When war was declared by Italy, Mussolini volunteered for active service, but his record as a revolutionary was too fresh in the memory of the authorities to admit of his acceptance. He was told to await the turn of his class, and went later as a recruit with the rank of a corporal.

"Tell Mussolini that today the duty of a good Italian is to put the pen aside and take up a rifle."

At the front Mussolini was seriously wounded by a shell. He was almost lifeless when taken to the hospital. The hospital was visited by the king, who scarcely imagined that the mutilated soldier before him would five years later be prime minister and virtual dictator of his kingdom.

When Mussolini recovered he was found unfit for further service and discharged. He returned to his newspaper in which he at first acclaimed President Wilson and later ridiculed him. He supported D'Annunzio's notorious Flume adventure.

First Fascisti Formed in 1919

It was in 1919 that he formed the first fascisti organization in Milan, consisting of war veterans pledged to combat the red peril. He tried his fortune as a candidate for parliament, on a platform of nationalistic republicanism, but those were the days of Bolshevism in Italy, and he polled an insignificant vote. During the regime of the Nitti government Mussolini was arrested for his incendiary articles and activities.

"On one of the most turbulent days of the red fever I happened to be with Mussolini in the offices of his newspaper," writes a friend of his. "It was a day of red flag processions and of yells, among which were the invariable, 'Death to Mussolini! Long live Russia!' Repelled by the troops, the reds invaded the side street where Mussolini's paper was published, singing the internationale. Judging by his face, his fierce smile, the look in his eyes, and his entire demeanor, I concluded that Mussolini's pulse was normal.

"He was seated at a small table, in a modest little room, almost bare of furniture, the main decoration of which was a large map of Italy with a tiny tri-colored flag pinned to the point where Fiume was indicated.

"A large glass of milk which Mussolini sipped occasionally and an impressive pistol, in striking contrast to the milk, were conspicuously set before him on the table.

"The cries, intermingled with the whistling of the police and the clicking of rifles, grew menacing. Mussolini, sipping his milk, spoke:

"They shout, yell, and make a world of noise, but behind the flags and flowing cravats are a herd of fools. Don't think they will corns up here. They were led to believe that I am done for, that I am finished politically, and they also know that if they came I would kill at least two of them with this pistol. And in Milan there are not two men among the members of the socialist organization—not two men with nerve enough to face me or to fight!' "

On the wall of his office was a sign which read: "The person who employs five words to say what can be said in one word is capable of little action." The indolence characteristic of his race is entirely lacking in him.

The fascisti movement developed around Mussolini's personality. The failure of D'Annunzio's enterprise augmented the ranks of the fascisti forces. The poet's legions, composed largely of soldiers of fortune, furnished Mussolini his shock troops.

Veritable Crusade of Destruction

With these he organized a veritable crusade of destruction against the socialist and communist parties. He terrorized the entire Italian labor body, sacking, burning, murdering all that was suspected of being red.

In 1921 Mussolini was elected to parliament at the head of a group of 30 fascisti deputies. In his first speech he emphasized his republican leanings. The discussion among the socialists and communists and their breaking up into several factions helped the fascisti.

The weakness of the government and the frequent cabinet crises convinced Mussolini that his opportunity had come to seize power.

The majority of the army officers were secretly fascisti. He proceeded to form an army of his own, the uniform of which was a black shirt. The fascisti troops were trained and officered by war veterans. Mussolini then plotted the conspiracy which so spectacularly brought him to the helm.

A week before the fascisti advance on Rome Mussolini addressed in Naples a vast gathering of his partisans. Having disavowed his republicanism completely, he appealed for iron discipline and preparedness for any emergency. "Every time in history," he added, "when strongly conflicting interests and ideas struggle for supremacy, it is force which ultimately decides the Issue.

"It is raining in Naples, what shall we do?"

The government, without suspecting its significance, allowed the transmission of this message to all parts of the country. It was the agreed signal for the execution of the conspiracy.

The action developed according to the plan. One hundred thousand disciplined fascisti advanced on Rome. The government tried to declare a state of siege, but the king refused to sanction it.

The cabinet resigned. The king invited Salandra on Saturday. October 28, to form a government. The latter officially asked Mussolini to participate, but received a blunt refusal.

"I refuse to participate," he replied, "because I do not want to impair the fascisti victory."

King Asks Rim to Take Reins

Then came the turn of the son of the locksmith. The King asked him to take over the reins. So it happened that Mussolini, who had experimented with revolution for years, finally succeeded in achieving his grand coup d'etat. In his first address to parliament he used this Cromwellian phrase:

"I am here to defend and to strengthen the revolution of the black shirts, infusing it into the history of the nation as a power for development, progress and stability.

"I refuse to conquer too much, although I can take care of the victory. I impose limits upon myself. I tell myself that the best wisdom is that in which the victor does not abandon himself after his victory.

"I formed a coalition government not with the intention of having the support of a parliamentary majority without which I can get along excellently. I do not want, as long as it is possible, to govern against the will of the chamber. But the chamber must understand its peculiar position, which makes it liable to dissolution at any time."

Parliament was scandalized by this insult to democracy, but subserviently bowed to Mussolini.

This Fascisti Business
American Legion Weekly/March 16, 1923

by Thomas Ryan

A great electric star blazes forth in broad daylight over the main piazza of an Italian city. The electric lighting may very likely fail this evening, but that is no reason why lights should not burn today. For the Fascisti have willed that there shall be festival, and this is a day of Fascisti triumph.

Up the narrow Corso comes a blare of brass music. The air is "Giovanezza" –"Youth"—the Fascisti marching song. It is well known in Italy as "Madelon" was in France five years ago It has a catchy, music-hall lilt.

Youth! Youth!
Springtime of Beauty!

Those are the words. They are a little incomprehensible if, as Italians say, this was the song of the Arditti, the shock-troops of the Italian army. There are many Arditti among the Fascisti.

110

Black banners come into view.

"The Gagliardi!" murmur the people along the sidewalks ,and they make ready to live their hats. It is wiser to do so. It is wise, too, to pause and smile dutifully at the skulls embroidered on the black flags. It is better still to raise a little cheer.

The column swings past, in good order. The men are coatless, and they wear black shirts, army-green breeches and tin hats. Their hair is long, after the style o Garibaldi. In their hands are loaded clubs and in their pockets revolvers. The police see the revolvers but say nothing.

If there are enough people to watch, the column breaks into a double-quick. And so it makes its way to the workingmen's quarters

The next day—but not from the papers—the café crowds learn that workmen were beaten, a co-operative store looted and a mutual aid premises burned.

It is taken for granted that certain scared persons were dragged to the Black Shirt headquarters. As they approached, they saw over the door the shield with the fasces—the bundle of axes and rods which symbolized the old Roman power to punish. The scared ones were still more scared, for to them the fasces have all the dread significance that the Lion's Head once had for the victims of the Venetian Ten.

Inside the building an army field-kitchen was smoking. Men were carrying in great sides of beef. Messengers darted past, bound for distant towns where comrades were on active service.

And here, in an inner room, knives were produced; the scared ones were prodded, and the alternative was set before them—three-quarters of a pint of castor oil, with a chase of tepid water. They took it, and hurried away.

These are daily incidents in the life of every Italian town.

What are these Fascisti? Are they an Italian version of the American Legion or are they a Ku Klux Klan strong enough to come into the open? Their friends put it one way, their enemies the other.

The story should begin with the Armistice, and it calls to the mind of a reporter a series f pictures—dramatic, tragic, and ridiculous.

In what seems now the dim past—nearly four years ago---a city on the Adriatic sweltered under the blue heat of summer. In its streets were Allied troops, mostly Italian, and in its port were Allied warships, including one of our own destroyers. Loafing along the quays, whispering in case, was as disreputable a rabble as ever disgraced a seaport. The town was Fiume.

The rabble was largely imported from Italy, though it numbered some local hotheads. Every evening it held demonstrations, which, considering the heat, was imprudent. Every few days it was addressed by impassioned orators who quoted D'Annunzio's poems and coined such phrases as "Fiume or Death!" "Down with American Capitalism!" Among these orators was one who was known to us inly as a newspaper editor, and whose paper frequently damned America, Britain and France for not giving Fiume to Italy.

He was Benito Mussolini, now the Italian premier.

It is doubtful if those orators meant all that they said. It was a very hot summer, and their purpose was obviously to create "incidents" in Fiume which might serve as arguments in Paris. They overshot their mark. French blood flowed in the streets of Fiume.

The rabble, which called itself Giovanni Italiani, handed on its torch to the poet D'Annunzio, who in turn delivered it to the Fascisti. They held it up to new problems, but they have never ceased to focus it periodically on Fiume, Dalmatia and other lands which Italy covets.

The spirit which animates the Fascist is not a new thing. It was the spirit of the Italian army in 1919, when it played for the east coast of the Adriatic and prepared for war with Yugoslavia. To grasp the continuity of the movement, you must see it through the eyes of a Fiuman. He makes no distinction between the old rabble, the Italian military, the opera-bouffe D'Annunzio and his present masters, the Fascisti. They all picked on the Fiuman. Men kicked and clubbed in the streets, police looking on with a smile, the election at the point of the bayonet—these things the Fiuman associates with all the Italian regimes.

And when he sees a Fascists saluting, in Roman style with uplifted right hand, or when he hears a Fascists say "Ave" or "Vale," the Fiuman remembers that four years ago the spellbinders talked o a new Roman empire.

"Whatever was Roman before we will make Italian," the officers used to remark modestly to their troops.

And the Fascisti today take Caesar's legions for their model. Words familiar to the high school boy—centurion, decurion, cohort, manipulum—occur in their orders. They have legions, not regiments.

Their battle cry is the one that the Romans used to shout—all in the same key, to make it carry—just as they hurled their javelins and got into the close-up business with short swords. This battle cry comes at the end of the Fascists marching song: "Eja alala!"

In 1919 Italy seemed cannoning into war with Yugoslavia. That was one of the grievances of the workers, who began to oppose the extreme nationalists. Not that the workmen cared about the ruin of Fiume, which Italian occupation had caused. Not that they shed any tears of Yugoslavs in Dalmatia deported in the dead of the night, or houses raided or women clubbed. They picked out the best grievance at hand.

When the Communists virtually ruled over Italy in 1920 and 1921 they set up a detestable tyranny. Railways could not carry troops. Officers were forbidden to wear arms and men with war medals were spat on and beaten. The national flag was never seen. Tenants seized the estates, workmen the factories, and produced only what they pleased. IN grappling with the Communist frenzy the Fascisti passed through an heroic stage.

A few Italians had never abandoned the dream of a Greater Italy, an empire which would embrace all outposts of the Italian race. Malta should be annexed from Great Britain; Nice, Savoy and Corsica might be taken from France some day, and Dalmatia from Yugoslavia. They didn't stop there. An Italian doge had once set his banner on Constantinople. There are plenty of Italians in Egypt. Djibouti, a French port in East Africa, would be useful to the Italian colony of Eritrea. And within easy distance of Sicily is the French protectorate o Tunisia, where Italians have migrated.

These Greater Italians patriotically mourned for the present state of their country. They realized that the slogan" "Mother Italy! Restore her at home and abroad!" would rally the decent citizens to their standard. These men were the same who had made Fiume a hell-on-earth and an unhealthy spot for Americans; but now they launched themselves on a nobler task—protecting their own firesides.

There have been in the Fascists war deeds of great sacrifice, lit by the Latin's sense of drama. At roll call, when the names of the dead were pronounced, the whole unit answered: "Here!" It took an Italian to think of that delicate token of loyalty to the dead. There is a legion called "The Most desperate" which had embroidered on all its uniforms—and even on its hospital dressings—"I don't give a damn!" And fifteen thousand

Fascisti of Piacenza have forsworn all jewels and other ornaments, which they have sold for the benefit of their country.

Such men take literally the dictum of D'Annunzio: "Other races are of human origin. The Italian is of divine."

What a power they are in the land may be judged by the act that they exchange salutes with the army and navy. Their officers have the power to force their obedience and to punish "by acts of violence."

Don't let the Ku Klux call themselves Fascisti. Italy's problems were almost desperate. She hung over the abyss; and her people, blind to their obligations, permitted a government in its dotage to do nothing The Fascisti ended all that. They employed some extreme methods—there were brutal murders for which no one was brought to trial, there were beatings and burnings—but they fought in the open.

They sing of youth, because the one hope of Italy is rejuvenation. She has a name for rising again. They pretend that they are Romans, because all Italians respect that name, and glory in their descent. The strutting of Mussolini was never like the bombast of D'Annunzio. There was some point to it.

Only the thing went too far. There was a brave fight for Dinna Italia, and the Fascisti won. The Communist menace was scotched. In Milan, Turin and Trieste—the worst large towns—not a red flag could appear; not a Communist dared speak in public. It was a moment for amnesty and elections, for most of the workmen had been forced into Communism. But while at home the Fascisti feted their victory by further bloodletting, abroad they went to the pains o giving Yugoslavia a hint of danger to come.

Yugoslavia is populated by fighting men and their mothers and sisters. In America Yugoslavs become miners because they are built like excavators. They don't really love work, but, Lord! How they do hanker after a scrap. History has not been ungenerous to them in this respect.

Such are the people who for over four years have submitted to every form of insult from their bigger, richer and better equipped neighbor, Italy. When the Italians began seizing Yugoslav territory that was vital to Yugoslavia, many officers in the Yugoslav army tugged at the leash. "One Serb is good for ten Italians," they argued. But the government said, "No, we must negotiate," and negotiate they did. Thanks to Italy's trouble at home, Belgrade secured the Rapallo treaty and the pact of

Santa Margherita, which, though they favored Italy somewhat, were more than Yugoslavia had expected. Then came the Fascists victory, and Fascists influence in Rome. The Italian parliament was no longer willing to ratify the pact. And meanwhile the Fascisti, like their comic forerunner, D'Annunzio, swooped down on Fiume, shelled it from an Italian warship and drove out the decentest government that it had had since the Armistice. The Fascisti speak of this treaty violation as the "Revolution of 1922."

So the movement that brought relief to Italy gave chains to Fiume and alarm to Yugoslavia. The Fascisti are still in the town, busily dosing its more public-spirited citizens with castor oil. Local physicians protested against this method of treatment; drug stores complained that they could not meet the demand. Meanwhile Hungary's erstwhile best port is without shipping. Yugoslavia will not let goods pass until Italy keeps her plighted word. The Fascisti will not let their opponents work on the docks, and as everyone is their opponent, and as the Fascisti don't swing a very mean crate themselves, no work is done.

On a wall overlooking the silent business street, like a grim commentary on the silence, somebody once painted "Fiume or Death!" Only the last word is visible today: "Death!" Fiume is dead and the Fascisti killed her.

Then came the coup which made Mussolini premier It was burlesque, in that it was illegal but that no firm resistance was made. Imagine the American Legion marching on Washington. The Fascisti marched. Then they returned to their homes with black banners, seized all the public buildings and shouted "Long Live the King!" Some troops lost their heads and fired, but mostly they handed over their carbines. The King saw the writing on the wall, and he yielded.

At first it looked as if all would be safe on the frontiers. The Fascisti who had mobilized there to watch Austria and Yugoslavia went home, and Belgrade papers spoke well00after government hints—of Mussolini. He seemed to justify their opinion of him by his new attitude toward Fiume. Some young Fascisti had raises across the border, seized a Yugoslav flag and burned it. Mussolini ordered another flag made and returned with apologies, and he even sent the youngsters to jail. When a handful of firebrand Arditti—some of D'Annunzio's—grabbed the Yugoslav club in Fiume, the government got them out by a clever trick.

115

Mussolini was learning that while an editor might call for a "strong" policy abroad, the premier of the nation must walk with caution.

But there were people behind Mussolini who did not want caution. They wanted Greater Italy, and they had hoisted Mussolini into the saddle for that purpose. So the saber had to be clanked, and Yugoslavia, weary of patience, began to mobilize certain classes.

If the Fascisti had only stayed at home! But like Pussyfoot Johnson and all enthusiasts, they had no sooner seen their cause triumphant at home than they set out to spread the gospel to all people. They took it into Bavaria, just where they shouldn't have taken it. In Bavaria Communism was not a danger. Fascism was. Every energy o the Bavarians should have been bent to working their way through the winter without much coal or bread. But Fascism turned their attention to Jew-baiting. Mussolini had never disgraced Fascism at home by anti-Semitism, but in Hungary, as well as Bavaria, that was the form that Fascism took.

There was a tactical reason for carrying Fascism to Hungary. That country is the enemy of Yugoslavia and her allies, Czecho-Slovakia and Romania. Italy has coquetted for years with the Hungarians, and now she is drawing tighter the bond between the two countries providing against the war which she foresees.

Then, too, the Fascisti are intriguing in Montenegro. They receive fugitives from that country who can be trusted to plot with their friends at home against Yugoslavia. And at Ancona there is a bureau whose business it is to watch the Yugoslavs in Dalmatia.

Even in Ireland the Fascisti are trying to organize branches. There they have met with a real check, for both sides claim to be the true government and neither will tolerate a third party.

There are signs that Italy herself is wearying of Fascism. Sardinia has virtually revolved against it, and elsewhere people are tiring of violence when the need for it seems past. Workmen of dubious character have been paid to march with the Black Shirts, to counterbalance the Communist workers. Yugoslavs in Trieste and Fiume claim that they have to pay tribute in order to stay and carry on business. And somewhere deep hidden in the Fascisti organism is a band called "Knights of Death," whose crimes the Fascisti disavows.

In medieval Italian cities history was a see-sawing—into power and out—of two hostile factions. Blood was spilled; neither side gained real advantage, and in the end Italy was ruined for hundreds of years. Will the modern Communists strike back some day? May not the war of Fascisti and Communists be like the wars of Guelfs and Ghibellines?

If there is an moral to draw—and morals are not safe when we write of our own times—it is that private citizens can not usurp the government's functions without weakening respect for all government. If the time comes when private citizens must act, they must lay down their arms as soon as order is restored. If they remain in arms and power, like the Praetorian Guards of Rome, they court their own ruin and ultimately that of their country.

Civil War By Murder
The Guardian (London)/June 27, 1923

Secret "Fascism" in Germany

A Terrible Example

Government Tolerance a Protest

The latest murder committed by the Fema or vendetta of the secret Fascist organizations has now come to light in all its details. Revolting as the details are, they are so characteristic of the present state of Germany that no apology is needed for relating them.

Last Friday two young men called at the editorial office of "Vorwarts" and gave information about the secret clubs formed by Lieutenant Rossbach in Mecklenburg and about the murder of a certain Walter Kadow. "Vorwarts" immediately informed the police and investigations were made. Five men have now been arrested in Mecklenburg and two in Berlin. The facts now established by the police are as follows:

Kadow was 23 years old. He had risen to the rank of first lieutenant in the war, but since then he had led an irregular existence. Latterly he had been employed on a big estate and was a member of the local Rossbach

Club. Some of his fellow-members suspected him of being a Communist spy and decided to get rid of him. On the evening of May 31 he was invited to an inn at Parchim, where they treated him to drinks. When he was half drunk they telephoned to the neighbouring estates and asked for reinforcements. By nine o'clock, twenty-five to thirty Fascists had collected. Towards eleven they loaded Kadow, who by this time had lost his senses altogether, on to a cart, and eight of them drove off with him. After a time he regained consciousness, but when a revolver was held to his head he remained quiet.

The Murder

After a drive of about five kilometers they dragged him out of the cart and beat him with cudgels and rubber life-preservers. He collapsed beneath their blows. They loaded him up again, and drove into a neighboring forest. Here they stamped his face into the ground. One of them, named Wiedemeyer, cut Kadow's throat with a hunting knife. Two others, Hoese and Zabel, fired three revolver bullets into his head. Then they all drove off to an estate near by, where they washed the cart.

Next morning Hoese and Zabel came back with picks and shovels and buried the body three feet deep. It was disinterred by the police last Saturday. It was found in a terrible condition. Besides having three bullet holes the skull was split across. Those of the murderers who have been arrested have made a full confession. The remaining murderers and their accomplices are being searched for all over Germany.

During the search in Mecklenburg a heavy machine-gun was discovered. Four days before the murder came to light the local Rossbach clubs held a celebration in honor of Schlageter.

Underground Fascist Movement

The crime is only one of several that have been committed in similar circumstances during the last fee months. Both the victim and his murderers are typical of the German Fascist movement. The secret organizations are recruited mainly from men who are in their twenties who were N.C.O.'s or subalterns in the war, since when they have been leading irregular lives, serving under Von der Goltz or Rossbach in the Baltic provinces, with Kappists in various parts of Germany, or with Selbstschutz in Upper Silesia. Their clubs supply volunteers for "the Ruhr front," where they commit acts of sabotage and murder Frenchmen.

It is also characteristic that so many of them should be spying both for reactionaries and Communists and be in the pay of both Germans and French (Schlageter appears to have been in the pay of the Poles as well). Together with Bavarian Separatists, they are the vanguard of Fascism in Germany and a menace that cannot be underrated. It is not mere sensationalism when this morning's "Rothe Fahne" prints the headline "Fascists begin civil war." The danger is increased by the fact that both the extreme Right and Left are gathering strength, as was shown by the elections recently held in Oldenburg, and as will be shown by the elections soon to be held in Mecklenburg-Strelitz.

Demand for Government Action

"Vorwarts," a paper not always very decided or bold in its utterances, speaks in the strongest terms this morning of the recent murders and acts of sabotage (including the dynamiting of the Socialist newspaper offices at Munster), conspiracies like the Munich plot, and the reactionary press campaign:

We must ask the Government of the Reich what it intends to do now. It must be said with all clearness that the reticence of Herr Cuno towards German Nationalists is no longer tolerable. We have waited in vain for Herr Cuno to utter sharp words condemning acts of sabotage and of violence in the occupied area. Herr Cuno has been silent all too long. We have vainly waited for Herr Cuno and his government to support Herr Severing in his arduous and difficult duties. Herr Cuno has been very careful to remain silent when he damned well ought to have opened his mouth. The government shares responsibility for the fact that things have now gone so far that a bombing offensive is being opened against our party. It is also Herr Cuno's duty to be more exercised than he has been hitherto in making a radical cut through the threads that are still spun between the Reichswehr and the Nationalist organization. Finally, Herr Cuno would be well advised to inform the Bavarian government that

*the tolerance it shows towards murder organizations and incitements to
murder are not compatible with the interests of the Reich.*

*As for the working class, the Socialist party, and the trade unions,
they would do very wrong if they did not pay the greatest attention to
helping themselves. Germany is not Italy, and German Fascists will get
broken heads for their trouble. Labor must not delay in taking counter-
measures and organizing the necessary defense. We are strong enough to
create our defensive organizations against the murder clubs and bombing
societies. We have the most urgent wish that the state will at last do its
duty with the necessary ruthless energy and keep the political fight clear
of murder and violence. But if the state fails we shall not be lost by a long
way, for we shall help ourselves, and that thoroughly.*

The Swashbuckling Mussolini
New York Times/July 22, 1923

*Latest Heir of the Caesars Has Conquered Because
His Countrymen Understand Arrogance*

Anne O'Hare McCormick

At the moment when dyspeptic Europe ceases to struggle with the
digestion of more unbaked democracy than any continent was ever called
upon to swallow before, when England recalls the Tories and France
remobilizes the chauvinists, when Prime Ministers of a German republic
begin to invoke the empire, when Turkey stands pat, when Albania
clamors for a Scottish King, when all the new republics are dying of
liberty and professional politicians resume everywhere a business of which
amateurs are sick and tired, Mussolini the Autocrat mounts the tribune of
the Caesars and creates one of those exciting diversions which sometimes
change the course of history.

He shouts aloud all the dark and stabbing doubts of democracy
that secretly assail those who have tried it. He plays up a hearty and
unsanctified nationalism against the pale virtue of co-operation which
the enlightened have been trying to cultivate as a super-national grace.

He dares to call a Legislature in public what all men call it in private. He arrives at the hour of the sharpest decline in the stock of the liberals and uses language about popular government that relieves the pent feeling of its best friends. He finds Italy self-governed to a deadlock, in a literal paralysis of democracy, and sets the machinery going by turning out the tinkerers and running the whole works himself.

His presence at the head of an enlightened State is therefore in itself a challenge. Is he a symptom of the disease of politics that infects civilization, or is he a remedy? Is he autocrat, liberator or merely demagogue? How far is he going, and where? After eight months of practically unlimited authority what has his Government accomplished? Enough to prove one-man power to be less dangerous than the powerlessness of many men, to show that a general-manager form of control may be applied to a nation as well as to a town? Is he, in a word, as right as he is popular in proceeding on the assumption that people really desire government more than they desire a voice in government?

These are questions that are drawing to Rome reporters and observers from the ends of the earth. Political reviewers, journalists, politicians, bankers, business prospectors, reformers, flock here to make their varying deductions from what they see of Italy under the Fascists regime. They gave it six months last October when the Black Shirt army made its sensational raid on Rome and seized the Government from a panicky Parliament and an eagerly acquiescent King. Now that it has stood that test they begin to suspect that there is something more in it than a scene in Italian grand opera, and inquirers arrive to satisfy what is apparently a universal curiosity in regard to its achievements and its intentions. They gather in the official and unofficial ante-rooms where one waits, sometimes vainly and always long, for different brands of ill-prepared information. They study the budget figures as presented in the recent statement of Minister of Finance de Stefani, perhaps the ablest member of Mussolini's rather too-personal Cabinet. They interview the President of the Council if they can catch him between his almost daily dashes to various points of the political battlefront. They talk to the officials who are primed for such inquiries, an industrial magnate or two, the handy head waiter, who speaks all languages. If their week's tour of inspection allows them to see anything they are not shown, or are not looking for, they take a glance around the country. Seldom by any chance have they the time of the words or the curiosity to talk to the people.

Yet in Italy even more than in most countries there is no use trying to study Fascism and its chances of success without some understanding of the Italians. I had not been in the country a week before discovering that what Americans find most difficult to swallow in Mussolini and his movement is what the Italians gulp down with the greatest gusto. They love his swashbuckling and blaguer. They delight in his impudence to a Parliament which they all despise. They are enraptured when he reminds the recalcitrant that it is only by his forbearance that they exist; when he threatens his enemies with an army held in leash only by his good pleasure. Boasts of force feed their love of power and their disdain of weakness.

Like Barrie's "Tommy," with whom they have no sentiments and many tastes in common, they adore a masterful man. They have always flourished under a strong hand, whether Caesar's or Hildebrand's, Cavour's or Crispi's. That is because they are not a people like ourselves or the English or the Germans, loving order and regulation and government for their own sake, however weak their Ministers. Experience has taught them to distrust all government and instinct makes them resent the intrusions of authority. They have never been united except by force or by disaster, and they follow a leader as long as he leads, and no longer.

Mussolini is secure while he shows no fear. When his critics accuse him of unconstitutionality they only recommend him the more to a highly civilized but naturally lawless people. The youth, the bravura, the political intrepidity which the old politicians call inexperience, are the strength of the Fascisti. Look at the great portraits that strut among the meek Madonnas and suffering saints of all Italian galleries—Caesars, condottieri, courtiers, Cardinals—and learn how these people understand arrogance.

Only last week a friend bitterly disillusioned with a Government that had promised the millennium and only increased his taxes came to me after a speech of Mussolini's in the Senate completely reestablished enthusiasm. "Magnificent!" he exclaimed. "He said that he made explanations but that he owed none. He declared that with sacrifice and solidarity in two years he would make over Italy. He snapped his fingers at all the barking canaille. He says he may be shot, but it does not matter if he is hit going forward instead of going back. At least a man can respect himself in following such a leader!"

Whatever Mussolini does not know, and there are said to be many things not dreamed of in his philosophy, he knows his own people. He knew when to turn on the drama, and I believe he will also know when to shut it off. No citizen of a strictly limited democracy like ours can imagine the relief of being ruled by a good, strong, forthright autocrat after the absolute, unbridled, impossibly logical form of self-government suffered in Italy. The people were already yearning for a dictatorship when Mussolini appointed himself a dictator. So far from a usurpation of authority against the popular will, his march on Rome was like an answer to prayer. The professional politicians had had their chance. They had all failed. Even the Fascisti could do nothing in the Chamber. They were a small group in a helplessly divided body—thirty-two members out of 535. Mussolini only made himself receiver for a Government in bankruptcy.

It must be remembered that in that crisis, when the Government acknowledged its incapacity to function, when anarchy was held down only by Mussolini's army, the Fascisti could have done anything they chose with the country. Everybody admits that the Government was to be had for the taking. Mussolini could as easily have led to power the Socialists or the Communists as his battalions of fighting nationalists and patriots. He had under absolute control the best young manhood of Italy, an armed force of half a million unpaid volunteers, mobilized by his magnetism, dedicated and disciplined to his will.

Wherever he led they would have followed. There are many who think that he could have overthrown the monarchy as easily as he reestablished it. Two-thirds of the army was already Fascist. There might have been a republic, even without civil war. Anything might have happened; all that did happen was that Victor Emmanuel hastened to make the Fascisti constitutional by inviting them to form a Government. The bankrupt Parliament conferred all its powers upon the Fascists leader for a year, and both King and Prime Minister were heartily cheered by the people for their resourcefulness in making the realities so different while leaving all the names the same.

That very night the Fascists forces were out of Rome. They marched to the Capitol and dispersed as soberly and exaltedly as they came. Many were country youths on their first visit to the metropolis; they were tired, dusty and dry after long marches over hard roads. Yet with all the cafes open there was not a case of drunkenness; there was not the slightest disorder and not a murmur against the unwelcome order to return at once to their homes. They showed themselves and departed, but they got what they came for and thus saved their country as thoroughly, and more neatly, than if any one of them had the poor judgment to oppose them.

The leaders of Italian constitutional liberalism, who are more anxious than the best American journalist scenting a story to find out just how far Mussolini is going, declare now that the Government was about to assort itself and the Parliamentary confusion was on the eve of clearing when he made his parade of revolution. They complain because he embarked and proceeded upon his unknown course without any guidance from political experts. They forget that he had watched the experts being expert for two years from his seat on the Right of the Chamber of Deputies; and the restraint he exhibited once he had precipitated the crisis they could not avert was hardly more remarkable than their instant docility to his demands.

They submitted to the most contemptuous lambasting any Parliament has ever received from the responsible head of a Government. Certainly nothing but the lack of any alternative could have induced them to endow their castigator with absolute powers. He continues to abuse the Parliament, but so far he has not abused the mandate he forced from them. He talks about upholding the traditional "jus murmurandi," a right as old as Roman law, but all criticism angers him and he will not have a word of contradiction in his own ranks. He does not suffer any opposition patiently, and though he cannot expel his political opponents, he does not placate or reassure the worried constitutionalists when he reminds them that except for his intervention there would be no Constitution to save. He is secure in the fact that, by whatever coercion of circumstances he arrived where he is, he is there by appointment of the King and consent of the Parliament, so that if he is a dictator he is so by all the constitutional authority there is.

Two-thirds of his grant of power has now expired and many of the observers who come to find out what he has done with it, to estimate how one-man rule works in a modern State, are inclined to be disappointed that he has not created the safe heaven the Conservatives hoped for or the despotic hell the Radicals predicted. I have heard more than one trained interpreter of events assert that the Fascists Government has been advertised for a great deal more than it is worth. It has done few of the things that look impressive in a report. But it has performed one miracle. And because miracles are rare in a world without magic, that wonder, I think, should be celebrated above all its failures and achievements.

The miracle is a miracle of conversion. Here at last is a Government that has transformed a people. If that sounds too strong, I can only say that it is the first and only term that does justice to the first impression made on one who left Italy two years ago and comes back today. Then it was a land visibly running down, with a kind of hand-to-mouth administration, so that one never knew today where tomorrow's Government was coming from. There was no assurance that anything was going to work—railroads, telegraphs, trams, posts, power plants, bakeries, any kind of public or private service. One tried a water faucet skeptically; one bet on the chances of getting a train. Life was a daily gamble, sporting enough for the traveler but pretty desperate for the native. The people were all either idle and rebellious or idle and dispirited. The war had left them bitter and poor; subsequent events had made them lose pride in their country and respect for their Government. Everywhere was slackness, despondency, recklessness.

One left confusion and fear, and under confusion and fear, apathy and discouragement. One returned to a country cheerful, industrious, interested and orderly. All the railroads were running and running on time. There was not even the threat or shadow of a strike. There has not been a single strike in any part of Italy since the Fascisti came into power. The streets were clean, the roads were being mended, the enlivening sounds of construction were heard everywhere. Workers were singing at their work. It was like a land recovered from a blight.

Was this Mussolini's revolution? I asked myself, contrasting the friendly dispatch of the customs inspection at Naples with my last hideous experience at the same port. "We have a Government now!" boasted a Neapolitan, and when I remarked on the transformation to the first Roman I met, he assured me that I would be more amazed the more I saw. "It is hard for a stranger to understand," he said, "but Mussolini has actually changed the minds and spirit of the people. He has dramatized work and sacrifice and national pride and made them popular. Go out to the San Lorenzo quarter, where a few months ago a man was shot for flying the Italian flag. Now they are all patriots there, all working, contented, shouting for Mussolini. I don't know what happened to all the revolutionists."

I sought out one of the still-existent Socialist headquarters for an explanation of the mystery. It was the quietest retreat I found in Rome, deserted except for the voluble and agreeable executive. He admitted that his comrades were dispersed, for the moment shorn of their thunder, infected by nationalism, and that some had basely surrendered to the bourgeoisie.

"Are you as free as ever to organize, to hold meetings, to make propaganda?" I asked, and when he answered with a qualified affirmative, I inquired if it was true, then, as I had heard in America, that the government had instituted a virtual censorship of the press and public opinion.

"Hardly that," he replied. "We publish our papers just the same as ever. The Government has a strong press, which specializes in daily advertisement and adulation of Mussolini and keeps the people stuffed with all his promises, like the reform of the budget and the proposed electoral iniquity. Mussolini punishes all his own people who open their mouths against him. There have been local examples of suppression of newspapers for criticizing the Fascisti, the most notable example being the powerful Corriere della Sera, which was suspended for a day in Milan. But there has been no general censorship. The Italians would never stand for it. And Mussolini won't go so far now as when he was making war on us. He is too anxious to stay in power. As for us," he shrugged, "well, we are out; we have been outraged and persecuted and weakened. But of course we will come back. Mussolini has the people hypnotized, but he has been given so much rope that he is sure to hang himself in the end."

The Fascisti have done things which the political reviewer finds more interesting than these trifles. They have ferreted out the tax dodgers and forced 400,000 citizens to pay income taxes who never paid before. They have simplified and reclassified taxation. They have made a valiant attempt to deal with the bureaucracy that stifles all European States. Several Government departments have been closed, the personnel of others reduced and various administrative economies have been effected. The number of State employees actually discharged, however, is much less than was promised. There is a limit to the number of enemies the most fearless leader can indulge in!

The new budget proposes to reduce the national deficit to one and a quarter milliards of lire, about four milliards less than it is today. Committees are working on educational reforms, on a reform of the electoral system, on new provisions for constant emigration which the few natural resources of the country and the rapidly growing population make necessary. But these are mostly in the future—great schemes which all Governments dream about in their youth and few ever grow old enough to realize. The project for electoral reform is interesting enough to be considered in another article. It will bring an issue to the fight Mussolini must have with the constitutionalists and measure the strength of the growing opposition to his policies. As outlined, it is a novelty, never tried before in any country, and it will probably never be tried again even in this if it succeeds in its purpose of putting the Fascisti in power for the next four years.

Not even if all the proposed budgets balance, and if Mussolini works out a formula of economic salvation for his country, a problem he has not even tackled, his greatest reform will still be the one he has already accomplished. He may in time find experts to create industries and outlets for trade; the creation of a national spirit and the restoration of order and confidence in Government will remain his personal triumph. Always remembering that Italy is full of Italians and not Americans or French or Germans, it is nothing less than amazing to watch the whole country trying to be like him. By working fourteen hours a day, by living hard and taking hard exercise, by talking always of courage, strength, law, discipline, he has inspired among Italians a cult of the strenuous life such as Roosevelt once popularized in America.

He calls himself "the trustee of the youth of Italy," and he makes the young men, the ex-soldiers, university students, schoolboys, farmers' sons, feel for the first time that the country is theirs, and that it is their job to work for it and their responsibility to see that it is well ruled. Discipline, the least favored of all virtues among his countrymen, is the favorite word of their leader. Not even a Church supposed to specialize in discipline has been very successful in imposing it on its Italian adherents. In other countries Catholics are orderly and well organized; in the center of Christendom, if a foreigner can judge by observation, they seem to take the liberty of worshiping God in the manner they please. The discipline of the Fascisti, now the national militia, is therefore no mean achievement.

It is true that in this army Mussolini wields a despotic power. He is called and is the "Duce"—leader whose word is law, who brooks no insubordination and expels his best friends for a whisper of contradiction or a gesture of disloyalty.

He includes the Church in his policy of restoring what he calls the "hierarchies," of bolstering up authority wherever he finds it. The first and not the least astonishing thing he did as Prime Minister was to take the King and all his Ministers to mass at the Church of Santa Maria degli Angeli, the basilica carved out of the Baths of Diocletian by Michelangelo.

"Mussolini was the first to make a Christian out of the Unknown Soldier," smiled a great Roman Cardinal, whom I asked how the ex-editor of Avanti was doing as an apostle of religion. "Until he ordered his Ministers to their knees to pray for the soul of the dead warrior, it has been in Italy a pagan cult, like the ancient worship of the god of war. I don't know how much is religion and how much is statesmanship," the Cardinal added, "but it is a popular novelty here to have a government which refers with respect to the Vatican, raises the image of Christ in the schools, and acknowledges what is, after all, 'the religion of Italy.'"

The new Government cultivates the spectator. One of the reasons for its popularity among a people smarting under a sense of being undervalued in the world is that it gives them at last a leader who is a headliner, so to speak, able to command public attention and keep Italy on the front page. And Mussolini concentrates most of his efforts on healing the wounded amour propre and building up the morale of the nation. He makes politics a kind of noble show and keeps enlivened and interested the audience, so bored by his predecessors. During the last few weeks, scenting that he is at the beginning of the second and most perilous phase of his regnancy, the phase of criticism, disappointment, reaction from the high mood, he has made triumphal excursions to all parts of the country.

He is far less arrogant in addressing the people than he is to the politicians and to the various financial, journalistic and Masonic rings that used to rule the country. He is wise enough to know that the chiefs of the old order will always be his enemies, and that it is among the people that he must find his friends. And nothing is more surprising in a skeptical race than the popular belief in this peasant who preaches aristocracy and this ex-Socialist who defends hierarchies. He started out with a following of the adventurous young of the middle class.

Now the middle class does not shout for him so unanimously as in the beginning. They find that Fascism is not a property defense league; it makes property pay. The workers are reassured by the same discovery. I suspect that a good many of the lost Socialists may be found among the Fascisti. On the other hand, there have been desertions as well as expulsions from the ranks of the Fascisti. The material out of which revolutions are made is not so good for making reforms. Mussolini is said to have confided to a friend that he will have to disgust 30 per cent of his followers in order to go on with what he has to do now.

In the United States we have a democracy, which means that the majority of people, acting on motives which often have nothing to do with government, freely elect officers who do not give them what they want. And in Italy a strong minority has elected itself and is giving the country the kind of government the majority want but did not know how to get. In other words, the will of the majority seems to be better satisfied in Italy at this moment than in the United States. The Italians certainly enjoy a personal liberty and freedom from regulation beyond even our conception of liberty.

I suppose peoples as well as Presidents and Prime Ministers can't be opportunists, and that the dictatorship of Mussolini, prevailing by the will of his people, may be classified as a democratic expedient. He is a reaction against nothing but inaction, and proves no more than that when a leader appears the people will follow. They will chafe after a while under his heavy pose of inflexibility; they will tire of the fascinating spectacle of watching him do everything himself. Perhaps, having performed one miracle, in that day he will have other incantations to work other wonders. It is not easy to say where he is going, but it takes no prophet to predict that two elemental and powerful popular appetites, the hunger for leadership and curiosity as to what happens next, will carry him at least beyond his year of trial.

Interview with Adolf Hitler
The American Monthly/October 1923

by George Viereck

"We might have called ourselves the Liberty Party. We chose to call ourselves National Socialists. We are not Internationalists. Our Socialism is national. We demand the fulfillment of the just demands of the productive classes by the state on the basis of race solidarity. To us state and race are one."

Asked to elucidate his program further, he said: "We believe in the ancient adage of "a healthy mind in a healthy body. The body politic must be sound if the soul is to be healthy. This is no less true of the individual. Moral and physical health are synonymous. The slums are responsible for nine-tenths, alcohol for one-tenth of all human depravity. No healthy man is a Marxist, for being healthy, he recognizes the value of personality.

"We contend against the forces of disease and degeneration. Bavaria is comparatively healthy, because it is not completely industrialized. All Germany, including Bavaria, is condemned to intensive industrialism by the smallness of our territory. If we wish to save Germany, we must see to it that our farmers remain faithful to the land. To do so, they must have room to breathe and room to work. We must regain our colonies and we must expand eastward. There was a time when we could have shared the world with England. Now, we can stretch our cramped limbs only towards the East. The Baltic is necessarily a German lake.... However we cannot expand commercially or territorially, we cannot regain what we have lost, until we find ourselves. We are in the position of a man whose house has burned down. He must have a roof over his head before he can indulge in more ambitious plans. We have succeeded in creating at least an emergency shelter to keep out the rain. We were not prepared for hailstorms. However, misfortunes hailed down upon us. Germany has been living in a veritable blizzard of national, moral, and economic catastrophes. Two years of democracy have lost us Silesia, the Rhine and the Ruhr.

"Our demoralized party system is a symptom of our disease. What can the present government do? Nothing. It has no permanent support anywhere. Parliamentary majorities fluctuate with the mood of the moment. Parliamentary government is the spawn of hell. It opens the gate to Bolshevism. Bolshevism," Hitler emphatically continued, "is our greatest menace. Kill Bolshevism in Germany and you restore seventy million people to power. France owes her [present] strength not to her armies, but to the forces of Bolshevism in our midst. The Treaty of Versailles and the Treaty of St. Germain are kept alive by Bolshevism in Germany. The Peace Treaty and Bolshevism are two heads of one monster. We must decapitate both....

"Our German workers," Hitler said, "have two souls. One is German, the other is Marxian. We must arouse the German soul. We must root out the taint of Marxism. Marxism and Germanism, like German and Jew, are antipodes." Here Hitler outlined his case against the Jews.... The Jew, Hitler asserts, is destructive by nature. Unable to lead a national existence of his own, his presence in the modern state provides the ferment of decomposition."

Asked, "What would you do with the Jew?" Hitler said, "We would disfranchise him. [Even if he is born in Germany, because] birth in itself is no sufficient qualification for citizenship. Citizenship depends upon a clear recognition of the duties implied in its rights. The Jews are not German. They are an alien people in our midst, and manifest themselves as such....

"The fact that a man is decent is no reason why we should not eliminate him. Our hand grenades [in the war] made no discrimination between decent Englishmen and others. Decent Jews will realize that it is necessary for us to protect the integrity of our race. I look upon the Jews," Hitler continued, "as you look upon the Japanese. Both are an alien race. Both are an ancient people. Both have an ancient culture. Nevertheless, you [in the USA] do not admit the Japanese to citizenship. Yet, the Japanese, unlike the Jews, are not a destructive force. They have ruined no state. They are not carriers of Bolshevism.... They constitute no problem.

"Mixed breeds lack vitality. We would forbid mixed marriages hereafter. We would treat the off-spring of mixed marriages according to their desert. If they were patriots, we would accept them, although we would not encourage intermarriage with them. The issue that confronts us is one between Jew and Aryan. The mixed breed dies; it is a valueless product. Rome fell when it ceased to keep its race pure. In literature, in

131

the movies, in science, the influence of the Jew is destructive. We are like a consumptive, who does not realize that he is doomed unless he expels the microbes from his lungs. Nations, like individuals, are apt to dance most wildly when they are nearest the abyss. Hence, I say, we need violent correctives, strong medicine, maybe amputation.

"Now, more than ever, we must differentiate between elements that make for weakness and elements that make for strength. Incidentally, no deed of violence against Jews is on record in Bavaria. Not even the windows of a single Jew were smashed by my followers. No one, not even the Jews, can deny our honesty of purpose. We wish to purge ourselves from the Jews not because they are Jews, but because they are a disturbing influence. We wish to reserve citizenship and a voice in the council of our nation only to those who are of pure German blood.

"Our slogan is "Germany for the Germans." Foreigners, whether Jews or not, will be permitted to live in Germany only by sufferance....

"When I take charge of Germany, I shall end tribute abroad and Bolshevism at home."

Adolf Hitler drained his cup as if it contained not tea, but the lifeblood of Bolshevism.

"Bolshevism," the chief of the Brown Shirts, the Fascists of Germany, continued, gazing at me balefully, "is our greatest menace. Kill Bolshevism in Germany and you restore 70 million people to power. France owes her strength not to her armies but to the forces of Bolshevism and dissension in our midst.

"The Treaty of Versailles and the Treaty of St Germain are kept alive by Bolshevism in Germany. The Peace Treaty and Bolshevism are two heads of one monster. We must decapitate both."

When Adolf Hitler announced this programme, the advent of the Third Empire which he proclaims seemed still at the end of the rainbow. Then came election after election. Each time the power of Hitler grew. While unable to dislodge Hindenburg from the presidency, Hitler today heads the largest party in Germany. Unless Hindenburg assumes dictatorial measures, or some unexpected development completely upsets all present calculations, Hitler's party will organize the Reichstag and dominate the government. Hitler's fight was not against Hindenburg but against Chancellor Bruening. It is doubtful if Bruening's successor can sustain himself without the support of the National Socialists.

Many who voted for Hindenburg were at heart with Hitler, but some deep-rooted sense of loyalty impelled them nevertheless to cast their vote for the old field marshal. Unless overnight a new leader arises, there is no one in Germany, with the exception of Hindenburg, who could defeat Hitler - and Hindenburg is 85! Time and the recalcitrance of the French fight for Hitler, unless some blunder on his own part, or dissension within the ranks of the party, deprives him of his opportunity to play the part of Germany's Mussolini.

The first German Empire came to an end when Napoleon forced the Austrian emperor to surrender his imperial crown. The second empire came to an end when William II, on the advice of Hindenburg, sought refuge in Holland. The third empire is emerging slowly but surely, although it may dispense with scepters and crowns.

I met Hitler not in his headquarters, the Brown House in Munich, but in a private home - the dwelling of a former admiral of the German Navy. We discussed the fate of Germany over the teacups.

"Why," I asked Hitler, "do you call yourself a National Socialist, since your party programme is the very antithesis of that commonly accredited to socialism?"

"Socialism," he retorted, putting down his cup of tea, pugnaciously, "is the science of dealing with the common weal. Communism is not Socialism. Marxism is not Socialism. The Marxians have stolen the term and confused its meaning. I shall take Socialism away from the Socialists.

"Socialism is an ancient Aryan, Germanic institution. Our German ancestors held certain lands in common. They cultivated the idea of the common weal. Marxism has no right to disguise itself as socialism. Socialism, unlike Marxism, does not repudiate private property. Unlike Marxism, it involves no negation of personality, and unlike Marxism, it is patriotic.

"We might have called ourselves the Liberal Party. We chose to call ourselves the National Socialists. We are not internationalists. Our socialism is national. We demand the fulfillment of the just claims of the productive classes by the state on the basis of race solidarity. To us state and race are one."

Hitler himself is not a purely Germanic type. His dark hair betrays some alpine ancestor. For years he refused to be photographed. That was part of his strategy - to be known only to his friends so that, in the hour of crisis, he could appear here, there, and everywhere without detection. Today he could no longer pass unrecognized through the obscurest hamlet in Germany. His appearance contrasts strangely with the aggressiveness of his opinions. No milder mannered reformer ever scuttled ship of state or cut political throat.

"What," I continued my cross-examination, "are the fundamental planks of your platform?"

"We believe in a healthy mind in a healthy body. The body politic must be sound if the soul is to be healthy. Moral and physical health are synonymous." "Mussolini," I interjected, "said the same to me." Hitler beamed.

"The slums," he added, "are responsible for nine-tenths, alcohol for one-tenth, of all human depravity. No healthy man is a Marxian. Healthy men recognize the value of personality. We contend against the forces of disaster and degeneration. Bavaria is comparatively healthy because it is not completely industrialized. However, all Germany, including Bavaria, is condemned to intensive industrialism by the smallness of our territory. If we wish to save Germany we must see to it that our farmers remain faithful to the land. To do so, they must have room to breathe and room to work."

"Where will you find the room to work?"

"We must retain our colonies and we must expand eastward. There was a time when we could have shared world dominion with England. Now we can stretch our cramped limbs only toward the east. The Baltic is necessarily a German lake."

"Is it not," I asked, "possible for Germany to reconquer the world economically without extending her territory?"

Hitler shook his head earnestly.

"Economic imperialism, like military imperialism, depends upon power. There can be no world trade on a large scale without world power. Our people have not learned to think in terms of world power and world trade. However, Germany cannot extend commercially or territorially until she regains what she has lost and until she finds herself.

"We are in the position of a man whose house has been burned down. He must have a roof over his head before he can indulge in more ambitious plans. We had succeeded in creating an emergency shelter that keeps out the rain. We were not prepared for hailstones. However, misfortunes hailed down upon us. Germany has been living in a veritable blizzard of national, moral, and economic catastrophes.

"Our demoralized party system is a symptom of our disaster. Parliamentary majorities fluctuate with the mood of the moment. Parliamentary government unbars the gate to Bolshevism."

"Unlike some German militarists, you do not favor an alliance with Soviet Russia?"

Hitler evaded a direct reply to this question. He evaded it again recently when Liberty asked him to reply to Trotsky's statement that his assumption of power in Germany would involve a life-and-death struggle between Europe, led by Germany, and Soviet Russia.

"It may not suit Hitler to attack Bolshevism in Russia. He may even look upon an alliance with Bolshevism as his last card, if he is in danger of losing the game. If, he intimated on one occasion, capitalism refuses to recognize that the National Socialists are the last bulwark of private property, if capital impedes their struggle, Germany may be compelled to throw herself into the enticing arms of the siren Soviet Russia. But he is determined not to permit Bolshevism to take root in Germany."

He responded warily in the past to the advances of Chancellor Bruening and others who wished to form a united political front. It is unlikely that now, in view of the steady increase in the vote of the National Socialists, Hitler will be in the mood to compromise on any essential principle with other parties.

"The political combinations upon which a united front depend," Hitler remarked to me, "are too unstable. They render almost impossible a clearly defined policy. I see everywhere the zigzag course of compromise and concession. Our constructive forces are checked by the tyranny of numbers. We make the mistake of applying arithmetic and the mechanics of the economic world to the living state. We are threatened by ever increasing numbers and ever diminishing ideals. Mere numbers are unimportant."

"But suppose France retaliates against you by once more invading your soil? She invaded the Ruhr once before. She may invade it again."

"It does not matter," Hitler, thoroughly aroused, retorted, "how many square miles the enemy may occupy if the national spirit is aroused. Ten million free Germans, ready to perish so that their country may live, are more potent than 50 million whose will power is paralyzed and whose race consciousness is infected by aliens.

"We want a greater Germany uniting all German tribes. But our salvation can start in the smallest corner. Even if we had only 10 acres of land and were determined to defend them with our lives, the 10 acres would become the focus of regeneration. Our workers have two souls: one is German, the other is Marxian. We must arouse the German soul. We must uproot the canker of Marxism. Marxism and Germanism are antitheses.

"In my scheme of the German state, there will be no room for the alien, no use for the wastrel, for the usurer or speculator, or anyone incapable of productive work."

The cords on Hitler's forehead stood out threateningly. His voice filled the room. There was a noise at the door. His followers, who always remain within call, like a bodyguard, reminded the leader of his duty to address a meeting.

Hitler gulped down his tea and rose.

Europe in Sore Need of League Guidance
Baltimore Sun/October 18, 1923

Corfu and the Ruhr are Examples of Europe's Troubles Which are Said To Have Proved the Present League Incompetent

by Harold E. Stearns

From all accounts the vigorous Fascisti manner in which Signor Mussolini told the League of Nations to go chase itself, when the question of that society's "competency" over his occupation of Corfu was raised at Geneva, has pretty effectively killed American interest in the organization that was to bring law and justice to the age-long contending nationalisms of this distracted continent.

The plea that all would have been different had the United States only been a member may be true to a certain extent, as a matter of fact, but I believe popular instinct back home is right in feeling that the plea comes with singularly bad grace from nations which have so long been asserting what great benefits would accrue to us by our joining. If the league is impotent to settle so comparatively trivial a flare-up as Corfu without our help, what particular moral advantage lies in our coming in? Are we to act as judges and—thanks to our economic and financial power—executioners in every petty European dispute? I do not wonder that we have turned down the invitation with thanks.

The recent operetta performances at Geneva, I fancy, have settled the hash of the league as a genuine political issue at home for some time to come; in addition, they have confirmed those who believe in a narrow "isolationist" policy. Hence, from a broad point of view, they are regrettable as encouraging the anti-cooperative spirit in international affairs—a spirit which the modern world will eventually have to abandon if it is not to repudiate all that modern civilization has won since the Dark Ages.

Corfu has dramatized to the United States all its fears and terrors, all its distrust of what it did not understand. It has put a premium on obscurantism in political action abroad and given a prize to those who, because the world currents of events are so tangled and so extraordinarily difficult to understand, make a virtue of their intellectual laziness and say, "Let us attend to our own affairs and the rest of the world can stew in its own juice."

Even liberals at home and "hard-boiled" American newspaper men here in Paris, who—though really they ought to have known better—had put all their faith in the league, have given up hope, as they mournfully see another illusion go crash. I know nothing more grimly pathetic than the laments of the moderately "left" French publicists, who had thought to find through the league some method of pulling France from the moral impasse into which, they vaguely sensed, the occupation of the Ruhr had brought her.

Now, if my purpose were merely to add to the chorus of "I told you so's" of the cynics, who have all along predicted the league's failure, I should not bother to write this article. It is precisely because the league did embody generous hopes and ideals, did focus the aspirations of peace-loving men and women everywhere, that I wish to point out once again how this failure illustrates an old, old truth which runs to the effect that good intentions are not enough.

The league had failed long before the Corfu "test"—and for the very good reason that the entire spirit in which it conceived was a false and hypocritical one. Almost all the big powers regarded it simply as a convenient instrument for furthering certain aspects of their own policies, and the moment the smaller nations, or their representatives, under any pretext whatever, permitted it to become just this thing its doom was sealed. It would have been better all round if the league had confined itself to the discussion of postage stamps and international parcel post rules, and kept its own skirts clean, rather than have mixed in political action unless it could do so honestly.

For a long time, perhaps for a century, all it might have been able to do would have been to protest against certain actions. The bigger nations might have withdrawn, leaving only the neutrals and those that could not be accused of selfish interest. All the better: the one thing the league needed was to build up a world reputation for disinterestedness.

This is not a counsel of perfection, whatever realists pretend. By trying to play both ends against the middle the league has emerged discredited and powerless, the laughing stock of Europe. It has accomplished less than nothing, and has actually done more harm than good.

If it had realized that its force was a moral force, that its power was in the power of ideas, that its effectiveness lay in its integrity and nowhere else, it might have been politely smiled at in the chancelleries of Europe, but it would have been feared. Now what it says or does is not even seriously considered.

One of the worst casualties of the World War—which this whole episode so clearly brings out—is the loss of any kind of moral sense about international relations. To America, as I have said, Corfu seems to have dramatized the battle of right and wrong.

I read with a sigh Col. Stephen E. Lowe's bitter condemnation of the Italian shelling of an undefended city. The supporters of Near East Relief back home will probably read his statements and glow with righteous indignation. To speak brutally, this indignation is sheer sentimentality. This episode is dramatic and exciting; it rivets our attention. And we grow sick with disappointment because some deus ex machina on which we had pinned our faith proves but a rickety fake. It is our own fault.

138

Ever since the Armistice, practically, Bulgaria—to take a simple example—has been living under a treaty almost and unmitigatedly bad from every point of view as the abortive one of Bucharest, in 1913. The Greeks hold many thousands of Slav-speaking Bulgarians in subjection; so does Yugo-Slavia.

Yet the moment Greece gets into trouble with a stronger neighbor like Italy, she runs to the league as a possible source of help. Public opinion, forgetting all about Bulgaria (or, perhaps, in the case of America never knowing anything about it), at once becomes agitated, and the affair becomes a "test" of the league and its power.

In other words, the little nations, like the big, have been perfectly willing to call on the league for help against oppression, but they have resolutely fought bringing the cases of their own oppression on still weaker neighbors to the attention of the league.

I shall not go on to point out innumerable further instances of the same kind of thing, but one is too glaring not to "jump to the eyes," as the French say. The occupation of the Ruhr, after all, was but the application on a broader scale of the principle of "sanctions" (or gages, as they are called in Paris), a fact which Signor Mussolini was not at all reluctant to point out. If the league is to pass on the "competency" of the Corfu issue in one case, why should it not do likewise in the case of the Ruhr?

Whether political orators back in the States saw this point or not, certainly French diplomats themselves were quick enough to see it, and it explains why they lost no time in insisting that the whole question should be passed over to the Council of Ambassadors.

Belatedly, yesterday, Professor Gilbert Murray, one of the league's strongest supporters in England, brought up precisely this question, but with the "surrender" of Germany now practically a matter of hours the problem of reparations and "sanctions" will of course be settled by France, Belgium, Italy and England without the league's beneficent intervention.

If the occupation of the Ruhr and all that that occupation implied morally had been brought up publicly by the league in the week that French forces moved into Essen, then it would have a case—though only a moral case.

Today it has no case at all. Nobody will pay the slightest attention either to its protests or to its recommendations, except in so far as these latter may conform with the wishes of the big powers. And the league will sit impotently by watching the disintegration of the Continent, which can now not be prevented, whether Germany formally capitulates or whether she does not.

The process of economic absurdity has gone too far for any gesture whatever by any political government to make that absurdity rational. The process of hate creation, by injustice, has gone too far for any accord, reached under compulsion, to dissipate that most disruptive of emotions.

All Europe will pay toll for what it has allowed to happen unprotestingly for the last seven months, and France herself hardly less than other nations. For a few days to come, probably, paeans of artificial joy at the famous "victory" will fill the columns of the French and Paris press. But when it comes to an exploitation of that victory it will be something else again.

The league missed its opportunity to become the one institution to which both France and Germany might look for a disinterested plan when—as I think inevitable within a month or so—the cost both of the occupation and of the resistance to it will prove more than Europe can bear. Civil war in Germany, Fascism scattered all over the Continent, the most highly organized industrial population of the world endowed with habits of no-work and of sabotage, financial chaos, bitterness on both sides—a fine balance sheet indeed!

No, this League of Nations is dead. But its death may make necessary a new birth, under cleaner auspices and more honest principles. The ideal itself cannot die; it is as old as civilization itself. But for years to come Europe must pay the penalty for being false to those ideals. It will not do to reproach the United States for staying out. Why, as we look over the nightmare, years since the Armistice, should she ever have come in? Some day, doubtless, we shall join a league. However, it will be a league of peoples, not of nations. And that day is not yet.

Monarchist Coup in Bavaria's Capital
The Daily Telegraph/November 10, 1923

Reported Fiasco

Leaders Captured

Ludendorff A Prisoner

As was announced in the late edition of The Daily Telegraph yesterday, a Nationalist revolt broke out at Munich on Thursday. The government of Herr von Knilling was overthrown and a sort of revolutionary junta was formed including Herr von Kahr, the so called "Dictator" of Bavaria; Herr Hitler, the Fascist leader; General Ludendorff; Herr von Poehner, ex-Chief of Police at Munich; and General von Lossow, the ex-commander of the Bavarian Divisions of the Reichswehr. Hitler's Fascist ("Oberland") troops occupied various public buildings and open spaces and seized the offices of the Muenchener Neueste Nachrichten, a leading Democratic organ.

Immediately the news of this coup reached Berlin, which it did at a very late hour on Thursday night, President Ebert issued a decree appointing General Von Seeckt Commander-in-Chief of the Defense Forces of the Reich, with full powers to adopt the necessary step for the security of the Reich, and Herr Gessler, the Minister of Defense, prohibited the publication of other than semi-official reports regarding the events at Munich. He threatened that any contravention would be punished under Paragraph 4 of the Exceptional Regulations, and that papers acting contrary to the order would be liable to suppression. Renter, who wires the above news, adds: "In consequence of the overthrown of the Bavarian Government, the Government of the Reich has cut off all communication with Bavaria until constitutional conditions are restored."

According to the latest news received from Berlin, the insurrection in Bavaria has been entirely suppressed, and Ludendorff, Hitler, and other prominent "Putschists" have been arrested. In a telegram received late last night, however, Reuters remarks: "It is still too early to regard the insurrection as ended."

Hitler 'Putsch' Proved Fiasco, Easily Ended
The Gazette/November 10, 1923

Leader, Badly Wounded, Reported to Have Escaped

Rebels Hold Knilling

Ludendorff Is a Prisoner—Martial Law is Reported Proclaimed

The great "beer cellar government," proclaimed in Munich
Thursday evening with the announced purpose of regenerating Germany
by demolishing the republic and restoring the monarchy, had a brief
existence. Tonight it lies in ruins. Its career ended ignominiously today
in circumstances quite different from those attending its inception, when,
amid the fumes of beer and tobacco, the burly general, Erich Ludendorff,
declared that he would not flinch in the task assigned to him, even before
the prospects of war with France, as Bavaria could immediately put
300,000 fully equipped men in the field.

Today Ludendorff was a prisoner of the government he aimed to
overthrow. His coadjutor, Adolph Hitler, leader of the Fascisti movement
in Bavaria, was also captured, but, according to a late report which has not
been confirmed, he succeeded in escaping. It is said Hitler was wounded in
fighting that followed the "putsch."

Sixteen men, including loyalists and rebels, were killed in the
fighting at Munich, according to the latest advices from the Bavarian
capital. Two members of the Reichswehr were slightly wounded and some
members of the security police were killed and six or seven wounded.

The dispatches add that order in Munich has been completely restored
and that the Reichswehr and the security police are masters of the situation.

Putsch Was Confined

Did Not Spread Much Beyond Beer House

Information dispensed by official quarters this evening would
indicate that Adolph Hitler's "putsch" in Bavaria scarcely got beyond the

confines of the Rathskeller where the Fascisti leader proclaimed himself dictator of all Germany and Gen. Erich Ludendorff his war minister.

Just what happened after that remains to be cleared up, although reliable versions of the incidents which took place in Munich last night indicate that Dr. von Kahr, the Bavarian dictator and General von Lossow, commander of the Bavarian Reichswehr, immediately disentangled themselves from the prevailing confusion and hurried to the nearest barracks and there ensured themselves of the fealty of the Reichswehr troops, with the aid of which they rehabilitated their dictatorship and the civilian authority of Premier von Knilling

Political quarters in Berlin incline to the belief that Hitler's giant firecracker exploded prematurely and that he and Ludendorff were its chief victims. Both men are reported to have barricaded themselves in the war ministry in Munich, but afterwards to have come out and surrendered.

At the Ministry of Defense it was declared this evening that the troops were standing by Dr. von Kahr, under command of Gen. von Lossow, and that Hitler's attempted coup, as far as its physical menace was concerned, should be entirely dissipated.

Munich experienced little of the "putsch," and the rest of Bavaria failed to react to it. In Berlin it provoked a minimum of interest and no alarm.

The Nationalist leaders in the Reichstag make no concealment of their chagrin over the fiasco, which they obviously view as having done irreparable damage to the swing to the right among a large body of the voters. Incidentally, the movement has seriously handicapped the negotiations proceeding between the members of the Nationalist party and the German People's Party for the formation of a bourgeois cabinet, a movement which had received fresh impetus today when Chancellor Stresemann's party adopted a resolution to suggest to the Chancellor the advisability of inviting the Nationalists into such a coalition.

Awaits Liquidation.

With the Munich debacle awaiting final political liquidation, the belief is expressed in political circles that the Nationalists in the present situation suggest a heavy liability to such a four-party constellation, which, were it formed, in all probability would demand the retirement of Dr.

Stresemann. Nether the Chancellor, the Democrats nor the Clericals thus far have indicated their attitude toward the proposed bourgeois cabinet.

Chancellor Stresemann's government today informally apprised the diplomatic missions in Berlin that its authority had not been impaired by the 'putsch' and that the Munich episode was considered as having been disposed of insofar as it threatened to become a menace to the Berlin government's stability.

French opposition to the establishment of a limited directorate, or even a dictatorship, which Premier Poincare is said to have expressed informally through the French Ambassador, is viewed in semi-official circles here as unwarranted intervention in German internal affairs. Admonition from the French Government, or support from that source, is not required by Germany in connection with her efforts to adjust internal affairs, and it may even be suggested that support from this source would rather discredit the cause of democracy, says the National Zeitung.

Hitler Has Escaped.

Adolph Hitler, who led the Bavarian putsch, is reported in late advices from Munich to have escaped despite the wounds he received.

General Ludendorff, the chief of the Oberland Association, and other leaders of the Nationalist-Socialist Party are said to have been jailed. Eight or ten persons were killed in the fighting. Munich is described as calm.

Knilling Detained

Still Being Held by Adolph Hitler's Followers

The followers of Adolph Hitler are still holding Premier von Knilling of Bavaria, who was placed under arrest by them during Thursday night's coup.

Former Crown Prince Rupprecht of Bavaria has declared himself as strongly against the insurrectionary movement in Bavaria.

Details of the events in Munich are still somewhat obscure, owing to the fact that only scant official reports are available. The two leaders in this comic opera revolt, which collapsed in less than 24 hours, apparently were left in the lurch by their supporters when it was seen they had no chance of success.

The role played by Dr. von Kahr, the military dictator, and General von Lossow, commander of the Bavarian Reichswehr in the coup, appears, according to the official accounts, to have been in the nature of a diplomatic maneuver. It is said they could hardly have refused to accept the posts allotted to them last night by Hitler, when Hitler had six hundred armed followers behind him, as they certainly would have suffered the same fate as Premier von Knilling and the other Bavarian ministers who were promptly arrested by the Hitlerites when they raided the Rathskeller. They accordingly decided that discretion was the better part of valor and pretended to concur in the rebel plans. As soon as they regained their quarters where they were out of reach of Hitler's band, they decided to have nothing to do with the "putsch," but on the contrary to oppose it with the utmost energy. This decision of von Kahr and von Lossow gave a death blow to Hitler's hopes, as the Reichswehr remained loyal to von Lossow.

Extraordinary scenes were enacted in the now famous beer cellar in Munich during the raid. Hitler and his supporters made free use of their revolvers to obtain order; bullets were fired into the crowd occasionally to remind those present that a revolution was in progress. Hitler's threats to destroy the Treaty of Versailles, depose President Ebert and the Berlin Government and march against Berlin were received with frantic applause. General Ludendorff, who entered the hall toward the close of the proceedings, was given a great welcome. He made a speech in his best "mailed fist" style.

There has been absolutely no repercussion in Berlin from the events in Munich. The populace generally appear to be taking little interest in the affair, being much more concerned with the increasing prices of food. The government, however, is adopting all necessary precautions.

Martial Law Proclaimed

A dispatch to the Daily Mail from Berlin says martial law has been proclaimed throughout Bavaria and that any death sentences pronounced by court- martial are to be executed within three hours.

The dispatch adds that, according to a communication from Munich: Adolph Hitler escaped and is believed to be at Rosenheim, near the Austrian frontier, trying to rally his followers.

Where Is Ludendorff?

The whereabouts of General Ludendorff and Adolph Hitler was a mystery tonight, Neither Dr. von Kahr, the military dictator, nor General von Lossow, commander of the Bavarian Reichswehr, have given any indication of their intentions toward the captured general and his Fascisti prompter.

In official quarters here it is declared both men gave Dr. von Kahr and General von Lossow and other Bavarian officials unequivocal assurances of their loyalty and also promised that they would not attempt a coup or embark upon any political adventure without duly appraising official quarters.

Hitler's aides and other leaders of the various nationalist units were warned by Dr. von Kahr, who informed them that he would employ military force to disperse them if this became necessary.

Temporary Headquarters

Temporary headquarters of the government of Dr. von Knilling, the Bavarian premier, were established here this morning by Dr. Matt, Dr. Neinel and Dr. Krausneck, who immediately got in touch with von Kahr, von Lossow and Premier von Knilling.

As von Knilling still is detained by the Hitlerites, Dr. Matt as vice-premier immediately assumed authority instructing all Bavarian officials to disregard the orders of the insurgents.

Von Lossow ordered all available troops garrisoned outside Munich and the local police forces to report to him for service in Munich. The situation throughout Bavaria is tranquil; trains are again running on regular schedule.

Declarations Are Null

A Havas dispatch from Munich says the Bavarian news agency has circulated a proclamation issued by General von Lossow, commander of the Bavarian Reichswehr, saying his declarations of fealty to the revolutionists when he was arrested in their raid on the Rathskeller were obtained from him at the point of a revolver and therefore are null. The proclamation says von Lossow has resumed his office and that the guilty in the revolt will receive the punishment they deserve.

The dispatch adds that the National-Socialist party and the Overlandwar Flag Association have been dissolved.

The Munich Trial
The Guardian/February 26, 1924

Ludendorff's Part

The Story of the Hitler Plot

The chief actors in the drama that took place in the night from the 8th to the 9th of November, 1923, were Ludendorff, Hitler, Von Kahr, and Von Lossow. The trial of Ludendorff and Hitler on a charge of high treason begins to-day. The minor actors (some of whom will also be tried) need not concern us here.

The proceedings will be conducted in an atmosphere that will make a just verdict impossible. The two chief accused are national heroes. Ludendorff is still regarded with the greatest veneration by German patriots, especially by the ultra-patriotic Freedom party. They argue that he led Germany in a great war against overwhelming odds, that he is the greatest military genius of our age, that he would have been victorious had not pacifists, Jews, and Socialists stabbed the German army in the back, that he is still the real leader of Germany, and that when she reawakens it is he who will lead her to victory against the French and re-establish the monarchy and the military caste system in all their former magnificence. The faith in Ludendorff is of the perfervid kind that cannot be shaken even by the most obvious facts.

Hitler

Hitler is rather more of a local celebrity. He has admirers, but few real followers outside Bavaria. But in Bavaria he eclipses even Ludendorff in commanding a blind, ecstatic, fanatical adoration. He is an Austrian of humble origin. He is a voluble and impassioned orator. He has what is popularly known as "personal magnetism." He belongs to a florid, emotional type not uncommon on the Continent but rare in England, though not perhaps in Ireland.

He is the leader of the National Socialists, who are the Bavarian counterpart of the Freedom party. They are, of course, not Socialists at all, although, like the Italian Fascists they attract workmen into their ranks. The movement is, indeed, quite definitely Fascist. Its aims are to enforce law and order and to destroy Bolshevism and the influence of the Jews. Emotionally, at least, its most powerful driving force is anti Semitism.

Ludendorff's Earlier Intrigues

Ludendorff is an old and ambitious intriguer. Soon after the revolution he prepared a scheme for the invasion of Russia. He made a special study of the Red Army and pronounced it to be a danger to Europe. He advocated a kind of holy alliance between England, France, and Germany. He himself, as the greatest general living, would take command of the three inter-allied armies, lead them across ground with which the Great War had made him familiar, capture Moscow, destroy the Soviet Government, and re-establish the Tsardom. If the Allies refused to see the danger with which the Red Army threatened Europe, so much the worse for them. And if they persisted in their folly he might even go so far as to offer his sword to the Bolsheviks, in which case the world would witness some startling events. His mouthpiece at the time was Arnold Rechberg.

The Allied Military Missions at Berlin were approached but they showed themselves unsympathetic, and nothing came of Ludendorff's plan.

Preparing the Hitler Coup

The Kapp Putsch found him in Berlin and in close touch with the Kappists. When it collapsed he lay low for a while. Eventually he settled down at Munich and became the nucleus of reactionary intrigue.

In 1922 he again prepared plans of a rather grandiose character. He got into touch with General Averescu and proposed alliances with Hungary and Romania. In Germany itself the reactionaries were growing stronger every day. Their policy was to remove their chief opponents one by one before the day when they would sweep the whole country. Walther Rathenau, the greatest benefactor Germany ever had since the end of the war, was their most distinguished victim.

In 1923 their plans began to crystallize. Secret military formations dotted the country. Hitler's battalions were numerous and well disciplined. They were not armed very heavily but well enough for civil war.

Early in November Ludendorff came to Berlin to complete a scheme for its isolation and capture. Groups of his armed followers were in readiness to concentrate at points along a wide semicircle round the city. Ludendorff himself was to take command as soon as the signal should come from Bavaria.

Wittelsbach or Hohenzollern?

He returned to Munich, where the main conspiracy was maturing.

There were differences of opinion amongst the conspirators themselves—some, especially the Bavarians, wanted to restore the Wittelsbachs, others, amongst them Ludendorff, wanted to restore the Hohenzollerns. Hitler seems to have cared little for any kind of monarchy. But on one thing they were all agreed—namely, that a "national dictatorship" should be proclaimed at Munich and that it should be the signal for a general armed rising that would overthrow the Republican Government and establish the dictatorship all over Germany. The monarchy and the war of revenge against France would follow as matters of course. They had distributed the most important offices in the coming dictatorship amongst themselves. They had also drawn up a long list of the leading Republicans, Socialists, Democrats, Jews, Communists, Pacifists whom they would execute as soon as the power would be theirs.

But disagreement on minor issues grew deeper every day. Hitler's impetuous temperament and his melodramatic instincts filled the phlegmatic, dull-witted Von Kahr with uneasiness. Von Kahr and Von Lossow, the mutinous general who commanded the Bavarian regular troops, began to grow lukewarm. Von Lossow's diminishing ardor was particularly serious, for his defection would also mean the defection of the Bavarian regulars, against whom, so it was thought, the regular troops in the rest of Germany would never open fire.

149

Hitler grew alarmed, but all the more impetuous. He began to feel that delay might mean failure, and that if he took precipitate action the others, already deeply committed, would be unable to abandon the cause in the supreme moment.

And so, on the evening of the 8th November; he and a number of his armed followers burst into a hall where Von Kahr was addressing a packed meeting and proclaimed the "National Dictatorship." The meeting was thrilled to the wildest enthusiasm by this piece of audacity. All Munich went crazy with patriotic rejoicing.

But Von Kahr and Von Lossow were very concerned. Hitler took them into an adjoining room and, with alternate threats and supplications, dissuaded them from abandoning the cause for which they had striven so long and so ardently.

All three then went back into the hall. Von Kahr mounted the dais and proclaimed his loyalty to "his Majesty the King." Von Lossow also made a satisfactory declaration. Ludendorff, who had arrived in the meantime, spoke, amid wild enthusiasm, about "the grandeur of the hour."

Nevertheless Von Kahr and Von Lossow, no doubt foreseeing disaster for all Germany, deserted Hitler during the night and so broke the back of the whole conspiracy.

When Hitler and Ludendorff and their armed followers marched against the Bavarian War Office on the morning of the 9th they were met by police and by Von Lossow's regulars.

The Collapse

The troops opened fire. The street was littered with dead and wounded. Ludendorff was arrested, Hitler fled. It was all over.

For days afterwards Munich was in a turmoil. Expectation had been worked up to giddy heights and now the bitterest chagrin and disappointment boiled over. Kahr was called a Jew and a Jesuit (he is a Protestant). Both he and Von Lossow were shouted down as traitors and perjurers, which, although to the salvation of Germany, they were.

Hitler was caught a few days later. What his defense will be no one can tell. It seems likely that he will try to incriminate Von Kahr and Von Lossow. There have been several indications that Ludendorff will pretend that he was taken by surprise and that he simply placed his services at the disposal of the "National Revolution" which had burst upon the German Fatherland in such a sudden and unaccountable fashion.

It seems most improbable that either, least of all Ludendorff, will receive severe sentences. Although theoretically under arrest, he and several of his accomplices who will also be tried have been enjoying complete liberty and have even been allowed to address Fascist meetings.

Prospects of the Trial

Much if not all of the weightiest evidence will be hushed up. The court is to be cleared as soon as any facts compromising to certain influential people are likely to come to light. It is probable that Prince Rupprecht (the Majesty to whom Von Kahr declared his allegiance) will be asked to give evidence. That Von Kahr is only a witness and not amongst the accused is in itself a devastating comment on the trial.

It is even possible that Hitler's gunmen will try to stop the proceedings by violence. They have already uttered threats in plenty, and the necessary precautions have been taken.

No judge will be able to go against the great mass of excited, perfervid opinion. If the two chief accused, especially Ludendorff, are not acquitted they will get only nominal sentences, or if the sentences are severe they will be commuted or alleviated later on. Had the insurrection been planned by Radicals of the Left, and had the leaders been arrested, sentences of death and of imprisonment for life would have been distributed with the greatest liberality. No such sentences will be passed, or at least carried out, on Ludendorff and Hitler.

German Treason Trial
The Guardian/February 28, 1924

Hitler's Frothy Defense

Inquiries From The Dock For Dictator And General

Hitler is the hero of the hour. His defense, which takes up columns in this morning's papers, has made a great impression. He does not leave the slightest doubt that Von Kahr, the late Dictator, and Von Seisser, together with Von Lussow (commander of the Bavarian Reichswehr) were in the plot against the German republican government. "For months," says Hitler, "they spoke of nothing else."

The more light that is thrown on the plot the more pitiable does Kahr appear. In reply to his excuse that he submitted to Hitler on the evening of November 8 because Hitler threatened to shoot him later, Hitler now replies: "I never pointed my pistol at Von Kahr. He was not a terrible fellow who could only be held in check by force of arms. On the contrary, he stood pale and trembling on the platform." Hitler does not deny the charge made against himself, he only points the question: "Why are we in the dock and Von Kahr and Von Lossow free?"

The question is, of course, unanswerable. Hitler is at least showing the courage of his convictions, or, rather, emotions. Yet Von Kahr is more guilty than he, seeing that while Hitler was only a private adventurer he himself held high office in the federal state of the German Republic and used his position to plot its overthrow and then betrayed his confederates because his nerve failed him at the last moment. Von Kahr's ignominy is now complete. He himself has put the last finishing touch to it, for to avoid giving evidence he has slunk into a sanatorium. Whether the plea of ill-health will be allowed by the Bavarian Court, or whether he will be dragged out of his refuge, is still uncertain.

By incriminating Von Kahr, Hitler has obscured his own shortcomings. His speech is a torrent of histrionic emotionalism, full of froth. He does not give the slightest clue to what he really wanted. In some ways he resembles the Communist chieftain Max Holz, who is now serving a life sentence, but unlike Holz, he is not filled with the consciousness that he is fighting for the downtrodden and oppressed. He plotted and risked his life and the lives of others for no intelligible motive. He failed. Many of his confederates suffered wounds and death. Germany only just escaped civil war and anarchy. But there is nothing in Hitler's defense, not even a sign of self-interest or personal ambition that provides the slightest shadow of justification for such perils and sacrifices; nothing except empty phrases from the vocabulary of nationalism, anti-Semitism, and fascism. It would be difficult to find a more glaring instance of the intoxicating power of phrases on the perfervid, histrionic demagogue than the career of Adolf Hitler.

Ludendorff Free, Hitler Guilty in "Putsch" Case
Evening Star (Washington, D.C.)/April 1, 1924

by Edgar Ansel Mowrer

Bavarian Fascist Leader Gets 5-Year Sentence; Amnesty Probable

Verdict Is Popular

War Lord Nominated as Candidate for Seat in Reichstag

.Justice, as conceived in Bavaria, has found at last an absurd conclusion with the virtual pardon of the accused. Gen. Eric Ludendorff, scot-free, has accepted candidacy for the Reichstag, heading the racial party list.

Adolf Hitler, who has been occupying three charming rooms in prison, although sentenced to five years in a fortress, will be released after six months for good behavior, and in the end probably will be granted amnesty.

This was the most severe sentence for acknowledged high treason and armed endeavor to overthrow the government.

The courtroom was packed, many people standing. In order to gain entrance, it was necessary to pass seven examinations by soldiers and to be searched for arms. These precautions and the stringent police regulations forbidding public assemblies or placarding of the verdict had made one expect a certain severity in the judgment, but when the judges entered and read the sentence it was seen that the Bavarian court is logical in its absurdity and that all of the accused were practically pardoned.

Hundreds of persons waited outside the courtroom and eagerly demanded details of the sentence from German correspondents who first left the courtroom. The verdict was greeted by loud cheering, demonstrations of joy and a chorus singing patriotic songs.

Hitler's Closing Address

The so-called Munich carnival is fruitful to the historian, student and politician in two senses, which might be called revelations and results. Of first importance is revealed the responsibility of the entente for the German attitude.

Hitler's closing speech proved conclusively his jingo stock in trade furnished him by the entente. He stated specifically that had the republic government upheld the "national honor" by defying the entente he and his followers would still he republicans.

Future Depends on France

Germany's immediate future may depend largely upon whether, by wise moderation, France chooses to support the German republicans, or, by continued pressure, goad a placid people into nationalist fury. The Bavarian monarchist has stepped forth into daylight. It is commonly believed that back of the opposition to Gen. Ludendorff there are Prince Rupprecht and the Munich cardinal.

Only two days ago the crown was officially restored to the Bavarian coat of arms. Several of the deposed German monarchs find shelter, and Bavaria glories in their presence, yet at the same time the incompatibility between the ideals of Hohenzollern followers and Wittelsbach partisans was strongly outlined.

Considered Farcical

The main streets of Munich and all approaches to the courthouse presented the picture of an armed camp today when Gen. Erich Ludendorff, former German field marshal, was acquitted of the charge of treason for his part in the unsuccessful revolt here last November.

Steel-helmeted troops and heavy reinforcements of Bavarian police patrolled the streets, dispersing pedestrians. An ordinance proclaimed late last night by the prefect threatened participants in riots or mob gatherings with penitentiary sentences or even capital punishment. These precautions were taken with a view to suppressing hostile demonstrations by the followers of the men on trial.

Hitler's Followers Restrained

Hitler's followers arranged to signal news of the verdict from the housetops by wigwagging, as the police authorities prohibited public posting of the verdict and severely restricted admissions to the court chamber.

It became known today that Hitler's nationalistic anti-Semitic party had nominated Ludendorff and Poehner for Reichstag seats.

The trial at Munich occupied more than a month and much of the testimony was taken behind closed doors. A strong feeling in favor of Ludendorff, who made no attempt to hide his nationalistic beliefs, marked the entire proceedings.

The former field marshal, in a remarkable oration on the witness stand last week, declared that the judges themselves sat "before the judgment of history, which does not send men who fought for the fatherland to a fortress, but to a Valhalla."

Made Egotistical Speech

His speech was full of self-praise and his description of himself was "the victor of Tannenburg and other big battles—a representative of the old army which was crowned with everlasting fame."

The revolt for which the men were tried has been called the "beer cellar putsch," as it was before a gathering of Bavarian government

155

officials in the Burgerbrau Kellar that Hitler and his followers suddenly appeared on the night of November 8, fired shots to obtain silence and dramatically announced the overthrow of the government, proclaiming a dictatorship over the entire country, with Hitler at the head of the government and Ludendorff as commander-in-chief of the army. Poehner was to be premier of Bavaria.

Ludendorff was quoted at the time in press dispatches as declaring that he would not flinch in his new task, even should it mean another war with France, as Bavaria could immediately put 300,000 fully equipped men in the field.

Flays Central Government

"The dictatorial" government, however, had no opportunity to try its hand. The central government at Berlin, described by Hitler as "Marxian" and "Semitic," refused to take the situation seriously, and the Bavarian dictator, Dr. von Kahr, repudiated his adhesion to the movement, which he declared was given under compulsion.

After twenty-four hours of great excitement, during which the Hitlerites held the war ministry building, Gen. von Lossow's Reichswehr troops were brought into play and Hitler's doughty legions, which he had patterned after the Italian fascisti, melted away with but brief resistance.

Ludendorff was apprehended, but allowed to stay at his own villa under parole, while Hitler led the Bavarian authorities a lengthy chase before he was finally captured and immured in a fortress with a stolid guard, who could not be seduced from their duty by his famous "magnetic personality."

The verdict was received with popular approval, the populace being inclined to view it as a rebuke to Dr. von Kahr, former Bavarian dictator; Gen. von Lossow, former commander of the Bavarian Reichswehr, and Gen. Seisser, former chief of the Bavarian police, who repudiated the putsch after joining it at its inception, as they claimed, under compulsion.

From a punitive aspect the sentences imposed on Hitler and his followers were generally considered farcical, as Poehner and his chief will be obliged to serve only six months of their five-year term, after which they may be paroled on good behavior.

Gen. Ludendorff appeared in court in full military regalia, wearing numerous orders and decorations. He and Hitler were deluged with a mass of floral tributes which had been sent to the courtroom in anticipation of the verdict.

Despite the widespread police precautions the streets leading from the courthouse were quickly jammed with mobs of joyous admirers of both leaders, who were greeted with deafening cheers, punctuated by cries of "Down with van Kahr, Von Lossow and Seisser." Recent dispatches reported that the three former Bavarian officials had gone to Italy "for their health."

Ludendorff Goes Free In Treason Case In Bavaria
Asheville Citizen-Times/April 2, 1924

Adolf Hitler Found Guilty and Must Serve Five Year Sentence

Several Others Sent To Prison

Acquittal of Former Field Marshal Meets With Popular Approval

General Erich Ludendorff, former German field marshal, was acquitted today of the charge of treason for his part in the unsuccessful revolt here last November.

Adolf Hitler and former Chief of Police Poehner were convicted and each was sentenced to five years imprisonment and fined 200 gold marks. Dr. Weber and Colonel Kriebel, accused of being Hitler's aides, received like sentences.

Dr. Frisch, former president of the Munich district; Captain Rohem; Lieutenant Henry P. Purnett, who is Ludendorff's stepson; and Lieutenant Brueckner and Lieutenant Wagner were given 15 months and fined 100 marks each.

The verdict was received with popular approval, the populace being inclined to view as a rebuke to Dr. von Kahr, former Bavarian dictator; General von Lossow, formerly of the Bavarian Reichswehr, and General Seisser, former chief of the Bavarian police, which repudiated the putsch after joining it at its inception, as they claimed, under compulsion.

From the punitive aspect the sentences imposed on Hitler and his followers were generally considered farcical, as Poehner and his chief will be obliged to serve only six months of their five-year term after which they may be paroled on good behavior.

The court required only five minutes to read the verdict and a few seconds later it was heralded throughout the streets by the jubilant followers of the indicted men, who had arranged a wig wagging system.

General Ludendorff appeared in court in full military regalia. He and Hitler were deluged with a mass of floral tributes.

Despite the widespread police precautions the streets leading from the courthouse were quickly jammed with mobs of joyous admirers of both leaders who were greeted with deafening cheers, punctuated by cries of "down with von Kahr, von Lossow, and Seisser." (Recent dispatches reported that the three former Bavarian officials had gone to Italy for their health.)

Up to noon the police had not been called upon to intervene and, barring some local outbursts resulting from satisfaction with the findings of the court, no disturbances had been reported.

The popular approval of the nominal sentences imposed upon the convicted and of the unconditional acquittal of General Ludendorff was prompted by the feeling that they were actuated by patriotic motives.

Resentment over the alleged treachery of von Kahr, von Lossow and Seisser, is considered to have been plainly reflected in the verdict and is believed to have influenced the court's decision, which is viewed in liberal political circles as a moral victory for the Bavarian reactionaries and a tacit disavowal of the German republic.

While General Ludendorff's acquittal was widely forecast, there was an impression that the trial court would order Hitler's expulsion from Bavaria on the ground that he was a foreigner and an active menace to Germany's internal political situation.

Fascism Faces the Ballot Box
The Living Age/April 12, 1924

Guglielmo Salvadori

The strange admiration which so many English papers and English people show for Fascism can be explained only by a want of knowledge. Fascism is taken as a synonym of nationalism and patriotism. But as for nationalism, there is an older party of that name, which, though having as its motto a greater Italy, and though representing the small imperialistic and militaristic current and the idea of State authority versus the individual rights of the citizens, has never tried to overstep the law, proceeding always by constitutional methods; only after the advent of Fascism has it fused itself with the new party. And as for patriotism, it is not too much to say that the great majority of Italian patriots look with great suspicion at the new state of things, and are extremely anxious as to what it may bring about, for no good patriot and law-abiding citizen can look with approval at illegality and dictatorship. The Red and the Black Shirts are antitheses — the one came to free, the other to bind.

The salient feature of Fascism is illegality. An incident has just taken place at the station of Florence which, though almost too common to excite remark here, I will cite as an example. The Corriere della Sera, the gravest and most widely circulated newspaper in Italy, published at Milan, was waited for at the station by some thirty Fascisti, all armed. As the bundles of newspapers were unloaded, at two o'clock in the early afternoon, the Fascisti seized upon them, carried them out, and in the piazza before the station made a bonfire of them, under the eyes of a gaping crowd that knew better than to interfere, since the Fascisti shoot at sight. The police made a feint of protesting, but knew that to arrive late would please the Government, and in any case the arrests they might make would not be maintained. That the police should stand aside for such reasons when the law is violated is enough to characterize and condemn any government.

Another recent incident is that of Cesare Sobrero, correspondent of the Stampa and Giorno di Napoli, two well-known daily papers, which, like the Corriere della Sera, indulged in some criticism, cautious perforce, of the party in power. Sobrero was called to the police station and admonished to be careful, for his remarks had not pleased the Prime Minister! The truth is the one thing one cannot now say or print in Italy.

Many other so-called episodes occur all over the country — which indeed are not episodes but a method. At Genoa an ex-deputy is hindered from speaking in a private house among friends — Fascisti irrupt. At Bari two members of Parliament belonging to that province are banished. In the neighborhood of Rome the Popolari Party — in opposition — is prevented from preparing for the elections. The Fascio of Friuli decrees that the opposition shall present no candidate for the administrative elections. These infringements of the most elementary rights of citizenship might be multiplied without end.

It was during the short period of aberration that succeeded the war, with its strikes and red flags, already on the wane by September 1920, when the occupation of the factories had proved to the workmen themselves that they could not get on alone, that the bourgeoisie decided to bind themselves together (Fascio = bundle, bound) to support the State in case of strikes, and combat the well-organized Socialists. So far, so good; when order, which was gradually returning, was established, the Fascio was to have unloosed itself, having merited well of a grateful nation. Everything was contributing to this end — time, which in itself calms and settles, the staid Catholic Popolari Party with its great influence among the peasantry, the tragic example of Russia, and, last but not least, the obvious uselessness of strikes when too often abused as a weapon. It was then that the ex-Socialist Mussolini saw his opportunity; or rather the clique that financed him did, using him as a tool to combat Socialism and its anti-capitalistic principles.

Mussolini had left his party at the beginning of the war, and with money paid him by France — as he cheerfully admits — started the newspaper, Popolo d'Italia, to make propaganda for Italy's intervention in the war. The Socialists wept for their lost leader, whom they knew for a man, if not of an elevated type, at least of energy and organizing talent, astute rather than intelligent, and they regretted him still more when they saw his success. He chanced, whether from luck or cunning, to base his influence on the generation of boys who had grown up wild, nervous, and idle, with their fathers in the trenches and their anxious mothers doing men's work away from home, with the schools and workshops in disorder, and the ways of war their daily food — with D'Annunzio's raid on Fiume as an object lesson in coups de main.

These boys were in their teens when the Fasci began and gave them an outlet for their restlessness. Mussolini pandered to their tastes, to the boyish love of make-up and adventure. He dressed them in sinister black shirts, with a white skull or some other darkly romantic emblem embroidered on the pockets; he encouraged mysterious nocturnal 'punitive' excursions in autocars packed as full as they could hold of excited youth, well armed, to burn down Socialist mutual-society clubs, and afterward private houses, for 'reprisal' if anyone rebelled, shooting at sight, partly for fear and partly for bravado, all who resisted — learning the manners and bearing of stage villains. He taught them to consider themselves above the law, and all their crimes glorious, for this, he said, was patriotism. A true corrupter of youth, our Mussolini! But his chief teaching was the contempt for law — the only obedience was to himself, and to the King in so far as he patronized him.

On Mussolini's accession to power after the masquerade of the March on Rome — permitted chiefly because it was not taken very seriously, and done to amuse the boys — it was hoped by many that the Fasci would be unbound, and that Mussolini would govern in the ordinary legal way, respecting the Italian Constitution. But, too vain and not great enough to do this, he preferred to keep his devoted satellites, who began to find it rather dull, with no more nocturnal excursions, no manhunts. Mussolini then invented another diversion: he changed his Black Shirts into a militia, with Roman names — consuls, decurions, centurions, and so forth — and the Roman salute of extended arm. Julius Caesar and his host!

The militia are 300,000, to be increased to 500,000, armed and more or less drilled — a real army. Yet they in no way depend on the army or the King, but on Mussolini himself. He may threaten civil war with them, and does threaten to have anybody shot who criticizes this creature of his making, La Milizia per la Difesa Nazionale. But, as we have the army and navy for national defense, the very name is false.

They are not a corps of volunteers to help the army in case of need, as foreigners probably think, but a means to terrorize internal opposition, and daily, systematically, they take the law into their own hands, and are never punished for crimes against life and property, although severely for disobedience to their own rules. We can imagine how they will behave during the excitement of the coming general elections in April — elections which will be a sorry farce, and which ex-Minister Orlando and other leaders of the Liberal Democratic Party declined to countenance, declaring their intention of withdrawing from public life.

After the most definite assertions of complete independence and intransigence, expressing in most impolite and vulgar language the deep disgust all other parties caused him, Mussolini has sent messenger after messenger to Orlando, begging, almost imploring him to join the list of government candidates, not as a representative of his party, but on his personal merits. After much demur Orlando, and a few other notabilities of the same Democratic Party, have accepted, making it a condition that the Constitution and Parliament shall be respected, and hoping doubtless in this way to curb the dangerous career of the present Government.

That it is dangerous there is no doubt. Strangers who come abroad see that the country seems quiet, but order imposed outside the law cannot be durable. When the image of order, with feet of clay, falls suddenly, as fall it must, those countries that have not taken the trouble to look below the surface will have done Italy an ill service in encouraging the kind of infatuation for Mussolini which has come over many people, even among the Italians; and chief of these countries is England, whose press and whose subjects abroad hail Mussolini as the savior of his country!

High Treason in Munich
The Living Age/April 26, 1924

by Stephan Weigelt-Gauting

The Munich trial strips the mask from Bavaria, from counter-revolutionary Bavaria that we long have known as a hotbed of political assassination, an asylum for political criminals, the breeding-place of secret conspiracies, the drill-ground for military leaguers and all other preachers of violence — in short, the stronghold of those who hate the Republic and advocate restoring the old regime.

Chauvinist organizations had acquired an authority in Bavaria comparable only with that exercised by Mussolini's Fascist hordes in Italy.

Since their conceptions of power and politics were those of the Fascisti, they sought to duplicate the march on Rome with a march on Berlin. This project was favored, fostered, and prepared not only by the condottieri bands of ambitious political conspirators like Hitler, Rohm, and Pittinger, but also by responsible officers of the government, and first of all by Herr von Kahr, the Bavarian dictator, who owed his exaltation to that position to the aid of these societies. So the present trial opens the way for a general settling with Bavaria, which has impudently defied the constitution for the past three years. The Republic has made its authority felt in case of Saxony and Thuringia. What does it propose to do in case of still guiltier Bavaria?

In the trial of Hitler and Ludendorff, real leaders stand in the prisoner's box and not mere tools, as was the case when the assassins of Rathenau and Erzberger, the assailants of Scheidemann, and the instigators of Kapp were brought to book. Furthermore, the accused do not present a united front, as they did in these earlier proceedings. For it has been clear from the beginning that the prosecution is directed not only against Hitler and Ludendorff and their underlings, but also against men not formally accused but morally culpable, who are the high priests of reaction in Bavaria. To comprehend the situation we must bear in mind that Herr von Kahr, the head of the Bavarian Government, General von Lossow, the leader of the Bavarian defense forces, Colonel Seisser, the Chief of the Bavarian Rural Police, and Captain Ehrhardt virtually stand in the prisoner's box with Hitler himself.

The long propaganda speeches that Hitler, Ludendorff, and Pohner, the former Munich Police Chief, have made in court show clearly upon what they count for safety. Pohner brazenly declared: "If what I have done is high treason, I have been committing high treason for five years." These men have tried to prove — and they have nearly succeeded in doing so — that their treasonable conduct up to the morning of November 9 was known and approved by the highest officials of the Bavarian Government, by Herr von Kahr and by General von Lossow, and that they were conducting a revolt as the agents of the Bavarian dictator himself. They sought further to prove that this revolt, planned and prepared in Munich against the constitution and government of the Republic, was conceived and directed by the Bavarian authorities. They were able to cite as evidence of this the preliminary measures taken in conjunction with Kahr, Seisser, and Lossow during last September and October, as well as the notorious meeting at the Munich Burgerbrau-Keller on the eighth of November. The latter evening, Kahr, Lossow, and Seisser not only professed themselves in complete agreement with Hitler's projected revolt, but they consented to accept important offices in the new national government that Hitler proposed to set up. This is not modified by the fact that during the same night they decided for reasons of expediency to repudiate this action, and the following morning defeated the very insurrection that they had helped set in motion.

Ludendorff plays a miserable role in this affair. His "complete surprise" at the Burgerbrau-Keller in Munich on the evening of November 8 is a perfect duplication of his "accidental presence" at Brandenburger Tor in Berlin on the morning of March 13, 1920, when Kapp tried to overthrow the Republic. Ludendorff in tow of Hitler, who in turn was the dupe of Kahr and Lossow, does not make a very imposing figure. If ridicule can destroy a reputation, his reputation is killed for all time. And Hitler? He is, as he always was, a little man, a subaltern, no matter how cockily he may stand on tiptoe and crow. He is a barnstorming hero to strut a village stage. The sole remarkable thing about him is his conceit.

The only moral advantage that Hitler and Lossow show in their defense is the evidence that they acted consistently throughout and faithfully followed the plans that Kahr and Lossow had so carefully prepared. The idea of a march on Berlin was not conceived merely by Hitler and Lossow; it was a move matured by Kahr, Lossow, the leaders of the chauvinist unions, and their North German allies. The project to overthrow German democracy and the German Republic from Bavaria as a base is an old one that goes back to the first days following the revolution. Active preparations to carry it out started, as Pohner's testimony shows, immediately after Kahr was made dictator of Bavaria, with the title of Generalstaatskommissar. The first overt step toward accomplishing this treasonable design was to invite to Bavaria Captain Ehrhardt, who was then under accusation for high treason in the Kapp revolt, for participation in other conspiracies against the Government, for founding and directing "Organization C," and for perjury, and to entrust to that precious traitor the organization of the so-called "Emergency Police" on the Bavarian-Thuringian border. The first move toward attacking Berlin was to station the Ehrhardt marine brigade in Franconia. The next step in that direction was to withdraw the Bavarian

National Guard from the jurisdiction of the commander-in-chief in Berlin and make it entirely dependent upon the Bavarian Government. The third step was to nullify in Bavaria the Law for the Protection of the Republic. The national Government tolerated all this, at the very time it was asserting its authority vigorously in Saxony and Thuringia.

The man responsible for these measures was not Hitler or Ludendorff, but Herr von Kahr. The Bavarian patriotic organizations had been worked upon by intensive propaganda until they were persuaded that a national uprising must begin in Bavaria, and were impatient to set it going. These organizations, however, were divided into two groups: the original "Patriotic Unions," whose honorary chairman and recognized leader almost since their organization began had been Herr von Kahr; and the Hitler-Ludendorff group, which embraced the National Socialist "assault" units and the allied militant bodies known as Oberland, Wikingbund, and Reichsflagge. For some time these two groups had been struggling with each other for ascendancy, although they were united in their hostility to the Weimar Constitution, the Republic, parliamentary institutions, and democracy in general. Their differences related to the way they would reorganize future Germany. Ludendorff and Hitler wanted a united greater Germany under a Hohenzollern Kaiser. Kahr and the Patriotic Unions wanted a federal Germany, the partition of Prussia, the hegemony of Bavaria, and a Wittelsbach Kaiser.

Herr von Kahr, in his position as Staatskommissar, succeeded, largely through the help of Ehrhardt, in detaching some units from the Hitler organization. Wikingbund, Reichsflagge, and several smaller associations deserted Hitler and went over to Kahr. They were persuaded that the latter's scheme, the advantages of which were carefully explained to them, stood a better chance of success than Hitler's plan. Kahr's position as Staatskommissar enabled him to favor the societies loyal to him with financial resources as well as official backing. His alliance with Lossow also placed the Reichswehr, or Bavarian National Guard, at his disposal.

However, Kahr could not carry out his ambitious plans of overthrowing the Republic against the opposition of the National Socialists, who remained loyal to Hitler. It was therefore necessary for him to win over Hitler and Ludendorff and to get them to cooperate. Pohner's testimony shows that he acted as the middleman in these negotiations, and gives us a clear and detailed account of how they were conducted.

Although these joint preparations for a march on Berlin, between the end of September and the beginning of November, brought the two groups into closer relations, they still mistrusted each other, and they could not agree which party should exercise the leadership. That wrecked the project. The different groups, wrought up to a high pitch of excitement by constant alarms and mobilizations, demanded action. Kahr hesitated; he waited for reports from North Germany, where plans were by no means so far advanced as in Bavaria. In that part of the country the Patriotic Unions were not so influential. Most important of all, the Reichswehr there had not been won over. The evidence has not brought out as yet who Kahr's agents in North Germany were. Kahr himself did not have so much confidence in the magic of Ludendorff's name as did that general and his satellites. Finally Hitler and Ludendorff, who were burning with impatience and had no intention of being pushed into the background, seized the first favorable opportunity to set things going. They hoped in this way to seize the direction of the movement. So they managed to sweep Kahr off his feet at the Burgerbraukeller. On the evening of November 8, Hitler seemed to have won. At noon, November 9, Ludendorff was under arrest and Hitler was a fugitive. But at the same time the Hitler revolt had punctured the Kahr revolt. Kahr was pilloried as a traitor by the chauvinist patriots. The gulf between the two insurrectionary movements was deeper than ever. The two parties now stand before the tribunal mortal enemies. Each is trying to throw the blame for failure upon the other.

The frankness with which Hitler and Ludendorff, Pohner and Kriebel have described the historical background of the revolt is most gratifying. Their speeches, to be sure, show more eagerness to win public sympathy for the 'Nationalist' cause than to prove their innocence to the court. They know that the letter of the law and the facts of the case demand their conviction. But they hope that the court will not dare to sentence them for political reasons, or that if they are sentenced the outraged Bavarian people will liberate them from prison. They may be deceiving themselves. Ludendorff's attacks upon the Catholics and the Catholic clergy have decidedly lessened that prospect. In a situation requiring political tact, the General has a hand like a ham.

But not only does Kahr sit morally in the prisoner's box by the side of Hitler and Ludendorff—the whole Government Party of Bavaria since March 13, 1920, is summoned before the bar of public judgment. At that time Kahr took advantage of the treasonable attempt of Kapp and his associates to overthrow the Government at Berlin to seize power in Bavaria, with the help of the Freikorps Oberland and the other Patriotic Unions, and to make himself Prime Minister. Public sentiment and the Landtag offered no effective opposition. From the time he seized office we have had a constant series of crises between Bavaria and the National Government. Democratic and republican ideas have been systematically suppressed. The Social Democrats have been hounded and harried. Even after he retired as Premier, Kahr utilized his influential position as President of the Council of Upper Bavaria and his control of the Patriotic Unions to continue a policy of sabotage against the National Government.

How did it happen that the Cabinet appointed him Generalstaatskommissar, or dictator, on the twenty-sixth of last September? This was not an act of free will on the part of the legally constituted authorities. It was done under the duress exercised by the Patriotic Unions. Since the beginning of 1923 these Unions had declared that if passive resistance ceased in the Ruhr all Germany must rise up and put in power a " truly National" Government. The Kustrin revolt in Brandenburg was a premature fragment of this plan. Even before passive resistance in the Ruhr was formally ended, a drumfire of public resolutions and secret ultimatums was directed against the Bavarian Ministry, to force it either to defy the Berlin Government or to resign. Both the National Socialists and the Patriotic Unions, with Herr von Kahr pulling the strings, made feverish preparation for action. The weak Bavarian Cabinet, thinking to choose the lesser of two evils, appointed Kahr Generalstaatskommissar. This blocked the National Socialists but gave free rein to the Patriotic Unions. After that, measures to overthrow the Republic were rapidly matured. The trial shows glaringly how far the Balkanization of Germany by reactionary Fascist organizations, secret societies, and irresponsible but ambitious leaders, has already gone. When Lieutenant-Colonel Kriebel boasts in open court that when he. was commander of the National Guard in March 1920, at the time of the Kapp revolt and Kahr's first appointment as Bavarian Premier, he "earned his spurs as an insurrectionist," and when the late notorious Chief of Police Pohner cynically admits that he has been plotting high treason for five years, these witnesses throw a vivid ray of light into the depths of Bavaria's political rottenness.

Fascisti Facing Big Scandal in Matteotti Case
Baltimore Sun/June 18, 1924

High Officials Of Black-Shirt Regime Said To Be
Behind Four Men Accused Of Deputy's Murder

Mussolini's Hold on Power Regarded As Doomed
Unless He Forces Full Exposure of Conditions

Rome, June 17. When Premier Mussolini declared only the bitterest foe could have planned so diabolical a crime as the murder of the Socialist Deputy Matteotti he spoke the truth, for the crime has thrown a fierce light on Fascist rank-and-file violence against their opponents. By the arrest of four Fascisti—Dumini, Viola, Mazzuaoli and Puntato—whom the police charge with abducting Matteotti in broad daylight in the center of Rome, they have brought out the fact, although they do not admit it, that high officials of the Fascisti regime are behind the four prisoners.

Body Reported Found

The police have not confirmed the report that the deputy's mutilated body was found on the shores of Lake Vico, 30 miles from Rome, though it is known to friends of the missing man. They, seeing the indifference of the police on the first day after the kidnapping, hunted Sgr. Matteotti in Rome in the environs and are said to have been satisfied the body is found. The reason for the police's delay is reported to be that Premier Mussolini took time to consider the best methods of proceeding. It is said a gigantic scandal is inevitable as the facts are brought out. Rumors mention Under Secretary of Home Affairs Finzi, who resigned to defend himself against the charges, as the instigator of Matteotti's murder.

Preparing to Expose Finzi

The Socialist was kidnapped as he was on his way to the Chamber of Deputies to give facts and figures touching on Finzi's supposed gains from the oil option the government recently granted to Harry F. Sinclair.

He also is said to have profited largely by the recent decree legalizing gambling. It is charged Finzi has been taking bribes for months; the rumors to that effect were widespread, but Matteotti claimed to have documents to prove the charges true. It is freely predicted that if Mussolini keeps his promise to bring the murderers to justice, he will also bring on the most sensational revelations of dishonesty on the part of his closest henchmen.

Mussolini's Prestige Hurt

The murder already has shortened the life of the Fascisti Parliament's first session. Mussolini decided to adjourn it the day after the body was found for fear too much would be said on the floor. Nevertheless, the closing of the Chamber, for whose existence he passed a special bill and on which he relied to consolidate his position, is in itself a heavy blow to his prestige. During its short life it held only 13 sessions, but the Fascisti members were so riotous that the oldest members say they have seen nothing to approach the disorder of the present Parliament. Not only the general public but the best of the Fascisti party as well declare that, unless Mussolini has the courage to unfold the entire network of violence, peculation and intrigue of which Matteotti's murder was the climax, his domination must end soon. But if he courageously cleans the party of the thousands of jailbirds who have joined since the march on Rome, which brought him into power in 1922, his followers think Fascism and the country will rise stronger than ever.

Culmination Of Series

The murder of Matteotti is the culmination of a long list of outrages. There was the devastation of former Premier Nitti's home by the Fascisti; the almost mortal wounding of Deputies Misuri and Amendola, who refused to become black shirts; the thrashing of village priests and the burning of Socialists' homes and workmen's clubs. Such incidents have become almost daily occurrences in Italy's provincial life. The public exonerates Mussolini of direct complicity in these crimes, but holds him indirectly responsible for the reign of hate. The Premier never hesitates to use the most violent threats when addressing his militia; his hottest phrases are deleted from the printed reports and censored out of foreign correspondents' stories. But the blackshirts, especially the large body of turbulent, idle militiamen, never fail to quote their leader to justify some act of violence. His scornful definition of liberty as a rotten corpse is one of the much-used quotations.

Former Editor Arrested

Signor Filippelli, former editor of the Corriere Italiano, was arrested by the police and lodged in prison at Genoa following an attempted flight in a motorboat. The carabineers pursued the former editor, who was accompanied by Signor Naldi, now on the staff of the Corriere Italiano, and caused them to surrender. Both Filippelli and Naldi are being held in Marsassi Prison, Filippelli on a warrant charging him with being connected with the kidnapping of Socialist Deputy Mateotti, and Naldi on the charge of attempting to assist in the escape of Filippelli. Signor Filippelli was brought to Rome from Genoa today and placed in prison, where he will await interrogation by Judge Grossi regarding the part the former editor is alleged to have played in the disappearance of Mateotti. Filippelli is said to have had a loaded pistol on his person when he was taken. The police are also declared to have taken from him a large bundle of important documents and a sum of money.

An Enemy of Fascism
The Guardian (London)/June 19, 1924

Mateotti's Political Activity

Italian Election Terrorism

(From our Political Correspondent.) London, Wednesday. As their indignant resolution and telegram show, the British Labor and Trade Union movements are deeply stirred by the assassination, as they believe it to be, of Signor Mateotti. On his visit to London Signor Mateotti addressed a private meeting of the International Joint Committee of the

Labor party's Trade Unions Congress, at which he described the methods of Fascism as he knew them.

He had a fear that something of this kind would happen to him, and he frankly expressed it. He told how comrades of his own had disappeared, and declared that the police always failed to make arrests and that the judiciary under the control of the Government would do nothing to protect them. He said that he never visited his home in the country at the village near Florence, because in a country place he might be kidnapped easily. In the great towns there was more security.

He had compiled a documentary history, "A Year of Fascism in Italy," giving a summary of the material he had collected from all over the country, largely a catalogue of kidnapping and seizures of private property. It is circulated privately in Italy, and will soon be published in English.

Fascist Election Methods

He described to the Labor meeting the circumstances of the elections. The United Socialist party, of which he was the leader, had the highest vote of all the Socialist parties, and he himself was elected for two constituencies in Rome and Florence. He pointed out that where any political campaign of any kind was permitted, as m the towns of the industrial north, like Milan, Fascism was defeated. But in the south and in country districts no public meetings, posters, or distribution of literature by the non-Fascist parties were allowed, and the Fascists won a doubtful victory.

He gave examples of what must have been the terrorism from the impossible size of the Fascist vote in such places. In one country district, for example, there was a hundred per cent poll and a hundred per cent Fascist vote. In Rome there was no freedom for holding meetings and no freedom of the press, so that they had to get private printing presses.

Signor Mateotti and his friend Treves, another Italian Socialist deputy, were believed to be the most hated men in Fascist Italy. They were the leaders of the Right Socialists, and with Turati had kept the Socialist movement in the path of democracy during the last few years.

The Passport Story

It had been stated in the press that Signor Mateotti came to England without a passport, but the fact is that any Italian citizen can come to England without a visaed passport. The point is that Signor Mussolini had decreed that no member of the Italian Chamber of Deputies might leave Italy without his permission. It was this permission that Signor Mateotti did not ask for. Italian Socialists have always found in the past that Mussolini's permission to leave the country arrives when it is no longer worthwhile to travel.

Mr. W. Gillies, secretary of the International Department of the Trade Unions Congress and Labor party, who saw a good deal of Signor Mateotti when he was over here, gives me this personal impression of him. "He was really a typical young intellectual. He was under forty, a man holding strongly to definite political convictions and expressing them fearlessly, but also a man of genial temper, with no violence of speech or manner. He was a man of wide culture. The last day I spent with him in London we lunched at the 1917 Club, and then at his suggestion we went to the Wallace Collection and the Tate Gallery. Two days afterwards he left London."

A Martyr at Fascist Hands

Socialist Tribute

The Secretariat of the Labor and Socialist International has sent to the Socialist party in Italy a letter from London in which they say "We kept up hope till the last moment, but now it is only too true that Mateotti is dead. Our pain is all the keener because only a little while ago he was here in London amongst us. We discussed with him the work of the proletarian campaign in Italy, and the better we knew him the more we felt that he was not only a brave worker, but a man through and through, ready to offer any sacrifice for the cause to which he had consecrated his life. In Mateotti lay one of the greatest hopes for the reconstruction of the Socialist movement in Italy, for courageous and unbending resistance to the dreadful terrorism of Fascism to which you are a prey. We had been looking forward to seeing him again at the meeting of the Labor and Socialist International Executive in Vienna. He was refused a passport by Mussolini, and compelled to remain within the grip of Fascists, and still they did not hesitate to add the worst to their string of misdeeds.

With the strict impartiality and critical exactitude of a scientist Mateotti collected accounts of Fascist crimes, grouped them under towns and months, and published them without comment. This calm collection of Fascist doings, however, contained in his book "A Year of Fascism," constituted a flaming attack on Mussolini's tyrannical government. He was in the midst of his work for the publication of a second edition, extended to the second year of Fascist government. Through his death he himself is now a martyr at the hands of the Fascists.

Resignation of Mussolini Now Reported Near
Ottawa Evening Citizen/June 19, 1924

Dispatch to Berlin Says Fascist Position
Shaken Following Disappearance of Socialist Deputy

British Labor Has Severest Censure

Declares Mateotti Had Evidence Incriminating the Fascism Leaders

BERLIN, June 19. The resignation of Premier Mussolini is believed to be imminent, according to a special dispatch received here today by the newspaper Vorwaerts from its Rome correspondent. The dispatch states that the Fascisti position is rapidly becoming more and more shaken as the result of the Matteotti revelations. No confirmation of the impending resignation of Mussolini has been received from Rome. Other dispatches are contradictory. Some declare the excitement over the kidnapping and probable murder of the Socialist deputy is subsiding while others claim the situation grows only more tense. The transmission of news is made more difficult by the Italian censorship.

Fascism on Trial
The New Republic/August 6, 1924

The assassination of Matteotti, the deputy to the Italian Parliament, has caused a radical change in the political situation in Italy. The Socialist deputy, who was expected to deliver a speech of financial criticism hostile to the Fascist government, was seized in Rome in broad daylight, near his home, carried far away in a motorcar and murdered—how is not yet known. As I write, his body has not been found. Faced with the indignation of the public, which spread even among the ranks of the Fascist parliamentary majority, after hesitation and delay which gave the impression of complicity, the police arrested several of the material executors of the crime. Still later, they arrested three of the instigators, but only after these had found time to destroy all their compromising documents. They are men who occupied confidential positions in the group of friends or officials of Signor Mussolini: Cesare Rossi, the chief of his press service; Marinelli, the manager of the Fascist party; and Signor Filippelli, the director of the Fascist newspaper. The chief of the assassins has proved to be a certain Dumini, a devoted personal friend and follower of the Prime Minister, a typical figure of post-war days, a brave soldier during the war—later, unemployed and unscrupulous—a participator in, or an organizer of, many of the "punitive expeditions" of the time that preceded the "march on Rome" and of many attacks upon members of parliament and journalists in the subsequent period. The voice of the public was also raised in accusation of complicity against Signor Finzi, undersecretary at the Ministry of the Interior, an intimate friend of d'Annunzio and Mussolini, intermediary between the two, and formerly a courageous aviator (he accomplished the raid on Vienna with d'Annunzio). Later he became a Fascist deputy and minister, grown rich in a very brief spell of power. General De Bono, one of the directors of the "march on Rome," soon to become chief of police and chief of the national militia—likewise a brave soldier and a miserable failure in politics—was also among the accused.

Mussolini, under the stress of outraged public opinion, and urged by a group of ministers, which we may call the group of gentlemen (Gentile, Federzoni, Oviglio, De Stefani, Di Giorgio), relinquishing the hope that the episode might resolve itself into a mere nine days' scandal, was obliged to give severe orders to the police, to allow the magistracy free play, to ask Finzi and Rossi to resign, to place a substitute for De Bono at the head of the police and to name Federzoni Minister of the Interior.

The excitement of public opinion has been in part an emotional phenomenon and in part a political one. The emotional element is due to the circumstances of the crime, which had a romantic aspect and was of a nature to awaken general pity and to stir all consciences. Signer Matteotti has left a wife and three young children—who do not even know where the body of their father is to be found. It is not known whether he was subjected to torture. For whole days the lack of precise information, the revelation of the conspiracy, the irritating nonchalance of the authorities, the growing complicity of eminent political personalities, had held the public interest taut. Crowds, eager, curious, stampeded the stands of the news-dealers; while in public places, and trains, as well as in private houses, nothing else but the "affare Matteotti" was spoken of. The compassion and sympathy of all, the sense of shame and resentment aroused in every Italian at seeing his country blemished by an act so foreign to the character of the race—all this augmented impatience and the anger against those who were the instigators of the crime and morally responsible for it.

A grave political and financial background was revealed, when Signer Filippelli, the Director of the "Corriere Italiano," was implicated in the affair. This newspaper had appeared in Rome for less than a year; it was extremely vulgar and sensational in the means that it employed to gain readers. It was prone to publish hectoring articles, and offered a meager news-service. It owed its existence entirely to generous subsidies. But the murder laid bare the fact that this newspaper was merely the financial base of a criminal association, whose means were unconsciously supplied by powerful industrial chiefs of northern Italy, especially of Genoa. The menaces of the journal against the opponents of the government were often followed by such an assault as ended in the Matteotti case with the death of the victim; and the direction of this organization lay, it would seem, in the hands of Rossi himself, its secret inspirer, the "homme de confidence" of Mussolini.

A strange coincidence has been noted: the assaults upon Mussolini's opponents took place whenever Mussolini, in his speeches, showed an inclination to come to an agreement with his adversaries and to inaugurate a political system based on legality! It would seem as though the little gang needed, in order to go on, to hinder Mussolini's success in that reconciliation with certain forces of the nation, which he at times desired.

They lived on disorder and strove to increase it.

The metamorphosis of public opinion has been rapid. Many other misdeeds had been perpetrated against the cause of liberty, but they had not made so great an impression. Many of these offenses were directed against political liberties (freedom of the press, of opinion, of assembly) for which Italians are not particularly avid; whereas this one was against personal liberty, of which Italians are extremely jealous.

This transformation of public opinion, as a consequence of which, in one day, thousands of Fascist emblems were seen to disappear from men's buttonholes, shows that the public assent to the Fascist regime had been considerably corroded and undermined. The steps taken by the government during a year and a half have increased the taxes, rendered the scholastic administration more severe, discharged thousands of employees and have, in consequence, created an atmosphere in which discontent lay near the surface.

The so-called "filofascista" press, that is to say the press which, without subscribing to the doctrines of Fascism, had preserved, either for love of peace or from interest, an attitude of great friendliness towards the government, at once raised its voice and constrained Mussolini to weed out the obnoxious elements of the Ministry of the Interior, which had fostered all the protectors and accomplices of the criminal clique.

Many misdeeds had been tolerated because they were held to be a necessary consequence of the Fascist revolution, but Mussolini was expected to discipline the perpetrators. When it was learned, however, that these rebels were liberally paid and that the disobedient disciples were living in daily contact with Mussolini, popular sentiment felt its trust betrayed. It rebelled against Mussolini himself. Either Mussolini was an accomplice in what had been done, and so unworthy to govern the country; or else he was blind, and had not noticed what was going on around him. Most significant of all, if he was weak, not daring to apprehend his accomplices of yesterday, Mussolini's mask of strength fell.

An important political event, the result of the moral discomfort in which Mussolini and Fascism find themselves, is the rise of the Nationalists. In February, 1922, the Nationalist party was fused with the Fascist party. But a real amalgam had not been possible. The men who had supported Nationalism were politically more cultured, more economically independent, more consistent, than the Fascists. The followers of Fascism who have been implicated in the Matteotti crime all belong to the ranks of the Left; they spring from revolutionary forces, and they attempted to urge Mussolini towards a second revolution of a demagogic character, with shady banking associations.

On the other hand the Nationalists have held themselves aloof from these contacts and tendencies; and so, after the murder, it is natural that they should have resumed their ascendancy. The appointment of Federzoni, for many years Nationalist leader, as Minister of the Interior is the product of this situation. He is an honest, able, cultured man, gifted with great tact, and has succeeded in beginning his work of restoration of law amidst the general approbation of public opinion. Hence it is that the personal position of Mussolini appears considerably changed. It may be said, in brief, that he is no longer "Il Duce." The aureole of infallibility and absolute will has vanished. His own majority protesting, as well as some of his ministers, he is now obliged to negotiate with the opposition, which has taken the initiative by abandoning the Chamber, and by showing its resolution to establish conditions which constitute an encroachment on Mussolini's absolute powers.

Moreover, the Crown apparently does not contemplate this diminution with distaste. On the other hand it must not be supposed that the position of the Prime Minister has been excessively shaken. Around him still converge many personal sympathies and ties. The Mussolini myth is ended; there still remains, however, the man. Moreover, as soon as the wave of emotion over the Matteotti case began to subside, leaving room for cooler political considerations, many asked themselves whether it was possible to allow Mussolini and his regime to fall, without inflicting serious harm to Italy.

To these reflections, which have become the dominant motif of the conservative press and of industrial and agrarian circles, the tone has been given by the Vatican. The Vatican had looked of late with a certain distrust towards Fascism. It had accepted all its concessions (religious instruction in schools, acceptance of ecclesiastical ceremonies in state functions, etc.) but it had never given its approval or adherence to the regime. But today, faced with the danger that the fall of the present system may mean the return of an anti-clerical or at least agnostic democracy, the Vatican has pronounced a word of tolerance. This attitude has also been adopted in the Senate by the chief representatives of the Catholics, who have supported Mussolini and voted in his favor.

And now that Mussolini no longer awakens fear, the entire middle class and the banking world support his rule as a transition to some other regime, on the theory that shocks that might prove dangerous to the country, may thus be avoided. The Matteotti scandal has profoundly modified the conditions of the political struggle in Italy. The press is now surer of itself, and politicians are more at ease regarding their safety; violence can no longer be counted upon to guarantee cooperation.

There are also several who belong to the so-called revisionistic tendency, and who have attempted to transform Fascism into a modern party, capable of thought and self-criticism, and of competition with the other parties in the field of ideas. There are still powerful interests in some regions, such as Emilia, lower Lombardy, Tuscany, and the Abruzzi which remain deeply devoted to Fascism., The excitement over the Matteotti murder has been above all in the cities; the rural districts have taken a much smaller part in it.

The groups of the opposition, which after the crime joined to form a committee, consist of the Constitutional Democrats (Amendola), the Social Democrats (Di Cesaro), the Republicans (Conti), the Unitarian Socialists or Labor party (Turati), the Maximalist Socialists (Nobili) and the Populars or Catholics (De Gasparri). These forces all vary in character and power. Among them only three parties have any influence with the masses throughout Italy: the Labor Socialists, the Maximalist Socialists and the Populars. The Communists left the committee because Moscow did not desire collaboration with the bourgeois parties.

As I write, the opposition is not agreed on the conditions to propose before returning to the Chamber; several members, especially the Socialists, are more uncompromising and demand the resignation of Mussolini; others would be satisfied with the dissolution of the national militia, which really forms the gravest obstacle to a return to normal constitutional conditions.

Fascism has shown its weakness too soon. The accident of the Matteotti case has prevented its accomplishing liberal education, which it was in the way of achieving.

The transition to another regime will be neither easy nor immediate. Fascism remains a hard bone to gnaw, and Mussolini may still have more than one string to his bow. GIUSEPPE PREZZOLINI.

Ludendorff New Head Of Fascism
Los Angeles Evening Citizen News/August 16, 1924

General Assumes Position Left by Hitler In Germany

General Ludendorff has taken over the actual leadership of Fascism in Germany.

He has commissioned Deputy Strasser, "folkist" druggist, as the nominal chieftain of the now disintegrating Fascist forces to replace the spectacular former sign painter, Adolf Hiller, who from his cell in the Landsberg prison, laid down his mandate as Folkist leader.

Hitler, the fiery bombastic "trumpeter" of a new "Tag" for Germany, has been beaten in an internal row in the Fascist camp, and the man Ludendorff, who went free in the beer-cellar putsch of last November while Hitler went to jail, now steps into the directing position.

The appointment of Ludendorff means the end of the hip-hip hooray methods that made the magnetic Hitler a popular idol in the beer-halls of old Munich. It means that the "proletarian" appeal idea in Fascism has been dropped to a large extent and that hereafter the group favoring accomplishing the new "Tag" party via parlimentarism will be in the saddle.

Hitler believed in no parliaments. He wanted them ditched, and he worked his followers up to a high pitch on this point.

But since the youthful sign painter sat in his Landsberg cell and could no longer stir beer-hall followers, another wing of the party came into power. This wing, composed largely of old military men and some intellectuals, argued that parliamentary work could be very effective in making Germany "Folkish." It argued, too, that the enthusiastic frenzy

Hitler stirred up in his nightly beer-hall rounds was not the lasting foundation needed for successful accomplishment of the "Tag."

Hence, Ludendorff and others finally read Hitler out of his place. And his announcement on July 7 that he was done, that he did not want any visitors in his lonely Landsberg cell and that he was now engaged in writing a book, meant a new turn in the Fascist movement in Germany.

It probably marks the road toward collapse of the Folkist movement.

Big industrialists, who hitherto gave heavily for support of the movement, are reported to have withdrawn their aid, thus leaving Ludendorff and companions "out on a limb". The industrialists who were interested in the Munich beer-cellar putsch are now reported to see clearly that the Putsch season is past, and that the acceptance of the Dawes report will mark a new era in Germany's national life.

Likewise, the general public is beginning slowly but surely to turn away from the beer-cellar heroes.

The prospect of good times under the Dawes scheme has cooled many hot heads, and has given the German again his wonted stolidity and sound sense.

This does not mean that Fascisti are completely done. They are far from that, and they intend to continue their operations. But the government leaders and neutral observes are convinced that the swing in Germany is against radicalism, and that a sane middle course will be the eventual route here.

Party Splits After Hitler Is Forced Out
The Miami Herald/September 12, 1924

German Reactionaries Facing Bolt of Large Groups;
Esser Stages Meeting

The "folkist" movement in Germany, one of the mainstays of reaction, is slowly splitting up.

The first indication of this fact was the resignation of Adolf Hitler from the presidency of the party. The second was given recently by the formation of a rival folkist party by Herr Esser, the most radical adherent of Hitler.

Simultaneously with the formation of Esser's "Pan-German-National-Community," another leader of the opposition, Herr Streicher, known for his rabid anti-Semitism, also formed a branch of his own at Nuremberg under the name of "Reichsadler." This branch will be conducted practically along the same lines as Esser's new party, but without forming a part of it.

Esser used for the formation of the new party, which he claims Hitler has approved, the old, never-failing paraphernalia of the great Adolfus.

In the largest Munich beer hall, accommodating 3,000 people with considerably more attending, he staged one of the old Hitler meetings with much shouting, cheering and beer drinking. Then he launched a formidable and fiery speech denouncing everything and everybody not swearing allegiance to the swastika colors of "true folkism."

Esser, however, added a new item to the list of things to be denounced. Without mentioning names, he accused the new folkist leaders of having "sold out" by leading the party into the "morass of parliamentarism much as the old parties do."

Esser declared amid frantic applause that the genuine folkists did not believe in "Hitler the Drummer" — an attribute that the man around Ludendorff invented for Adolf in attempting to make him powerless in the movement. The real folkists, according to Esser, still believe in "Hitler the Statesman."

"This belief," he added, "gives us the energy to unsparingly put aside all those who think they can eliminate Adolf Hitler."

These plain words, unmistakably addressed to the new executive of the party that had eliminated Hitler, mean ensuing war within the folkist movement.

Hitler, whose opponents said he needed a rest, does not believe in their prescription. It is generally assumed that, after his release from prison, he will lead the feud against the parliamentary faction of which Ludendorff is the head. He will be aided by quite a number of the old leaders who did not obtain "soft jobs" as delegates in either the Reichstag or one of the numerous Diets. These men, hailing mostly from the rank and file and knowing the psychology of the masses, will rally many adherents to the fight for re-establishing the old folkist party.

Through this fight the erstwhile "bugaboo" for German politicians may disappear. Stabilization of conditions here will rob the movement of many of its followers, it is believed. Thus, the battle for the supremacy among the different factions may become a matter of no importance except for those directly involved. The movement also lacks funds, and without funds, it will be difficult to conduct the propaganda campaigns which in past years have attracted a great number of people and induced them to become members of the folkist party or voters on its tickets.

Foes Draw Up Proclamation Condemning Fascist Rule
The Evening Independent (St. Petersburg, FL)/November 12, 1924

Two years from the time he led the Fascisti black-shirts in the triumphant march to Rome, Premier Benito Mussolini finds the opposition to himself and his party so formidable that the hitherto invincible Fascisti parliamentary phalanx may be shattered when the chamber reconvenes.

While Mussolini pleaded for continued support before a meeting of government deputies Tuesday, members of the opposition drew up a proclamation to the country condemning Fascist rule and reiterating the determination of the opposition deputies to refuse to participate in the Fascist-bossed parliament which meets Wednesday.

"Fascism has forced Italy to concentrate all her energies in conserving public and private liberty and representative institutions," the opposition deputies declared in their message to the people. "Italy cannot overcome this crisis until power is restored to popular sovereignty and the opposition cannot abandon the fight until Italy knows how to redeem her liberty."

Situation Precarious

Mussolini's situation is precarious because his majority in the chamber is not composed entirely of members of the Fascist party. There are Liberals and former-combatants among his supporters and if these could be coaxed over to the side of the opposition, the Italian dictator would find himself stripped of a parliamentary quorum and the choice of governing without a parliament, or of entering into a doubtful general election which would be thrust under the government's nose.

The opposition deputies are making the most of the incidents of Nov. 4, the Italian Armistice day, when regimented Fascisti and members of the ex-combatant organized by a descendant of Garibaldi fought in a public square in Rome following a misunderstanding for which each blames the other.

Mussolini's 24-month dictatorship has caused tremendous dissatisfaction among Liberal elements who were gradually alienated from his cause as he unfolded his political theories including the famous tenet expressed in a speech several months ago that democracy is a futile thing with which Fascism would not toy.

Continuous Bloodshed

There has been continuous bloodshed in Italy, culminating in outrages perpetrated by hoodlum bands of Fascisti and opposition supporters. The Fascisti themselves had pointed the way to summary and unlawful punishment of dissenters to their scheme of government with the famous castor oil cure which many Romans and provincial Italians suffered.

Neither Mussolini's nor his authority of government nor his authority can be compared with the almost chaotic situation that is resolving itself out of the dictatorship of General Prime De Rivera in Spain, but it is significant that the two great south European dictatorships are simultaneously experiencing opposition which may topple them from power.

The Italian opposition demands a general election to be held without the interference or dominance of the Fascist party which has developed an uncanny ability to influence the trend of balloting.

Whether Mussolini will accede to this request depends upon the attitude of his extra-Fascist supporters who hold the balance of power in the Italian parliament.

Try America, Adolph
Baltimore Evening Sun/May 25, 1925

Adolph Hitler, he of the beer-cellar revolt, is a man without a country. Bavaria refused him citizenship. He went to Austria and now the Austrian Government has announced his expatriation.

What to do? Hitler's chief crime, if memory serves, was that he was the leader of the Bavarian Fascisti. Fascism, as everyone knows, is the antithesis of red revolution and communism. If Hitler is in search of a place to lay his head, there is no very good reason why he should not look to the United States. If Hitler wages war against the Reds, he should find a kindred spirit in the State Department, whose officials more than once have shivered at the prospect of the red flag being run up over the White House. Hitler himself could have conceived no more perfect gag than the State Department placed upon Count Karolyi. Nor was the suspicion ever completely dissipated that Editor Carlo Tresca's imprisonment and his attacks on the Fascist Mussolini were not a mere coincidence.

Diametrically opposed to Karolyi and Tresca, the logical conclusion is that Hitler would receive a hearty welcome provided he promised to pursue his Fascism anywhere except in beer cellars.

Mussolini a Real Napoleon in Mastery Over His Country
Toronto Daily Star/November 19, 1925

Has Complete Power Over Every Citizen
Under New Reforms Backed by Power

Is Like the Head of Gigantic Factory With Forty Million Employees

Rome, Nov. 19 — Mussolini who, when parliament closed its session last spring was thought by his enemies to be about to fall, reappeared at the opening of the new session before madly cheering fascist deputies as the undisputed ruler of Italy. During the last six months, while living abstemiously, not touching a drop of wine and fulfilling the duties of five and sometimes six ministers, presiding at innumerable ceremonial functions and delivering speeches which will remain permanent contributions to Italian political literature, he has been silently and methodically reorganizing the entire Italian political structure through laws decrees and constitutional reforms which will be confirmed unhesitatingly at the present sessions of the chamber and the senate.

Complete Master of Country

Mussolini has extended the executive powers of the government to embrace every activity of national life — social, economic and intellectual. He now is more completely master of his country than any statesman of Western Europe since Napoleon. His present position is unlike that of any other prime minister. He is like the head of a gigantic factory of forty million workers which he is seeking to administer according to scientific efficiency methods, more intensive production, greater earnings and increased competitive ability.

Instead of the rights of man Mussolini has proclaimed the duties of man, holding each citizen to a prescribed task. Under the new laws he can dismiss any employee — government clerk, teacher or judge — who is inefficient or who does not work for the firm's interest; can dictate wages and conditions of work through state monopolized labor unions; can maintain the balance between agriculture and industry through tariffs, subsidies and government loans; can administer local affairs directly through executive control over small towns, perhaps later over cities; can in some degree control the cost of living through governmentally organized co-operatives; can sustain loyalty and guide the thoughts and emotions of citizens through a virtual monopoly of the press.

Has Force Behind Him

If such measures are inadequate in certain instances, he has 300,000 fanatically obedient fascisti organized along military lines in every city and village in Italy prepared to execute his commands directly. Mussolini's position differs from that of a factory director only that he is not working for private gain. If he died today he would leave his children nothing except his reputation

Mussolini Jolts Italian Editors; Must Limit Papers to Six Pages, Newest Fascist Order

The (Spokane) Spokesman-Review/July 2, 1926

Revolutionary transformation of all Italian newspapers, so that nothing but the barest of facts of democratic happenings and virtually no foreign news may be printed, is the goal of the new fascist economy plan, of which the cabinet's order reducing all newspapers to not more than six pages in the first step.

This intention is announced almost unanimously by the fascist newspapers in approving comments on the proposed changes. In addition to the elimination of detailed foreign correspondence, sporting, art and literary news, and accounts of court cases, particularly crimes, will gradually be dropped, the semi-official Tribune declares.

Fascist Editor Ironic

"We will have dry newspapers, restricted to the most essential comments," says El Tevore, extreme fascist organ, adding ironically: "Also, we won't know whether the new sect of worshipers of tapeworm started on the banks of the Potomac; we would not be able to read the prose of the special correspondents in Pernambuco."

The Impero sees the cut in the size of newspapers as the work of a genius, declaring that daily journalism has become a scandalous waste of paper.

The Tribune says that fascism desires faithfulness to fundamental central ideas and brief, succinct basic considerations.

Discussing the newspapers outside the large cities, Signor Turati, secretary-general of the fascist party, said in the course of an interview:

"Each province cannot have more than one newspaper, in which will be published the party's orders, and the political acts of fascism will be briefly illustrated; all the rest of the space will be devoted to things which are being constructed and work which is being carried out."

Personal Journalism Doomed

Personal journalism, Turati declared, is doomed, and he asserted that fascism is determined to bring out the educational and the moral aspect of the press.

"I am also determined," he continued, "to destroy the innumerable weeklies, which although dealing in national problems and spreading fundamental fascist ideas, represent solely the personal acidity and literary impatience of their editors.

"Some of our comrades have already set a good example by suffocating their own creatures. I will cite in an order of the day those following this example."

The secretary general concluded by remarking: "We may have surprises to offer in this field."

Nine-Hour Work Day

The lengthening by one hour of the laborers' work day, is permitted in a new decree by the fascist government, which recently forbade strikes.

The decree is one of a series designed to strengthen the lire and offset last year's unfavorable trade balance.

No new cafes, hotels or dance hall may be opened. New housing is restricted. The cabinet has authorized a fund of two million lire for prizes to encourage authors.

Restrictive measures even more severe than were prevalent during the world war days are still contemplated by the government, according to the semi-official Popolo di Romano. The sale of soft drinks, tea and coffee, as well as alcoholic beverages and of food of any kind, after 10 p.m., will be forbidden in forthcoming decrees, the paper says.

Even daytime coffee drinking will be hit by the imposition of a 300 lire direct tax on each coffee percolator in cafes, bars and restaurants.

New Mussolini Surprise

The newspapers today hail the decrees, which were entirely unexpected by the public, as another of Premier Mussolini's strokes, characteristic for its surprise at the "opportune moment."

Answering objections concerning the increase of the normal working day from eight to nine hours, Popolo di Roma says that it is preferable to use this method to prevent a possible economic crisis with its subsequent serious unemployment, than to drift along aimlessly.

How I Do Not Love Italy
Vanity Fair/October, 1926

An Extremely Unorthodox View of a Widely Celebrated Section of Europe

by e.e. cummings

EDITOR'S NOTE:—The receipt of this article in the offices of Vanity Fair caused a high degree of perturbation and anguish. Why? Because the Editors were nurtured on Italian culture, achievements and ideals. Our first thought, therefore, was that the author of this essay should be reprimanded, not to say chastised. Then there came to us this thought. What if Italy should become efficient? What if automats and five-and-ten-cent-stores and slot machines and Ford factories and quick lunch counters should definitely succeed the sonnets of Petrarch, the paintings of Mantegna, the learning of Pico della Mirandola, the sculptures of Giovanni Bologna and the large, easy-going, colorful grandeur of the Medicis? Merciful heavens, what weighty pain in that thought! With that direful prospect in mind we saw the need of publishing Mr. Cumming's article forthwith, in toto, with the idea of saving Italy from imminent disaster, from modernity, and from (what is most terrifying of all)— American efficiency.

Once upon a time, when we were incredibly spirited, helpless, and otherwise young, the singing teacher of a New England public school induced our throat to utter the following fraudulent ditty:

"O, Italia, Italia belov-ed
Land of beauty, of sunlight and song,

188

When afar from thy bright skies remov-ed
How our fond hearts for thee e'er do long"

...or something like that. We were amazed, at the time, by the asininity of the words and the triteness of the tune. But amazement is temporary. We sang other songs and we grew up and we forgot all about *Italia.*

Not until full fifteen years later did the land of sunlight, etc., actually loom upon our horizon—when, becoming bored with Paris, we purchased a bicycle and rode all the way to Napoli with a patient friend. This little jaunt (and the reader is strongly advised to consult a map ere attempting the same) taught us altogether too much about Italia. We became so disillusioned, in fact, that when afar from her bright skies remov-ed our very far from fond hearts decidedly did not do any longing.

Yet what is disillusionment to a healthy person? *Niente.* Only a year or so after the Paris-Napoli venture, we found ourselves getting shoved off all the sidewalks of Roma by enthusiastic cohorts of Black Shirts. A revolution, or something, had just happened. We sought refuge in a stationery shop. Before our eyes reposed a series of colored post-cards celebrating the recent cataclysm. The first card at which we glanced depicted Mussolini, in the role of Christ, raising *Italia,*in the role of Lazarus, from the dead. Shocked to our aesthetic foundations, we left hurriedly both the shop and Italia.

Shocks, however, cannot discourage really inquisitive people. Our third visit to *Italia* belov-ed has just been completed—and completed successfully, thanks to a hypertranquil disposition plus, at times, a superhuman digestion. All things considered, we feel that we are now entitled to express ourselves publicly re the home of beauty, etc.; therefore (in the limpid language of that notorious nation) *"avanti"*!

Italia, without any doubt the most overestimated country in this world, consists of a peninsula which is shaped like a leg that has been caught in the act of kicking Sicily. This naughty leg, whose chief industries are ruins, religion and automobiles, is technically a monarchy ruled over by a king (S.M.Il Re) but is actually a pawn in the hands of the onorevole Benito Mussolini. The king nevertheless retains two extremely important functions, which are (a) to be photographed with Mussolini and (b) to pose for postage-stamps.

Signor Mussolini, whose singularly uncheerful visage appears all over *Italia* at the present moment—not only in rotogravure, but painted on houses, fences, railroad stations, etc.—was, just a few years ago, a wicked radical. But one day this wicked radical turned a complete backward somersault and landed an ultra-conservative. Shortly afterward he bought up all the black shirts in sight, hurriedly put a great many young men into them and captured Rome without difficulty. He then informed everybody that *Italia* had been dead for some time and that his program, il fascism, consisted of nothing less than a revivification of the corpse. If *Italia* swallowed the dictatorship pill, Mussolini positively guaranteed that she would rise from the dead and be alive even as she was alive in the days of the Caesars. In other words, she would be alive at the expense of everybody else and would rule the modern world very much as Rome ruled the ancient world.

After a number of Mussolini's former comrades, the Italian bolsheviks, had been beaten up, compelled to drink castor oil and sent to other planes, the corpse took her medicine and Mussolini was acclaimed as "Caesar". But Mussolini was no ordinary man. He could not possibly be satisfied with being merely Caesar. He also wanted to be Napoleon. This was easily arranged. A photographer "shot" him in Napoleonic costume, the photograph was printed on thousands of post-cards and the post-cards were circulated all over *Italia*. Taking the bull by the horns, Mussolini now rushed into international politics and mixed them up "something awful," as we say back home. But while the world at large recoiled from his exploits, *Italia* applauded with both hands and both feet—and exactly what the Hon. Caesar Napoleon Mussolini will attempt next, nobody knows. The French people guess that it will be the annexation of France, since he says quite frankly that *Italia* is overpopulated and must have a lot of brand-new territory—in a hurry. So much for the shepherd. And now a few words concerning his flock.

In our humble opinion, there is no word big enough to suggest, or describe, the bigness of the contemporary Italian inferiority complex. To understand the origin of this national misfortune, we must remember that for some time previous to "*il Duce*'s" somersault, the inhabitants of *Italia* had lived in a tranquil doze. But with the thunderclap of fascism, they awoke to a consciousness of themselves; or, more truly, they awoke to a realization of their weakness and apparent unworthiness. Practically the entire nation, stricken with a sense of shame, thereupon set in motion within itself what psychologists term a "defense mechanism"—that is to say, all *Italia* (with a few exceptions) began to swagger and boast and pose; dozing meekness was superseded by insolence; and vanity, never a negligible Latin characteristic, bulged to colossal proportions. Luckily, however, the official military headgear consists of a cap so high in the crown as to permit of considerable head-swelling. From which painful subject, let us turn to *Italia's* scenic glories.

Concerning the innumerable catacombs, cathedrals, museums, ruins, etc., which recall an illustrious past and which have inspired so much bad and good poetry, philosophy and criticism, we beg to opine (1) that the ceiling of the Sistine Chapel is worth all the rest of Italia dead and undead; (2) that we love Venice much but that we love Coney Island more; (3) that one small church at San Tomé (Spain), which contains El Greco's The Burial of Count Orgáz, houses more aesthetic intensity than does the whole Galleria degli Uffizi; and (4) that the world is still looking for an unidentified man who disappeared after partially expressing a desire to show us the coliseum by moonlight.

Concerning the famous scenic glories of the unillustrious present, we have the following remarks to make. First of all, nobody can possibly comprehend better than ourselves the real meaning of the celebrated mot "see Naples and then die"—for when we saw Naples we very nearly did die; and Naples at its worst is certainly no more depressing than are the other famous Italian cities at their best. Secondly, while it is true that certain much-touted portions of Italia's landscape, such as Fiesole, are distinctly attractive, it is not true that said portions are any more remarkable, in and of themselves, than is most of the unadvertised country called Portugal. Finally, be it known that there exists, somewhere in the Italian Riviera, a perfectly cracker-box-shaped edifice (known as a villa) with twenty windows, of which nineteen are painted while one is real— and be it further known that the painted blinds of the nineteen painted windows all cast painted shadows and that in one of the nineteen painted windows is a painted potted plant which also casts a painted shadow and that on what remains of the villa's walls are a number of painted statues, each statue casting its own private, separate, individual, particular painted shadow. No wonder *Italia, Italia* belov-ed is described as a land of sunlight!—Incidentally, all the painted shadows are very, very wrong.

They are not, however, any more intrinsically wrong than is the sign "SOMETHING NEW, CHEAP AND BEAUTIFUL" which, ostensibly, is an attempt to lure unwary Anglo-Saxons into a shop off the Piazza San Marco in Venice, but which actually—unless we very deeply err—is an epitome of the whole fascist program for Italy in particular and the world in general. Nor do we, as an American, write the foregoing sentence without shame; for we realize that the glittering slogan just quoted reflects, all too well, our own nation's slip-shod method of thought. The sad fact is that Signor Mussolini has invented nothing. He has simply, as a means of purging his compatriots of their unworthiness, borrowed from America her most unworthy credo (the utterly transparent and lifeless lie: Time is money) and the results of this borrowing are already apparent.

Assuming the continuation of *Italia's* present régime, America will find herself playing second fiddle to Italia in more unlovely ways than either Napoleon or Caesar could shake a stick at. Already *Italia* is up to America's tricks of "progress" and "morality". If you doubt this, get in touch with the fascist representative in your home town and find out for yourself. Already the Piazza Venezia is dark and dreary. Already you cannot buy a glass of cognac on Sunday. Later, or sooner, everybody in the "land of beauty, of sunlight and song" will be minding everybody else's business as thoroughly as everybody does in the dear old U. S. A.— at least, so your correspondent decided one night, when (being unable to sleep on account of a deafening racket) he lifted up his weary eyes and beheld, emblazoned on the door of his microscopic room at the Albergo Somethingorother, the following moonlit sentiment: *In the generally interest, the Visitors are requested to observe the extremely quiet.*

Fascism: For the Italians
The New Republic/January 12, 1927

H.M. Kallen

At a distance of three thousand miles, and through the perspectives of a press limited in its reports by propaganda or by censorship, Fascism and its Duce are not phenomena to inspirit the liberal mind or to make it hopeful of the future of Italy. Bondage of body and spirit reeks too strongly; there are marks of tyranny, of rapine and sudden death; of paranoid magniloquence that knows no decent restraint of speech and no effective technique of realization. Fascism seems, at that distance, the synthesis of all that the liberal spirit condemns and rejects.

Yet, after one has lived in Italy awhile, one learns that there can be an intolerance of liberalism also. With the things that liberalism rejects go, as their obverse, things that liberalism recognizes as requisite to the good life of the masses of men. One begins to doubt whether, in a world so mixed as this, there ever can exist the unmixed goods that liberalism requires, or the unmixed evils it rejects.

For on the intimate testimony of many people living long in Italy, Italians and foreigners both, Italy has become a better country to live in since, through the accident that the King refused to empower his ministry to disperse the historic "march on Rome," Fascism replaced "democracy" as the government of the Italian people. The ministry, being constitutional, resigned, and the King called upon Mussolini to form a government. The episode constituted a political revolution, and is leading to a social one. It is a curiously paradoxical revolution, as such events go, unusually bloodless and free from violence; especially free from the interruptions of the customary activities and pursuits of life such as occurred during the French and the Russian revolutions.

This quality is not to be attributed to the notion that Fascism was financed by big business which naturally wants to get affairs into its own hands. Affairs are not today in the hands of Italian big business. They are in the hands of Mussolini, and big business is doing his bidding, not he, its.

The reason, I think, is to be sought first in the history of modern Italy, then in its economy.

Reading the unrestrained oratory of Il Duce we are likely to forget that modern Italy is little more than half a century old, and that there are thousands of men alive who fought in the army of Garibaldi. On the anniversary of the march on Rome I saw in the Roman streets scores of old men in the red shirts of the Garibaldista, mingling with the hundreds of young men in the black shirts of the Fascists. The Italy which these men in the red shirts established was a comminuted Italy; its territory was divided in large part between foreign conquerors; its native states were sect one against the other; there were—there still are—sharp rivalries between the very villages perched on separate hills. To convert this piecemeal, too-localized life into a single political organization, and to animate it with a unity of national feeling and action became the dearest ideal of Italian patriotism. The classic exponent of this ideal was Mazzini, and his break with the socialism of his day on account of it is historical. Italian nationalism provides the thread of feeling on which are strung the separate beads of the Risorgimento. It is the dynamic ground of that sacro egoismo of which the liberal was called to take unpleasant notice during the War. It is what accounts both for the rise to power and the popularity of Mussolini. The King of Italy spoke with perhaps better insight than he was aware of when he referred to the Duce as a combination of Garibaldi and Cavour.

For the ideals of these men, of Mazzini, of Garibaldi, or Cavour, seem to me still far from realization. They are still very much ideals. Italy is still far from being the united Italy, single in spirit, strong in government, rich in achievement that Mazzini foresaw. Fascism is formulating and executing in the early twentieth century what the prophets of the new Italy sought in the nineteenth. Its acts and utterances are to be best understood in the light not only of what it positively wants and achieves, but in the light, even more, of that against which it is a reaction. How important the latter is, any student of the history of ideals knows. What an ideal rejects colors profoundly whatever it proposes, impels it often to an extremity of negation which is never attained, and is in fact unattainable, in reality.

Although, as a student of the life-cycles of ideals, I was well enough aware of this, it came home to me with insuperable force when I discussed the philosophy of Fascism with Mussolini. I had read in an American paper that he claimed to be a pragmatist, and I was curious to hear more about it. I didn't, but I heard other things far more illuminating.

The audience took place in his office, with Miss Lillian Gibson of the New York Herald-Tribune and the Marchese Paoluci de Calboli acting as interpreters. In figure Mussolini is not unlike the late Colonel Roosevelt—a powerful, cubical torso, with enormous shoulders, on rather short legs. The face is, of course, familiar from the many pictures; but no picture can render the extreme mobility under the play of feeling; or the recurrent effect as of one of those Japanese devil masks when he would fix you with his dark protruding eyes under hairless eyebrows; or the extreme sensitiveness to the slightest variation in the social climate; or the vivid force and magnetism of the man.

The discussion about pragmatism was a fizzle. The Duce was clearly far more aware of William James's name than his teachings. "Fascism was," he declared, "turning the activism of James's philosophy into facts'"—which might mean anything. But when I asked what inner experience had converted him from socialism, there was a light. "I gained the conviction," he said, drawing himself up in his chair and beating the desk forcefully and rhythmically with his forefinger, "that there is no such thing as equality in life. We seek to bring out more and more the inequalities."

Fascism as a philosophy must be seen in the light of socialism. It formulates in the extremest terms possible a doctrine of human differences against the socialist teaching of the sameness of men with one another. It formulates an extreme doctrine of authority against the socialist teaching of democracy. "The state," Mussolini said to me, "must be paramount. The state above, for all, and, if necessary, against all." He held Machiavelli's view of the state as the correct one.

In the minds of the Fascists and their leader, the state is, I think, the concretion of United Italy. Education is largely devoted to impressing Italy as Italy upon the minds of the Italian young. Fascist "Cultura" is an extreme overstatement of Mazzini's national culture. The schools—church and national alike—have been set under a single standard and the standard has been raised. If I guess aright, it is designed that the Church itself be mutantis mutandis, being absorbed into the texture of the state as the trades-unions were, with the difference in treatment that the circumstances and power involved seem to require. The national podesta is replacing the village mayor, and the peasant is being urged by precept and example, including Mussolini's, who ran a tractor for two hours, to use agricultural machinery, and to enrich his way of life. Italy, it must be remembered, is and must remain an agricultural country. She is without resources in coal and iron, and such water power as she can develop is not adequate to maintain great industry. The status of the peasant is the critical test of the achievement of Fascism, and even in the very short period of Fascist power the beginnings of improvement are noticeable. Mussolini himself does not favor, he told me, city life. Nor, as a realistic statesman, should he. Italian industry is far from standing still. Indeed, it is the industrial changes that are the spectacular ones. Transportation is steadily being improved; and the resources of water power and electricity being made available. The Fascist vision of Italy is kept constantly before the eyes and minds of the Italian people with that exaggeration and overstatement which the consciousness of opposition, the necessities of education and very skillful publicity seem always to require. There is an intellectual as well as an economic vitality: not so much in the arts as in the philosophic and sociologic disciplines. When I remarked upon this fact to Mussolini and called attention to the presence of a similar activity in Russia, he gave grudging assent. I don't think he relished the parallel, but he acknowledged it. Italy, indeed, by contrast with other European countries I have been visiting, does seem alive. I said so to Mussolini, in answer to a question about my impressions, and he exclaimed, "In Italy today everybody is twenty years old, including myself, and I work twenty hours a day!"

Which, in fact, may not be so, but which does express a state of mind whence facts arise. It is a state of tension and eagerness; it holds a touch of febrility. There is an unqualified candor about desires and purposes, such as the makers of the New Russia showed at the beginning. And things are doing.

How long, how well, depends on the life of the Duce. Mussolini is today the essence of living Italy. He is a dictator. He holds the portfolio of all the ministries, and determines internal and foreign policies. He is also the head of a somewhat secret political organization with military features. The force of this organization of Fascists is what first lies behind his power as dictator. It is a power of force majeure, still the deadly enemy of all differences, all oppositions, all freedom. On the day that I saw the Duce, the Communist members of the Chamber had been arrested; a couple of days before, at Bologna, another attempt had been made on his life. If Fascism may be said to rule by fear, it also is ruled by fear. Its coercions are a measure of its sense of insecurity. Free speech and the other freedoms are a product of security, and the degree in which they become possible is a gauge of security. What happens about these matters in Italy will prove how firmly the makers of the new Italian dispensation feel it to be established. At present he is himself the dispensation, the voice of the great hunger of the Italian people. For Mussolini has another ground for his power that, it is by no means inconceivable, he may need to call upon against the first ground. This is his popularity. Whatever he may have started with, today he is indubitably the most popular figure in Italy, a hero of the masses, by his courage, his very evident sincerity, his simplicity of the Latin, his arts of the demagogue and the statesman both, and his marvelous energy of speech and action. There is an attitude, in the sixteen-year-old elevator boy at the hotel, in the sixty-year-old prince of the Church, both of whom spoke to me of the attempt on his life at Bologna, that only very warm and very kind feeling for a public leader can evoke. The wise and suave Cardinal who mentioned it said—"He is but one man, and we cannot tell what the future will bring—"

This, of course, is the penalty for dictatorship as a form of government. Institutions cannot go without the dictator. This is why wise dictators strive to render dependence on just one man unnecessary. But these reflections are aside from the point. The point is that the spirit of Fascism is continuous with the spirit of Mazzini's Young Italy and Garibaldi's army. The point is that the compenetration of its grotesquely exaggerated nationalism of idea with the grotesquely comminuted localism of feeling will, in the nature of things, result in a decent national self-respect. The point is that administrative reform, the educational program and economic enterprise all make for a safer, more comfortable and more vital Italy. In these respects the Fascist revolution is not unlike the Communist revolution. Each is the application by force majeure of an ideology to a condition. Each should have the freest opportunity once it has made a start, of demonstrating whether it be an exploitation of men by a special interest or a fruitful endeavor after the good life.

Il Duce Declares Violence is Fundamentally Moral--
Says Parliamentism is Paralyzing Force Upon Governments
Charlotte Observer/January 23, 1927

No Forward Step Possible in Evolution of Politics
Without Leaving Victims

Says "Personal Liberty'" Is Variable Concept Which Mast Change to Fit
Needs and Emergencies of the State—Considers It Possible That Present
Suffering Is Merely Effect of Superior Living Standards of Mankind—An-
ticipates Wars That May Burst on Humanity With Suddenness

by George Sylvester Viereck

"DO YOU THINK," I asked Mussolini, "that the skies for mankind are brightening, that the war that slew ten million men was not entirely in vain?"

Mussolini's lips curled. The rest of his face remained cold and impassive, as if it were chiseled from marble.

"It seems to me," he remarked, "that the twentieth century people are destined to live in a gloomy period of history, in an age clouded by tragedy. It is our duty to accept that fact like men."

"Your excellency," I replied, "is a pessimist. Briand…"

"Intelligent pessimism," the duce replied, without waiting for me to finish my sentence, "is much better than unintelligent optimism.

A Dangerous Father

"Do you really believe,'" he added with considerable acerbity. "that the war which devastated Europe, if not the world, between those terrible years of 1914 and 1918 is to be the last of which history will bear record?

"I am glad to say that many do not share this fine and splendid but dangerous faith that everything is to go well with the world in the future."

"Do you then consider war a necessity?"

"All the wars of which history bears record can be explained upon

198

the basis of the historical facts. But war itself, the fact of war, which seems to permeate the story of mankind since the days of Cain down to our own—that cannot be explained. At any rate it has never yet been explained.

"Perhaps war is one of the inscrutable things, one of the facts which like so many other inexplicable facts must remain too much for a merely human wisdom to account for. It may be that war is the origin of all things great, as an ancient Greek philosopher once said, or it may be of divine origin, as the French thinker Prudhon has affirmed.

Calls Statement Timely

"War may be the root from which human progress springs, as Renan said. Whatever one chooses to say about war as a fact, it continues to me to be certain that war is not exterminated. The war through which we have all lived and through which I fought as a humble private in the ranks does not seem to me to have characteristics of finality about its settlement that suggest it will be the last.

"At any rate," he added with a sarcastic drawl, "after the big world war we had a little war between Russia and Poland and then another between Greece and Turkey.

"War," the duce continued "is like a hurricane. It may burst upon us suddenly. The statement may lack novelty but it does not lack timeliness."

"It Is sometime claimed," I interjected, "that excessive armament is in itself a cause of war. Germany's highly organized military machine has been accused of being responsible for the holocaust of 1914. Powder magazines are apt to lead to explosions. Your excellency too is sometimes blamed for increasing the war power of Italy on land and on sea as well as in the sky."

Nothing Sinister

Mussolini smiled somewhat contemptuously. "There is nothing sinister about preparation for war There is something very sinister about certain phases of pacifism. In a sense every assertion of the will to live in a nation or in an individual is a preparation for war.

199

"The electrification of a railway is a preparation for war. An increase in the means of communication of a country is a preparation for war. A ship that takes the sea for the first time adds to the resources of a nation for war. The teaching of a nation's history is a preparation for war. The glory associated with the name of Napoleon's tomb is a preparation for war by the French.

"But all these preparations for war are insufficient if a people plunge into the sensualism of a peace that is hedonistic and selfish and self-satisfied, leaving them soft in body, weak in mind, shrinking from physical exertion no less than from mental effort. Preparation for war involves too many ideas that are economic, social, cultural, to be denounced wholesale by pacifists who talk about war as if they knew what it was and knew how to avoid it. It is a duty to avoid war whenever possible but it takes the highest genius as well as the highest character to do that.

Essential Factor

"Every people that is fit to live must prepare itself to defend its existence," the duce continued. "The spirit is more important in that respect than the mechanical means."

"You do not think that it is possible in the twentieth century to disarm a people by restricting the tools of war?" I interjected. "If so, the makers of the peace treaty of Versailles were sadly mistaken when they attempted to disarm Germany."

Mussolini smiled. "You cannot," he replied, "disarm a people unless you destroy its manhood. The war misled some into the belief that machines are more important than men.

"Society, government, social systems, exist not for the production of material things as an end. The end is the production of men and women in the highest state of efficiency and well being.

"All governments, all rulers, come in this conclusion in the end. I thought of this when not so long ago I read the intensely Interesting memoirs of Gallieni. He was, you know, military governor of Faria in the early days of the world war.

"Nothing can be conceived more stirring than the pages Gallieni devotes to an account of the crisis in Paris. The city was an entrenched camp. The territorial militia, the only force available with all the others on the firing line, was absolutely unarmed in the face of the approaching Uhlans.

"Although Paris had become an entrenched camp there were no weapons to hand out. There were no shells, there were no bayonets, there were no guns of any caliber. There was nothing to signal with. The mobilization had stripped the arsenals and the magazines.

"They were terrible days for France, those in which from the twenty-sixth of August until the sixth of September the plans of the German general staff were in full development. The Germans had crossed Belgium and were turning upon Paris. The Germans had reached the edge of the forest of Compiegne.

"One might Infer from the record of those days that there could be no such thing as enough weapons and enough ammunition. The same idea was at one time in the mind of the German General Ludendorff. He despaired of victory until at the second battle of the Somme he happened to look towards the hills and he saw the prospect made pleasing by quantities of tanks."

Mussolini's words rang out resonantly. He evidently envisaged the scene he described.

Cannot Make Men

"So far," he continued, "the facts seem to suggest that machines and weapons are more important than men. In due time, the discovery is made that men are more important than machines. Men can make machines but machines cannot make men.

"Machines can be standardized and turned out upon a pattern one after another in a series. Man cannot be turned out like that. The effort is sometimes made. It fails. Then there is the factor of time.

"A machine can be made in a year. Frederick the great calculated that it took 18 years to turn out a man for his army in the lowest grades. And it takes more than 18 years to turn out the right kind of man. Men make machines but machines do not make men.

"Woe to a world that sets out to produce men and ends only in producing machines!"

"But does not fascism tend to reduce life to the uniformity of a machine? Does it not exact machine-like obedience from men?"

Liberty Not Absolute

Mussolini smiled this time indulgently. "Fascism is opposed to excessive individualism. It is not opposed to individualism. On the contrary, we believe in variety, differentiation, the essential inequality of man.

"What impresses me about our own country in history is the sameness it has established in life all over the world. In past ages, when man went from one country to another, they were impressed by the differences they discovered. Today they are astonished by the points of resemblance between countries, sometimes very remote from one another.

"The folklore of the races is being obliterated because capitalism, as it is called, tends to make the life of the whole world uniform. There is a general leveling. We seem to live all over the world in terms of news We eat the same food, even if some of us avoid meat. We wear the same clothes or we tend more and more to do so.

"We believe in the right of the individual to lead his own life so long as its interests do not conflict with those of the state."

"Is It possible to find a formula to reconcile fascism and personal liberty?"

Conception of Liberty

Again a smile, this time somewhat cryptic.

"The conception of liberty is not absolute beaus there is no conception that can be absolute. Liberty changes its form as time changes the face upon civilization. What is liberty in time of peace is not liberty in time of war. There is a liberty in good times when all things can be gained easily, but this is not the same as the liberty enjoyed in hard times.

"Liberty is even at times a struggle between the individual and the state, between the state that seeks to centralize and the individual who seeks to remain unhampered by authority.

"For the individual, left to himself, is one who, unless he is a saint or a hero, will pay no taxes, will obey no laws, will enlist in no war. He calls this insubordination by the name of liberty.

"Liberty does not exclude discipline until it imposes its rigors upon themselves.

"Democracy," Mussolini continued, "does not really know half the time what it wants, but when it knows what it wants it is irresistible. The problem of democracy is to find out what it wants.

"The 18th and the 19th centuries experimented with democracy. In the 20th century, democracy should reach its maturity. It must find out what it wants. In Italy, fascism is the self-realization of democracy. The 20th will be the century of fascism."

Will Lighten Gloom

"Will fascism lighten the gloom which you predict for the immediate future of our country? Will it make the fate of the average man less hard?"

"It will," Mussolini replied. "Moreover the statement that times are hard may only indicate an increase in the scale of our wants. There may be greater prosperity than ever before in the world's history neutralized by the rise in the standard of living.

"The standard of living may be the unsuspected cause of hard times. To maintain the 20th century family standard of living, it may be necessary for husband and wife both to labor. In the morning he may leave the home early to go to the factory. She may leave the home just as early to go to the office.

"Some people complain that this state of things is taking the poetry out of life.

"Never!

"There is simply a new kind of poetry. The poetry of the middle ages made the marriage tie a matter of staying at home. The new poetry puts life upon another plane.

"Life in the 20th century may be hard, but it will not be lacking in romance."

The Part of Woman

"You believe that woman will have to bear a larger share of the world's economic burdens?"

"Undoubtedly."

"If such is the case, how can you or any one deny woman complete equality with man?"

"I am not afraid of increasing the political influence of woman. Some alarmists fear that the increase in the political power of woman will lend the world to a catastrophe. That I deny.

"In considering the woman question we must ask ourselves in what century do we live? In our own. We must settle the woman question then in the fashion of our century and not In the fashion of a century long past.

"I see little to gain from discussions of whether woman is man's inferior or man's superior. That is because woman is so different.

Woman's Intuition

"I should say of woman that she does not display man's capacity for what is called synthesis, that she is not a great creative artist. On the other hand, intuition always seemed to me a quality finer and better than intelligence. Any horse can display intelligence but only a woman has intuition. But that very intuition makes her distrustful of politics and politicians. It is to me doubtful if more than half the women in the world will ever exercise their right to vote even if all the women in the world win the right of suffrage."

"Whether," I remarked, "woman avails herself of the privilege of the vote is her affair. But I fail to see how any democracy, and you claim that fascism is democratic, can deny complete equality to both sexes?"

"The question of votes for women," the dictator replied, "is not a question of democracy or aristocracy. You ask me for proof? I believe that one of the most democratic countries in the world — a land more democratic than the democrats — is Switzerland. Yet Switzerland has not given votes to women.

"I suppose no one would deny that Spain is a land rigidly Catholic, proudly aristocratic, wedded to the traditional form of the family. Yet Spain has granted woman suffrage and there has ensued no general destruction of society there.

Suffrage Unimportant

"I have no objection to woman suffrage, but I do not think that it is of the utmost importance. Woman suffrage will not change the face of the world, if only because woman, while different from man, is not after all so very different from us. More important than suffrage for either sex is self-discipline, the ability to live and to die for an ideal. The course of history of the human race in the 20th century will not depend upon how men and women vote. It will depend upon what they do."

"What," I asked Mussolini, "is the contribution of fascism to civilization?"

"Fascism," the dictator of Italy replied, with flashing eyes, "leads mankind out of the blind alleys. It reconciles capital and labor in a new synthesis. Capital and labor had grown too strong for the state. Parliamentary government proved itself a helpless nurse, unable to control those unruly young giants until fascism stepped in.

"Society was sinking into a bog of rhetoric. Fascism compels the age to surrender the nursery tales of liberalism. For futile strife and self-seeking, fascism substitutes: Discipline. The world is indebted to fascism for the new discipline.

"Today fascism is a party, a militia, a corporation, a society. That is not enough. Fascism must become something more. Fascism must be a way to live, a manner of existence.

"What is that mode of life? Courage, first of all. Love of adventure, dislike of mere talk about peace wen there is no peace, readiness to do and to dare contempt for all sitting down and taking things easy—these make up fascism."

"Do you think," I replied, "that fascism can redeem other countries as well as Italy? In Germany, in Austria, in France, even in England, I have heard the 'cry for Mussolini.'"

Fascism Purely Italian

The duce smiled without amusement.

"Fascism Is a purely Italian product. Other countries must work out their own salvation. Every form of government must be indigenous to its own soil. Other states cannot adopt fascism, but they may evolve a system like ours based on their own idiosyncrasies. They must put an end to excessive parliamentarism if the world is to survive. Too much parliamentarism is the bane of modern civilization.

"The United States does not need fascism. The United States like every democracy, must create its own safeguard against the evils of excessive parliamentarism. The moment for such action arrives when parliamentarism paralyzes the forces of government. Fascism has tamed parliamentarism in Italy. The representatives of the people discuss, approve and make laws in Italy. That is what a parliament is for.

"What fascism really has done," the duce continued, "is to vindicate the executive power. Your constitution with its checks and balances reserves the co-ordinate powers of the executive. In many European countries, including Italy, the executive has become the plaything of parliamentary factions. The head of the state stands for all, not for a party. To that extent I agree with the kaiser.

Must Do Things

"The executive system in any system of administration should not be left impotent. The executive, as its name implies, exists to do things, to get things done, to translate a program or a policy into an accomplished fact.

"What is more contemptible than an executive power impotent to do, incapable of action?

"The restoration of the executive to its rightful place in the government was the head and front of our platform. The executive power is the agent of the national existence and the proof of the power of the national will. The executive is always faced with problems that it must solve.

"Now this executive power, the symbol of the national sovereignty, cannot be ground down under the heel of any other department of the government. The executive must set the wheels of government in motion and oil them with systematic vigilance.

"Never can the executive power in a state be brought down to the level of a set of puppets worked by men behind the scenes who only pull the wires.

"That is the doctrine of fascism and that doctrine fascism has made an accomplished fact."

Fascism is Revolution

"It seems to me," I remarked, "that fascism is as revolutionary in its way as Bolshevism."

"Right you are," Mussolini fired back at me. "Italy had the choice between Bolshevism and fascism. It chose fascism. Of course fascism brings innovations. Woe to the revolution that doesn't. Those who have been entrusted by destiny with the conduct of a revolution may be likened to those generals who have had command of an army in war. Revolution and war are two words that in a sense go together.

"War determines the course of a revolution unless a revolution brings on a war. The strategy of both has much alike. As in war, so in a revolution, it is not invariably the case that things are carried by direct assault.

"Sometimes in the course of a revolution it becomes necessary to beat a strategical retreat. Sometimes it becomes imperative to pause long upon the points of vantage already won.

"The goal is this: Government.

"The foundation of a city, the establishment of a colony, the inauguration of an empire—these are the prodigies of the spirit of man.

"And a government is not territorial merely. It may be the government of an empire that is economic or political or spiritual.

"It is an ancient adage," the duce continued, "that every people has the government it deserves. A government is a mirror in which the people may see reflected their own power and their own capacity. It is the duly of a government to last, but it is even more the duty of a government to make itself respected.

Bolshevism Theoretical

"Russia, as an experiment in communism, is interesting. Everybody now admits—and even the Bolshevik chiefs agree in admitting—that the communist experiment has failed. That is because communism, because of its equalizing tendencies, is contrary to life and to the teaching of history. There is the further fact of nature—she is profoundly opposed to equality and she may he said to exist upon the basis of the inequalities she establishes."

Mussolini rose from his desk. Walking up and down the room, he added, pronouncing each syllable with slow deliberation: "Fascism is based on reality. Bolshevism is based on theory. What do we fascists want? We want to be definite and real. We want to come out of the cloud of discussion and of theory and stand upon the solid rock of fascism.

"We must always realize the necessity of converting our theories into fact at last.

"Otherwise we shall go through life as helplessly as do those generals who command their armies on paper. We all got to know that kind of strategy of men who can sit at a table and conduct an army by putting pins in a map.

"These generals favored us with their pin prickings while we soldiers were eating our rations in the trenches. When we told these strategists of the pin prick that the time had come to leave the map on the wall and take the field, they considered the hardship of such a course, they thought over the peril of defeat, they looked at the grim reality of the trench and they held back.

"That Is how men are tested. The weak cannot transform theory into fact; they cannot translate an idea into a reality. The strong are those who do as well as dream.

"When," the Duce continued with quiet emphasis, "two elements are contending and prove in conflict they are irreconcilable, the one way out is by force.

Victims Inevitable

"To me violence is fundamentally moral. But the forces of violence must he wielded by those competent to guide their energies. Violence is more moral than compromise. The fact that violence is justifiable on the basis of its lofty motive renders it indispensible that those who use violence are guided by lofty morality—never by interested calculations of personal satisfaction. Violence should be avoided in all dealings with the innocent and with the upright, with the merely ignorant or the merely fanatical."

"What of the crimes of violence attributed to the fascisti?"

"No forward step in political evolution is possible without sacrifices and victims. It also involves certain errors. Such errors if they have been committed do not reflect on the fundamental principles of fascism. An occasional act of cruelty cannot be avoided in even the holiest crusade. The fascisti are black shirted, but believe me they are not black hearted. The black shirt cannot be worn legitimately by anyone who has not a white heart."

"There are," I said, "rumors of dissension in your own ranks. Is that the penalty you pay for practically displacing all other parties?"

"There are no dissensions. We believe in discipline. We apply this discipline not only to others but also to ourselves. Never was the party of the fasclsti more granite-like in its solidarity or more harmonious in its single-mindedness than it is today and today it is a unit."

Merely a Mouthpiece

"Is it not," I asked, thinking of the six would-be assassins who had attempted the life of Mussolini, "dangerous to concentrate too much power in one man? If the one man falls, the entire structure crumbles."

"Every great movement," replied the Duce, "must have its representative man. He must endure all the shocks of the movement and assume all its risks. He must be burned in its fires and he must be consumed with its passions.

"The banner of the fascist revolution is still aloft in my hands and I will hold it high against all comers at the price of my life and the shedding of my blood.

"But I am not fascism. I am merely its mouthpiece. The whole is greater than any of its part. Fascism is greater than Mussolini. My work will outlive me."

What is Fascism—And Why?
Chattanooga Daily Times/February 6, 1927

Is fascism the invention and weapon of Mussolini or is Mussolini the creature of fascism? Is fascism something that would die if he died, or is it something that would have played its part in the world if that eminently theatrical figure had never been born?

No doubt that under its present name and as an organization fascism from its very beginning has been most intimately associated with Mussolini. But, though it has kept its name and its leader, it has changed its nature very completely since its appearance seven years ago. Beginning as something of a novelty, it has abandoned every novel pretension it ever made. This reality that has now taken on the name and organization of fascism was fully vocal in Italy before the war, and its spiritual father is d'Annunzio. It was active and armed for the Fiume raid, while Mussolini was still encouraging crowds to loot shops and preaching "the railways for the railwaymen" and land for the peasants.

This spirit in Italy, which Mussolini did not create but which he has studied, adopted and used to clamber to his present fantastic position of Italian tyrant, had already found literary expression in the "futurist" poetry of Marinetti as early as 1912 and 1913. I can remember that rich voice in London at some dinner of the Poetry Society long before the war, reciting, shouting, the intimations of a new violence, of an Italy that would stand no nonsense, that adjured the past and claimed the future, that exulted in the thought and tumult of war, that was aristocratic, intolerant, proud, pitiless and, above all, "futurist." In those days Mussolini was just the sort of fellow the present-time fascist would spend a happy evening in waylaying and beating to death. He was a pacifist, a socialist of the extreme left, and he had made himself conspicuous by leading an agrarian revolt, the Red Week, in Romagna.

Even in 1919 Mussolini had not found the real soul and substance of his party, and the youthful violence of Italy had still to discover its organizer and god. The early fascist program read over again now, seven years later, is almost incredibly contradictory of all that fascism now proclaims; it was republican, pacifist, it demanded the abolition of titles, freedom of the press, freedom of association, freedom of propaganda, a census of wealth, confiscation of unproductive capital, suppression of banks and stock exchange, grants of land to peasant soviets and so forth. It was, in fact, a new organization of socialist extremists, outside the trade union and peasant classes.

But its strength lay not in its ideals, but in the ability with which it was organized. It set about its work from the beginning with a melodramatic picturesqueness that seized upon adolescent imaginations; it was aggressive, adventurous, quarrelsome and implacable after the heart of youth. It was, in a word, a great lark. But it put the rampant Italian futurists into a uniform and taught them a Roman salute. It developed a feud with the socialists and the populist party. It grasped an immense opportunity at the municipal elections of 1920 when it supported, and in return had the connivance of, the Giolitti ministry. It supplied convenient bands of young roughs to intimidate electors. It got arms in some secret but effective fashion, and a properly instructed police dealt with it in a spirit of friendly laxity. And when next year it had become an actual party represented in the chamber, it turned against its foster father, Giolitti, which served that venerable statesman right.

The early program had dropped out of sight by that time—it would be forgotten altogether were it not for the obstinate memories of antagonists like Sturzo and Nitti—and Mussolini was feeling his way steadily toward the poses and professions that would most fully satisfy the cravings of the more energetic and adventurous sections of Italian youth. He has emerged at last in a role that d'Annunzio could have written for him fifteen years ago, the role of the unscrupulous, magnificent savior and remaker of a hairy, heroic Italy.

As late as 1919 he had still been flirting with extreme socialistic ideas: it was only with the fall of Giolitti that he moved definitely over to patriotism, nationalism, religious orthodoxy and conservatism. I would not charge him with a cunning and calculated self-seeking in this change of front. He seems to have been guided by the quick instinct of the born actor and demagogue for what would "take," rather than by any intelligible reasoning; to throw himself and all his resources into the forms demanded by romantic reaction.

The forces of romantic reaction had been incapable of producing an organization, but they were prepared for melodramatic devotion. They had no great leader, except an elderly poet of literary habits, unhappily lacking in hair and a little exhausted by aviation and Fiume, and they cried out for a hero in the full vigor of life. The fascist organization, with the very little modification needed to scrap all the original principles, gave them the first, and Mussolini was only too ready to take his cue and come forward into the limelight as the second.

One need only study a few of the innumerable photographs of Mussolini with which the world is now bespattered to realize that he is a resultant and no original. That round, forcible-feeble face is the popular actor's face in perfection. It stares, usually out of some pseudo heroic costume, under a helmet for choice, with eyes devoid of thought or intelligence and an expression of vacuous challenge. "Well, what have you got against me? I deny it."

It is the face of a man monstrously vain and at the mere first rustle of a hiss—afraid. Not physically afraid, not afraid of the assassin who lurks in the shadows, but afraid, in deadly fear, of that truth which walks by day. The murders and outrages against opponents and critics that lie like a trail of blood upon his record are the natural concomitants of leadership by a man too afraid of self-realization to endure the face of an antagonist.

Roll Call of Critics

Away with them! Nitti, Amendola, Forni, Misuri, Matteotti, Salvemini, Sturzo, Turati! Away with all these men who watch and criticize and wait! What are they waiting for? Not one of these names of men beaten, exiled or foully done to death which is not the name of a better man than this posturing figure which holds the stage in Italy. And the supreme sin of each one of them has been the quack-destroying comment, the chill and penetrating eye.

In truth Mussolini has made nothing in Italy. He is a product of Italy. A morbid product. Italians ask: "What should we have done without Mussolini?" And the answer is: "You would have got another." What is now drilled and disciplined as fascism existed before him and will go on after him. If he were to die, fascism would not have the least difficulty in finding among the rich resources of Italy a successor as dramatic and rhetorical; its difficulty would be that it would probably find too many successors.

212

What, then, is this reality of fascism, which inflates this strange being and allows him for a little while to do so much violence as the tyrant of Italy? What complex of forces sustains him?

One power of fascism is that it is the first entrance of an organized brotherhood upon the drama of Italian politics.

It is only apparently a one-man tyranny. There is considerable reason to suppose that organized brotherhoods, maintaining a certain uniformity of thought and action over large areas and exacting a quasi-religious devotion within their membership, are going to play an increasingly important part in human affairs. Secret societies there have always been in Italy, but fascism is not a secret society: it is an association with open and declared aims. It discusses its activities in big meetings and regulates them through a press.

The Communist party which dominates Russia, the Kuomintang which is rescuing China from anarchy and foreign dominion, are other such associations, broader and more completely modern in spirit, but structurally akin. Their ideals and those of the fascists are in the flattest contrast, and their procedure is freer from furtive violence, but they have much the same material form. The contents of the vehicle differ, but the form of the vehicle is similar.

And, while in the Communist party we find Marxist theories struggling with practical reality and in the Kuomintang the conception of consolidating and developing a modernized, but essentially Chinese, civilization, in the fascist vehicle there seems to be the ideology of a young and essentially ill-educated Italian, romantic, impatient and, at bottom, conventional, wanting altogether in any such freshness or vigor of outlook as distinguishes the Kuomintang and Communist vision. Fascism as compared with these movements presents a mentality which cannot conceive new things, but which wants old things and itself made glorious. The Italian futurism it succeeds was never more than a projected return to primitive violence. It is a modern method without a modern idea.

This fascist mind demands workers who work with pride and passion and accept what is given to them cheerfully; soldiers eager for the prospect of death; priests who are saints without question; and teachers who teach but one lesson: Italy. It can face no doubts nor qualifications. It sees taking thought in the light of treason, discussion as weakness, and the plainest warnings of danger as antagonism to be beaten into silence and altogether overcome. So long as Mussolini sings its song it will lavish upon him a medieval loyalty. Should he by some miracle be smitten with intelligence and self-criticism, it would sweep him away. Its honesty, as a movement in general and disregarding the manifest cynicism and commercialism of some of its older leaders, is indisputable. Mussolini, before the cameraman as hero, is the caricature portrait of young Italy before the world as hero.

Now, how comes it that Italy has produced this sort of youthful mind in sufficient abundance to fill the ranks of fascism and make it for a time at least a great and powerful machine? Why has Italy bred her own servitude and degradation? To answer that question completely would demand a long and intimately critical study of the development of Italian secondary and higher education, and of the quality and supply of reading matter to the inquiring adolescent during the past half century.

For my own part, I do not even know if it is a case of bad schools or of insufficient schools, of inaccessibility of education, of religious or anti-religious tests for the teachers, of aloofness or cheapness of quality in the universities, of a pervasion of teaching by propaganda, or a defective distribution of books. But bad education there has surely been, and Italy reaps the consequences today.

The Italian intelligence is naturally one of the best in Europe, but in some way or in several ways it must have been underfed, under-exercised and misdirected for this supply of generous, foolish, violent young men of the middle classes to exist. This mentality could not be possible without a wide ignorance of general history or world geography, without the want of any soundly scientific teaching to balance the judgment and of any effective training in discussion, fair play and open-mindedness to steady behavior. It is the mentality of the emotional, imaginative, intellectually undertrained hobbledy-hoy.

Good Fascists

For the most tragic thing of all, to my mind, in this Italian situation is the good there is in these fascists. There is something brave and well-meaning about them. They love something, even if it is a phantom Italy that never was and never can be; they can follow a leader with devotion, even if he is a self -deceiving charlatan. They will work. Even their outrages have the excuse of a certain indignation, albeit stupid sometimes to the pitch of extreme cruelty. Mixed up with this goodness there is, no doubt, much sheer evil, a puerile malignity and the blood-lust of excited beasts, as when so hideously they beat to death and out of recognition the poor child who may or may not have fired an ineffective pistol at their dictator. But the goodness is there.

Yet I do not see that the alloy of generosity and courage in fascism likely to save Italy from some evil consequences of its rule.

The deadliest thing about fascism is its systematic and ingenious and complete destruction of all criticism and critical opposition. It is leaving no alternative government in the land. It is destroying all hopes of recovery. The king may some day be disinterred, the Vatican may become audible again, the populist party of Catholic socialism hangs on: but it is hard to imagine any of these three vestiges of the earlier state of affairs recovering enough vitality to reconstruct anew a shattered or an exhausted Italy.

Fascism is holding up the whole apparatus of thought and education in Italy, killing or driving out of the country every capable thinker, clearing out the last nests of independent expression in the universities. Meanwhile, militant gestures alarm and estrange every foreign power with which it is in contact. Now, through Tyrol, it insults the Germans to the limits of endurance; now it threatens France monstrously and recklessly; now it is the turn of the Turk or the Yugoslav.

Yet no European country is less capable of carrying on a modern war than Italy; she has neither the coal, steel nor chemical industries necessary; and equally is she incapable of developing a modern industrialism without external resources. Her population increases unchecked; no birth-control propaganda may exist within her boundaries. So beneath all the blare and bluster of this apparently renascent. Italy there accumulates a congestion of under-educated and what soon will he underfed millions. British and other foreign capital may for a time bring in fuel and raw material to sweat the virtues of this accumulation of cheap low-grade labor. We may hear for a time quite a lot about the industrial expansion of Italy. We may be invited to invest in Italian "industrials." But one may doubt whether the more intelligent workers of western and central Europe will consent to have the standards of European life lowered by Italian cheap labor without a considerable and probably an effective protest.

So it seems to me that the horoscope of Italy reads something after this fashion: This romantic, magnificent, patriotic fascist party, so exalted and devoted in its professions, will continue to grip the land, but of necessity it must become more and more the servant of foreign and domestic capital, and more and more must it set itself to reduce its dear and beloved Italy to a congested country of sweated workers and terrorized peasants, until at last it will be seen plainly as the industrial slum of Europe. I do not see any force in Italy capable of arresting the drive to degradation and catastrophe that the fascist movement, for all its swagger, has set going.

Italy is now the sick land of Europe a fever-patient, flushed with a hectic resemblance to health and still capable of convulsive but not of sustained violence. She declines. She has fallen out of the general circle of European development: she is no longer a factor in progressive civilization. In the attempts to consolidate European affairs that will be going on in the next decade Italy will be watched rather than consulted. She has murdered or exiled all her Europeans.

Many things may happen ultimately to this sick and sweated Italy, so deeply injured and weakened by its own misguided youth. Her present flushed cheeks and bright eyes and high temperature will presently cease to deceive even herself. She may blunder into a disastrous war or she may develop sufficient social misery to produce a chaotic social revolution. Or one of these things may follow the other. And either war or revolution may spread its effects wide and far. In that way, Italy becomes a danger to all humanity. But as a conscious participant she ceases to be great and significant in the world drama. She is now, for other countries, merely Mussolini. She may presently be his distracted relic.

But Italy is something more than a huge river valley and a mountainous peninsula under a fascist tyrant. Italian intelligence and energy are now scattered throughout the earth. Who can measure the science and stimulation we in the rest of the world may owe presently to the fine minds, the liberal spirits, who have been driven out of Italy by the fascists? How many men must there be today, once pious sons of Italy, who are now learning to be servants of mankind!

Winston Churchill's Approval of Fascism
The Literary Digest/February 26, 1927

"IF I HAD BEEN AN ITALIAN, I am sure I should have been entirely with you from the beginning to the end of your victorious struggle against the bestial appetites and passions of Leninism," declared Mr. Winston Churchill, the British Chancellor of the Exchequer, in an interview he accorded at Rome to a number of journalists at the time he visited Premier Mussolini. This frank avowal of Mr. Churchill greatly distresses some British editors and makes some of them hopping mad, but others praise Mr. Churchill, although with reservations. He went on to say that in Great Britain they have not had to face the danger of Bolshevism as it appeared in Italy, but he added that of one thing he had not even a doubt, namely, that "in the struggle with Communism we shall succeed in strangling it." As further quoted in the press, Mr. Churchill remarked:

"I will, however, say a few words on the internal aspect of Fascism. Your movement has abroad rendered a service to the whole world. The great fear that ever tormented every democratic or Socialist leader was that of being outbid or surpassed by some other leader more extreme than himself. It has been said that a continual movement to the Left, a kind of fatal landslide toward the abyss, has been the character of all revolutions. Italy has shown that there is a way to combat subversive forces.

"This way can recall the mass of the people to cooperation that is loyal to the honor and interests of the State. Italy has demonstrated that the great mass of the people, when it is well led, appreciates and is ready to defend the honor and stability of civil society. It provides the necessary antidote to the Russian virus. Henceforth no nation will be able to imagine that it is deprived of a last measure of protection against malignant tumors, and every Socialist leader in each country ought to feel more confident in resisting rash and leveling doctrines."

The Manchester Guardian concedes that without doubt Mr. Churchill meant to serve some serious diplomatic purpose by calling together a number of journalists at Rome to hear him give "a certificate of character to the Fascist Government." But any such gain, it thinks, is bought at too great a price in loss of credit to Mr. Churchill's country, from which he can not be wholly separated in the eyes of the world. This daily then remarks: "The root fact about Fascism, as it is the root fact about Bolshevism, is that it rests on a basis of murderous violence. Neither Fascism nor Bolshevism denied itself the use of just as much murder and terrorism as were needed to set up its domination. Nobody doubts that both Governments now rely for their security on a general conviction among their subjects that to oppose them manfully would be to incur a great risk of being murdered, with or without formalities.

"Whether government resting on a reserve of contingent murder, arson, and looting is a good institution or not, it is certainly not an English institution, and an English statesman gives a false idea of his country to foreigners when he asks to have it reported that he thinks 'a service to the whole world' has been done by the Fascist repudiation of every English political idea, and by its recourse, after the Leninist manner, to murderous intimidation as a means of seizing and keeping political power. A few English politicians may sometimes, when in a particularly bad temper, have a passing desire to bludgeon their opponents, but the general and inveterate feeling of this nation is that the bludgeoning trick is both base and futile. Mr. Churchill libels his countrymen when he encourages the wild men of poor Italy to entertain the delusion that England admires them, or that she regards the criminal politics of Fascism as a serious alternative to her own methods."

The Guardian expresses its belief that some extremist politicians— whether of the Left or the Right—in all European countries view the political future as a probable wild-beast fight between the Fascist and Bolshevik forces of disorder. Some of them even speak as if they liked this prospect, we are told, and they are already carrying on the war of verbal abuse which would no doubt accompany the squalid bloodshed to which they look forward so eagerly. Like Mr. Churchill, they see in their dreams a "victorious struggle against the bestial appetites and passions" of Bolshevism or Fascism, as the case may be, this newspaper charges, and it proceeds as follows:

"But we hope it is not too Chauvinist of us to harp on the fact that Englishmen have a characteristic objection to being dominated by the bestial appetites and passions of anybody, no matter how fine the sentiments that he professes. Englishmen have now a somewhat long record of tough resistance to that commonest of bestial appetites and passions—the passion for bullying other animals or persons into abject submission to one's own will.

"And they are quite sharp enough to diagnose that passion equally easily under a black shirt and under the presumably red shirt worn in the excessive Army of Soviet Russia. In Italy there is no free press to save Italians from the wildest delusions about public opinion outside their country. Many Italians may innocently imagine that in England we are all tired of our Englishness and on the point of turning either 'Englishmen Italianate' or 'Englishmen Muscovite.' Mr. Churchill's speech will strengthen any such unfortunate delusion. The truth—however poor 'copy' it might have made for the assembled journalists at Rome—is that we are, with few exceptions, quite English still, quite obstinately attached to civilized politics."

British criticism of Premier Mussolini has often been harsh, inconsiderate and not particularly intelligent, observes the Belfast Northern Whig. This must have deeply offended the Duce's legions of fervent admirers, says this daily, who no doubt, like the inhabitants of many Continental countries, imagine that the British press is the mouthpiece of the Government of the day. So it is claimed that Mr. Churchill's reasoned and evidently sincere tribute to Premier Mussolini will go far toward removing the unpleasant impression caused by less tactful persons. But we are also told that:

"It will be noted that the British statesman did not, like some of Signor Mussolini's eulogists in this country, who are at least as unwise as his detractors, hold up his policy as one to which the British Prime Minister should 'play the sedulous ape.' On the contrary, he laid stress on the fact, so frequently ignored, that no policy could be independent of atmosphere and environment. The political atmosphere of Britain is very different from that of Italy. The national temperaments have more points of unlikeness than of likeness. We have, as Mr. Churchill said, our own way of doing things—including the combating of the evil forces which Signor Mussolini crushed with Draconian severity.

"Mr. Churchill, and his fellow-Ministers, and their supporters abhor those evil forces as thoroughly as do Signor Mussolini and his faithful Fascists. They rejoice over the victory that Fascism won, recognizing that it was a victory for civilization, for humanity, all over the world, and not in Italy alone. They are not prepared to condemn any of the methods which Fascism employed to gain that victory, conceding that its leaders understood the situation, and how to deal with it, far better than any alien observer could do. But they are not necessarily of opinion that the same methods could advantageously be adopted here, even if—which may never be the case—a crisis closely resembling that which developed prior to the historic march to Rome were to arise in Britain."

From the French standpoint, as indicated by Andre Chaumeix in the Paris Figaro, the dominant fact in Mr. Churchill's declaration to the journalists he received at Rome is that Fascism vanquished Bolshevism in Italy, and this writer goes on to say:

"England, which is imbued with liberal ideas and Puritan influences, has no particular leaning toward Fascism considered as political discipline. But England, strong in its diplomatic traditions and in its experimental methods, can see without partisanship what succeeds, and can take from it a useful lesson. Fascism is an Italian phenomenon which does not seem to be assimilable by other nations. But such as it is, history shows that it has saved Italy from Communism. Mr. Winston Churchill, who holds himself above all quarrels of domestic politics, therefore was able to recognize publicly at home the truth of this fact."

This contributor to the Figaro then notes that there is much importance in the remark of Mr. Churchill that Italy's fight against Communism was of service to the entire world, because Communism is a menace to the entire world, and he adds:

"Every day events reveal the objectives of Moscow and the activity of Soviet propaganda throughout the world. Only lately Europe was astonished to discover into what dangers Moscow undertakings had plunged Poland. England more than any other nation is cognizant of Soviet aims and actions, because everywhere she turns she finds the Soviets in her way. She saw them working against her at the time of the general strike and during the miners' strike. She has seen them in action in Egypt, in India, and now in China. Therefore her mind is made up and she proclaims the fact."

England understood, we read then, that Moscow's aims were directed against all Western civilization, and that the conflict was on between civil society and Communism. England hopes to triumph by its own methods and according to its own means, but it is pointed out—

"England knows how to value the effort of others, and that is why

It must also be remembered that, with the increase of the number of fascists in the factories it has become more and more difficult for the employers to give them privileged positions. All these points must be born in mind when the partial successes of the fascists in the factories are spoken of.

Fascism Degenerates

German fascism has degenerated into an armed battalion of the big bourgeoisie. It supplements the machinery of capitalism in the state and the army. This, in the main, explains the fact that the Reformists, a few years ago breathing fire against the fascists, no longer wage against them even an oral campaign. This also explains the attitude taken up by the reformist unions and S. D. Party during the last "Steel Helmet" demonstration in Berlin. This demonstration, during which the fascists were admitted even by the capitalist press to have "run the gauntlet of the hostile Berlin workers," proved a fiasco entirely owing to the brilliant anti-fascist campaign waged by the Communist Party. The failure of the 8th of May Fascist demonstration shows that the broad masses are alive to the dangers with which fascism threatens them and ready to struggle with them. Fascism, springing up in a capitalist state is inherently incapable of being implanted in the masses of the workers for long. In the daily class struggle it is forced to show its true features, and stands unmasked as the traditional foe of the working class. None the less does the struggle with fascism become the most urgent task before the German working class, any blow struck at fascism being at the same time a blow at the whole capitalist state.

Realism: The True Challenge of Fascism
Harper's Monthly/September 30, 1927

by Lothrop Stoddard

THAT Fascism militant challenges our times is generally understood. Yet the full extent of the challenge is hardly appreciated. Most persons see in Fascism a disturbing political portent. Few observers perceive that it also interrogates certain established ideas and ideals in startlingly novel fashion.

The reason for this inadequate appreciation is that, outside Italy, Fascism's critics and admirers alike err in neglecting its intellectual side. Fascist acts and policies are closely watched, and pronouncements of Mussolini are carefully read. But the logic of Fascist thought is seldom accorded the attention it deserves.

The prevailing opinion in the world to-day is that, while Fascism can act a-plenty, it has little new or constructive to say. In America, for instance, many people visualize the Fascisti as a bunch of political rough-necks, violently assaulting the Goddess of Liberty, and then adding insult to injury by giving her a dose of castor oil. Others look at Fascism as a strictly one-man show, with Mussolini cast in a role varying between Napoleon and the Kaiser. Still others regard Fascism as a sort of 'White' Bolshevism, and see no essential difference between the present governments of Rome and Moscow. Even those who heartily endorse Fascism usually do so because of material benefits such as order and efficiency, and not because of any novel contribution to the stock of human ideas.

To the writer all this seems shortsighted, because his studies of Fascist thought and his personal contact with Fascist leaders have alike convinced him that Fascism has something to say which is bound to challenge our traditional thinking, regardless of how the present Fascist regime in Italy turns out. Mussolini may lead his people to disaster, and the Fascist government may collapse. Nevertheless, the intellectual challenge of Fascism as an attitude and philosophy of life will remain, and will have to be reckoned with throughout the civilized world.

II

What, then, is this novel element which constitutes Fascism's true challenge to our times? It can be expressed in one word: Realism. The keynote of the Fascist philosophy (as distinguished from mere propagandist screeds or popular outbursts of emotion) is a thoroughgoing revolt against the sentimentality and phrase-worship of our age. Indeed, no better illustration of this realism can be given than by stating that, should any of Fascism's accredited spokesmen read these lines, they will undoubtedly register a mental protest against my use of the word 'philosophy'; because so sternly realistic are the Fascisti that they deny having any such thing! Opposed to theorizing as they are, they consistently try to keep their minds from crystallizing around formulas of any kind, except as working hypotheses which they may scrap tomorrow. Similarly, tradition and emotion are recognized as useful tools and powerful stimuli; yet these are to be valued in a relative, not an absolute, sense. That such uncompromising realism should enthrone itself in Italy may to many persons appear a singular paradox. Yet a moment's reflection should make it seem less exotic. Realism is not foreign to the Italian spirit. Beneath the luxuriant emotionalism of the Italian temperament there runs a strain of hard-headed practicality which often disconcerts those who do not know their Italians really well. Italian history is full of striking examples, from the cold diagnostics of Machiavelli to the shrewd Realpolitik of Cavour. And in the late war, when the other belligerents vied with one another in high-sounding slogans like "Kultur," "Rights of Small Nations," and "Making the World Safe for Democracy," was it not an Italian statesman who announced that "Sacred Egoism" determined his country's policy?

No, the Fascisti are genuine Italian products. What renders them especially noteworthy is that they stress and exalt one aspect of the national temperament which had hitherto been deemed of minor or occasional import. Yet their intellectual significance transcends Italy, since in formulating their realistic doctrine they have borrowed freely from other lands—from thinkers as far apart as Bismarck, Georges Sorel the syndicalist apostle, and our own William James. It is interesting to note the effect of James' "pragmatic" philosophy upon Fascist thought. James tersely defined pragmatism as: "Does it work?" Now that terse phrase is precisely the acid-test continually employed by Fascist leaders in considering their problems. Indeed, it largely characterizes Fascism's intellectual attitude toward the entire scheme of things.

Let us see how Fascist thinkers view our age. In their eyes the world has long been going on a wrong tack—especially since the days of Rousseau and his fellows. For the past century and more, say the Fascisti, we have become increasingly obsessed by theoretical abstractions condensed into phrases or single words which we have set up like idols and to which we have superstitiously bowed down.

Consider some of our present-day idols. Their names are Democracy, Liberty, Equality, Inalienable Rights, Parliamentary

Government, and more besides. Look at them closely. What do they really mean? In themselves, they mean nothing. Theoretical abstractions that they are, they have no concrete significance. Yet there they sit, like Gods in a heathen temple, paralyzing the creative thought and energy of mankind! Before them we meekly lay our problems.

Is this not so? Look you! A situation confronts us. What do we do? Do we study the special facts of the case and then act according to those facts in the light of our common sense? We may do this in our private lives, but we rarely act thus in public matters. Instead, we seek the will of our idols! In other words we strive to find a solution which shall be "democratic" or which will not offend such "sacred principles" as liberty and equality.

"What arrant nonsense!" cries Fascism. "And—what dangerous nonsense, too! Such idolatrous blindness gets us nowhere; or, rather, lands us in a bog of troubles. Wherefore: Down with our idols! Down with Democracy! Down with Equality! Trample the somewhat decomposed body of Liberty! Out with the word 'Rights'—save, perchance, when coupled with the word 'Duties'! Sweep these false gods into the dust-bin along with the other fallen idols of the past! Thus, and thus only, may we clear our vision, free our common sense, and regain the path of true progress."

Such is the uncompromising "pragmatism" of Fascism—a fierce revolt against precedent, formal logic, doctrinal authority, and phrase-worship of every kind. To be sure, the Fascisti do not hesitate to use such things for propagandist purposes, to arouse popular enthusiasm and subdue the fickle passions of the crowd. But they do it with the tongue in the cheek, and this cynical disregard of consistency is, after all, another proof of their basic realism.

Here, indeed, is something new! For stark realism has often characterized closeted philosophers, and has even been enthroned in the person of an "enlightened despot" like Frederick the Great. But when has it inspired the ruling class in a modern State? There is a phenomenon with which our world must seriously reckon. It is a portent of far-reaching significance.

In the light of all this, how absurd appear current assertions that Fascism and Bolshevism spring from the same root. Despite certain similarities in method, the two movements are philosophically far asunder. For the Bolsheviks are not realists—they are subject to the most rigid dogmatism. No medieval Schoolmen were more bound by Scriptural texts and the authority of the Church Fathers than the Bolsheviks are by the gospel of Karl Marx, the glosses of Lenin, and the doctrine of economic determinism. Here again we see how necessary it is to go behind the acts and propaganda of the Fascist Government if we are to grasp the underlying spirit of Fascist thought and understand Fascism as a movement in the intellectual realm.

III

With this aim in view, let us consider some of the matters wherein Fascism most sharply challenges traditional ideas. Perhaps the most striking instance is the Fascist attitude towards the doctrine of Nationalism. The outstanding feature of traditional nationalism has everywhere been a tendency to become a doctrine, suffused with patriotic mysticism and buttressed by ex-parte historical precedents. From Ireland to Anatolia, your typical nationalist recognizes no historical "statute of limitations" and sublimely ignores present-day realities. A French nationalist eloquently arguing his "right" to the left bank of the Rhine by citing the geography of Ancient Gaul and Charlemagne is just as dogmatic as Greek, Bulgarian, and Serbian nationalists "proving" their rival claims to Macedonia by dragging in everybody from Alexander the Great to Stephen Dushan. And the extraordinary thing is that these folk usually so persuade themselves by their own arguments that they really believe what they say. Amid this general trend, Fascist nationalism presents an interesting variation. Of course, Fascism's nationalist aspirations are as grandiose as any others. The Fascisti are nothing if not patriotic; the power and glory of Italy are ever in their minds. And equally, of course, the Fascisti realize the emotional appeal of traditional methods and use them freely for propagandist purposes. The whole classic panoply today spread over Italy, with its symbolic fasces—the axe bound with rods, its legions, and its continual evoking of the imperial past are skillfully employed to get and keep the Italian people in what Fascist spokesmen describe as "a Roman mood."

And yet, despite all this, the fact remains that here as elsewhere the Fascist attitude is rooted in realism, so that at bottom Fascist nationalism is neither mystic nor dogmatic like that of its neighbors. To illustrate the difference I cannot do better than quote the remarks of a Fascist thinker, made to me during a conversation on this very point.

"I will explain to you," said he, "how our nationalism differs from the nationalism of most other peoples. Elsewhere you will find nationalism largely based upon abstract rights and historical precedents. We Fascisti disregard all that as beside the point. For us there are no abstract rights—not even the right of a nation to bare existence. A nation, like an individual, must deserve its existence and must continue to deserve it. For example: We Fascisti do not claim that our Italy acquires any special rights because, on this geographical area, there was a Rome, a Cinquecento, a Risorgimento; because its soil nourished a Dante or a Julius Casar. No. Our belief in Italy's present and future greatness rests upon what we living Italians are, do, and will do."

Cynical? "Machiavellian"? Certainly. But also—how bold-and how refreshingly novel! Here again we encounter a strain of original thinking which the world must take into account.

From Nationalism, let us turn to another field, that of Government. Here again we find Fascism entering the temple and laying profane hands upon another cherished idol—Parliamentary Democracy. During the past century popular representative government came to be regarded as a panacea for all political ills. Best developed and most successfully practiced by the English-speaking peoples, this type of government gained immense prestige throughout the world. In Continental Europe, in Latin America, and in the Orient it was the same story. Everywhere peoples aspired to set up legislatures elected by popular suffrage as the goal of political well-being. England was termed "The Mother of Parliaments," and the American Congress furnished a kindred model which was widely copied.

Unfortunately, many of these copyings did not yield the success of their Anglo-Saxon models. With some, the political machinery creaked badly, while others were obvious failures. In Italy parliamentarism was not a brilliant success. Political life was at once usurped by a caste of professional politicians who evolved the system known as trasformismo—a sublimated "pork barrel" which ate the heart out of the parliamentary regime. Divided into a number of political cliques based on personalities rather than principles, ministries were made up of shifting blocs—temporary party groupings, bound together more by desire for the spoils of office than by intention or ability to do anything constructive once they were in power. The upshot was that Italian political life was extravagant, inefficient, and, above all, purposeless. As for the general public, it became increasingly bored and disgusted, but for a long time no practical alternative to the parliamentary regime suggested itself.

The war and its aftermath showed up the hollowness of Italian political life. Deeply disillusioned, Italy fell a prey to profound disorders threatening civil war or social revolution. The old political caste did nothing but temporize and play politics, thus proving itself wholly unable to cope with the situation. Then the Fascisti took a hand, overthrew the tottering government, and established a frank dictatorship.

Nowhere is Fascism's stark realism more strikingly exemplified than by its reflections upon government. Discarding phrases and getting down to the brass tacks of actuality, it asserts the following propositions: That the true aim of and reason for government is to do things and do things worthwhile; that the test of "good" government is, not abstract forms or particular institutions, but a government that will work in the above-stated sense; that the parliamentary regime adopted from England has not worked in Italy, but got steadily worse over more than half a century until the Fascisti threw it into the discard; that this long record of failure apparently proves that Anglo-Saxon parliamentarism is not suited to Italy; finally, that the only hope for the future is to face facts, study them, and try to evolve new political ideals and institutions more in harmony with the Italian mind and temperament. For the present, add the Fascisti, their dictatorship must continue, not only in order to imbue the Italian people with the Fascist philosophy but also because the post-war world is such a dangerous place and Italy is so badly situated therein that only a strong, patriotic regime can put Italy where she belongs or even save her from disaster.

IV

Now, whether the Fascisti are right or wrong in their particular diagnosis of Italian politics does not here concern us. What we are interested in is the pragmatic, realistic view of government in general which is implied. To most Anglo Saxons, especially, such a view is apt to come as a rather startling novelty. Down to a few years ago, shortcomings

235

in democratic institutions anywhere were wont to be ascribed, not to limitations in the idea itself, but to faulty or partial application. To critics of the democratic theory one stock answer was ordinarily made: "The remedy for democracy is more democracy!"

Today we are not so sure. The ill-success of our institutions when transplanted to Latin America, the Orient, and even many parts of Europe, culminating in the downright repudiation of parliamentary democracy both in Fascist Italy and Bolshevik Russia, gives much food for reflection. After all, why should we assume that what is politically good for us is necessarily good for everyone else? May not the truth be that the world is big enough for several distinct types of government, suited to the respective temperaments and capacities of the various human groups? In other words, is not the pragmatic attitude toward government the only sound one to assume? But, once we adopt that attitude, the old shibboleth about the remedy for democracy being more democracy will (as applied to peoples of different caliber) be about as sensible as to assert: "The remedy for fits is more fits!"

Certainly, a dispassionate survey of the world would seem to show that capacity for our sort of government is really marked only in those peoples among whom it spontaneously arose. These are the peoples of North-European stock—the stock today best represented by the Anglo-Saxons, the Scandinavians, and the Dutch. Throughout their history the North European peoples have shown an instinctive tendency towards democratic self-government. The constitutional history of England is a commonplace, and wherever Anglo Saxons have gone it has been the same story. One of the most significant lines ever penned on this matter is the casual remark of an early English colonial official that, a few years after the colony was founded, "a House of Burgesses broke out in Virginia." No legislature had been specified in the colony's charter, but, almost immediately, one happened! Those transplanted Englishmen broke out into self-government as spontaneously and inevitably as a bird breaks forth into song.

Furthermore, this political tendency is not confined to Anglo Saxons, but is shared by their blood-relatives of kindred stocks, as is abundantly shown by the history of the Dutch and Scandinavian peoples. Indeed, the most extreme example of democratic self-government in all human annals is furnished, not by the Anglo Saxons, but by the purely

Scandinavian people of Iceland.

Iceland is by nature about the last place that one would look for a record in democratic self-government. This strange island of snow-fields and volcanoes, lying far away in the recesses of the Arctic Ocean, is so poor and barren that it might seem offhand as though its sparse, scattered population would be too oppressed by the struggle for bare existence to have time for corporate life or thought. Also, the first Norse settlers were culturally on a very primitive level. They were rude viking-farers, addicted to piracy, worshipping heathen gods, and quite out of touch with European civilization. Yet those rough barbarians who landed on the bleak Icelandic coasts over a thousand years ago had in their blood a strain of political efficiency which enabled them to found a republic of a most extraordinary kind. This republic had as its sole organs of government a legislature and a court. Neither an executive nor a police force was needed. The elected representatives of the people met and decided what should be done and how the law should read. The court interpreted disputed questions arising under the law. The people voluntarily did the rest. And this extraordinary government endured successfully for several centuries.

Let us now consider yet another instance where Fascism invades the temple and assails perhaps an even more cherished idol: Equality. "All men are created equal!" That is a slogan which has stirred the enthusiasm of countless millions and which has profoundly influenced our ideals and institutions. Yet against this popular doctrine Fascism raises an uncompromising challenge. To "Equality!" the Fascisti oppose the watchword: "Gerarchia!"

Gerarchia. That is the Italian word for "hierarchy." And it implies a theory of society which flouts egalitarian democracy in no uncertain fashion. Instead of preaching men's equality, Fascism stresses their inequality. Men being thus unequal, democracy, in the ordinary sense of the word, is an unrealizable absurdity. The Fascisti's ideal social structure takes the form, not of a level plain, but of a towering pyramid. They glimpse a society in which individuals shall be graded according to their natural capacities and limitations. Over a year ago the Fascist Government announced a policy of careful selection of the most talented youth in the schools and colleges, who were to form the nucleus of a new Fascist aristocracy destined to rule Italy.

Now here again, has not Fascism said something which must

reverberate portentously in the intellectual sphere? For, whatever may be the outcome of the Fascist Government's neo-aristocratic experiments, Fascism's challenge to doctrinaire egalitarianism is in accord with the trend of scientific discovery. Modern science proclaims in no uncertain tones that men are not created equal; that, on the contrary, men are born with an infinite diversity of inherited abilities and deficiencies ranging all the way from the genius to the idiot, and that however important environment and training may be, these can only work within the limits of the inborn capacity which the individual inherits from his ancestry. Of course, this is recognized and appreciated by scientists and well-informed laymen the world over. But in most countries these scientific findings have had little effect on politics, which is still swayed by the egalitarian, environmentalist notions of past times. Italy is the first instance of a modern nation ruled by men who have definitely repudiated the egalitarian tradition. If Italy's rulers become correspondingly alive to the importance of scientific discoveries of human values and translate them into positive legislation, Fascist Italy may show the world some surprising results.

Such are the outstanding items in Fascism's challenge to our times. Can any dispassionate observer deny that here is a real challenge that must profoundly affect modern thought, whatever may be the destiny of the Fascist Government installed in Rome today? Errors of judgment, blunders, excesses, even sheer bad luck, may bring "Il Duce" and his followers to disaster; nevertheless, the group of thinkers and doers headed by Mussolini have "started something" in the intellectual world more far-reaching, perhaps, than they themselves imagine. Eppur si muove!

Fascism's realistic, pragmatic temper, brutal and cynical though it may sometimes be, has a distinct tonic value. Lastly, even if Fascism be considered an exaggerated protest, it is at least a healthy, virile protest against the sentimentality and phrase-worship of our age.

Fascism Wrote a Bloody and Magnificent Page in History, Says Mussolini

Brooklyn Daily Eagle/October 23, 1927

Insists There Was Red Resistance and Revolution of Italians Was Real—
Resents Efforts of Adversaries to Belittle Overthrow of Labor.

Benito Mussolini

Adversaries of the Fascists have for a long time past attempted to deny the revolutionary character of events which occurred toward the end of October, 1922, bringing the following arguments in support if their claims: First, there was no real resistance and there were no conflicts leading to bloodshed. Second, all the anti-Fascist parties withdrew, leaving the road open because Bolshevist danger had already disappeared when the occupation of the factories under Giolitti ended in a soap bubble.

In face of these untrue assertions aimed to diminish the generous bloody effort of the Black Shirts, we must never tire in affirming and riveting the facts which led to the Fascist revolution. It is false that the danger menacing our country, Bolshevist or subversive or by whatever name you choose to call it, had disappeared from the Italian horizon in the year in which the Black Shirts marched on Rome.

Bolshevists Challenged Black Shirts.

Contrariwise it is true that the Bolshevist activity was most intense throughout Italy even after the occupation of the factories proved a failure. It is true that the Bolsheviks resorted to the general strike with murderous ambushes as a challenge to a general muster of Black Shirts.

It is true that two years after the occupation of the factories, only three months before the march on Rome, Bolshevism still considered itself strong enough to attempt the formation of a labor alliance in order to seize power. The fundamental character of this labor alliance was antifascist. It had a clear objective, namely to uproot Fascism through a tumultuous movement backed by a political parliamentary maneuver on one hand;

through a general strike on the other; by assumption of power by the socialist leader FilippoTurati.

Every indication sufficed to prove that the general strike was meant to develop a supreme attempt at insurrectional movement, barring the way to the onward march of Fascism.

Bloody Struggle

A bloody struggle began April 15, 1915, and reached a culminating point beginning in August, 1922, exactly four years in which the Nation was practically in a state of general civil war.

With the utter defeat of labor's last general strike in 1922, Fascism wrote one of the bloodiest and most magnificent pages in history, breaking the last efforts of its adversaries and proving to Italians that they were able to replace even government in order to guarantee the continuity of the nation's life.

After the defeat of the Socialists and subversives, there remained two forces in Italian politics, namely the democratic liberals and the armed Fascists. Subversive antifascism was crushed at the outset. It can never rise again. It would never dare to manifest itself. Its survivors have become fugitives from Justice. All remnants of the red army appeared simply non-existent, their men, newspapers and organizations smart under the terrible beating they received in August, 1922. They hardly dare breathe, gazing with a sort of stupefied resignation on an accomplished fact. There is now no such thing as the famous "appeal to the masses." Not a seditious cry is heard, not a gesture seen. Where are they hiding? Fascism will only catch a glimpse of them on the benches of the chamber where old parliamentary names and corridor Intrigues are over and done with.

Duel Became Acute.

This third competitor having disappeared, the duel between old, antiquated Italy and Fascism then became acute. Returning to Fascism's insurrection, it is a tale of the martyrdom of youthful Fascist lives. The moment between the success of insurrection and seizure of power was tense. Eleventh hour governmental combines failed. They were simply

240

ruses to gain time. The very soul of the nation seemed in suspense. Insurrection reached its culmination in success. The government which preceded Fascism tried to use the celebration of the Italian Armistice Day as a lure to Italian patriotism in order to defeat the insurrection. But the government and the old regime were overturned.

Their carefully prepared trick to profane the tomb of the Unknown Soldier on Armistice Day failed with a celebration by triumphant Fascism which lasted three months and culminated on Oct. 27, 1922. Our insurrection went straight for its objectives while various columns concentrated in Rome. There was a general occupation all over the country. Armed Fascists took possession of all vital centers of the nation—railways, post prefectures, barracks and other public buildings. The proclamation of a state of siege by the old government came when, had it been possible to succeed, success would have involved enormous bloodshed.

Leaders Were Generals

The theory has been advanced that the regular army could easily have overcome the Fascist columns. This is completely unfounded. The leaders of our columns were generals, many times decorated for their prowess in war, while the great majority of men under them were veterans. These constituted the sinews of the Fascist insurrection army, which was not an amorphous crowd, which a few volleys would have sufficed to scatter, but well organized, fully armed legions, led by men of sterling valor ready to give their lives for the cause.

Fighting in October

During the fighting from Oct. 28 to Oct. 31 there were a dozen Fascisti killed, more than fell in the taking of the Bastille, a conquest which has been exalted during the last 150 years as one of the greatest insurrectional episodes in history, and which did not result in the liberation of political prisoners, because there were none at the time in the Bastille, but only four common malefactors.

Black Shirts Left Rome.

When the insurrection was victorious there was almost an immediate departure of the Black Shirts from Rome. This great military achievement was due to Fascist discipline. There was no aftermath overshadowing the victory, such as pillaging, violence and disorder. That day was pure. The insurrection closed superbly.

Having accomplished their duty, the legionnaires returned to the factories and fields from which they came. The insurrectionist period was historically closed, the revolutionary period commenced. The basis and instruments of this revolution were created with the Fascist Grand Council and Fascist militia. A definite break between the old and new regime has taken place irreparably.

Deep-Rooted Revolution

For five years the revolution has been going on. No one further dare or doubt that it is a deep-rooted, authentic revolution. There are changes in men and transformation of institutions. The radical change of spirit, the moral temper of the people work out laws. The fact is that all antiquated parties, without a single exception, from liberalism to anarchy, were anti-Fascist, and constituted a counter-revolution. This in itself is proof of the formidable innovation which the Fascisti introduced into Italian life. That we are in the presence of a really great revolution is further shown by the fact that the vendeans of anti-Fascism, the bourbons of anti-Fascism, the emigrants of anti-Fascism, all unanimously agree, as manifested in their literature, in recognizing the impossibility of a return to the old regime, which Fascism definitely laid in the grave. In the opinion of its enemies, therefore, Fascism has accomplished something definite in the history of the world.

That we are in the presence of a great revolution is again proved by the fact that in every country of the world a battle is being waged for or against Fascism; that tendencies having strong resemblance to Fascism are making their appearance in many lands, and that Bolshevism regards Fascism as its most redoubtable enemy.

No Ephemeral Phenomenon.

So much interest would not be aroused if Fascism were purely an ephemeral phenomenon without any future before it. That it is an authentic revolution is demonstrated by the fact that it has tackled the problem of the modern State as its natural function. In the creation of a new state, which is authoritarian, hierarchical and organic, lies the great revolutionary originality of Fascism, carrying a lesson perhaps for the whole modern world, which oscillates between authority of State and that of individual, between State and anti-state.

Like all other revolutions, the Fascist revolution has had a dramatic development, but this in itself would not suffice to distinguish it. A reign of terror is not—revolution; it is only a necessary instrument in a certain determined phase of revolutions. At a distance of five years no Fascist entertains the delusion that his task is finished or about to end. We must say to ourselves and to each other that we shall never have a year of rest. 1928, our sixth year, will not be less full of problems and difficulties than the fifth year, but it is as well that it should be so, for it keeps us awake and sharpens all our faculties. I am convinced that so long as we are not allowed to linger by the way-side we shall accept this necessity as a reward for our labors.

Mussolini Dreams Of Empire—His Eyes Turn To The East
Brooklyn Daily Eagle/June 10, 1928

Dictator Will Not Be Satisfied With Colonies, but Seeks an Empire—The Finger of Destiny Points Eastward. Italy's Penetration of the Balkans Already Has Progressed to a Remarkable Extent, and Is Being Extended— Every Balkan Capital Swarms With Agents of Il Duce—They Are Amply Supplied With Money

Dictator Is Confident of Overcoming Yugoslav Resistance, but Finds in France a Barrier to His Advance Into Dalmatia, Just as She Bars the Way to North Africa—Mussolini Realizes His Challenge Will Be Met, but Hopes for Victory.

Because for the last seven years Mussolini has set himself up as an infallible oracle on the science of government, incidentally predicting the course of the world for the next two or three centuries, it must not be concluded that he is altogether ridiculous.

The son of the Romagna is athirst for fame and glory, bursting with energy and ambition and wholly free from scruples of any sort, but he also possesses in an extraordinary degree the quality of perseverance. Perseverance is a passion with him as well as a virtue. His constant admonition to the true-blue Fascisti is duraro—"hold fast." One of his oft-repeated mottoes is mete lontane, meaning "distant goals." Only the other day he inscribed these words in the album of one of the numerous artists who are called to the Palazzo Chigi and the Villa Torlonia to assure posterity of an ample supply of Mussolinian busts in bronze and marble.

One of His "Distant Goals."

Among the "distant goals"—distant less than a decade, if his own word be taken for it—is the expansion of Italy—an increase not only in her prestige as a factor in international politics but a substantial accession of territory. Colonies are but a small and subordinate part of his program. Mussolini is thinking of an empire which is to correct the injustice of peace treaties and assure to Italy a dominion over inhabited and civilized portions of Europe. Mussolini has never hesitated to express himself clearly on this subject.

In his parliament he spoke only a short while ago of the founding of an empire as a task worthy of Roman statesmanship.

Where Is Future Empire?

Where is the future empire of Rome to be found and founded? Is it intended to resurrect the empire of Caesar or Augustus or Trajan? Will fascism seek to revive the Eastern Empire of Constantine, which extended from the Hadrian (Adriatic) Sea (Mare Hadriaticum) to the Pontus Euxinus (Black Sea) and thence toward the shores of the Mare Caspium (Caspian Sea)? Attempts to rebuild the Western Empire have not been unknown in history from the days of Charlemagne to the virile race of the Hohenstaufen and to Henry VII, the "alto Arrigo" of Dante.

After that the empire declined to a mere name and an empty shadow until the more recent adventures of Napoleon revived the ancient faded memories. All the attempts to restore the vast structure of the Western empire failed—glorious dreams that never came true.

True, the Western Empire had by far the more glorious career, but as a political entity it is as hopelessly dead as the Egypt of the Pharaohs or the Athens of Pericles.

Destiny's Finger Points East

The finger of destiny points to the East, through the living remains of the Austro-Hungarian Empire and beyond to the ancient conquests of Titus, Tiberius, Trajan and Diocletian. Here is the line of historic precedent and, all things considered, possibly the line of least resistance.

To its dying day the Eastern Empire asserted its jurisdiction over what today are known as the Balkan States and over all of Asia Minor to the sources of the Tigris and the Euphrates. Centuries before the Eastern Empire perished before the onslaught of Islam all these countries had been conquered by Roman arms and had accepted Roman laws and Roman culture.

The veterans of the Trajan legions who, under grants by the state, settled in what today is known as Romania even preserved the Latin dialect, which forms the basis of the modern Romanian tongue. Pannonia, Macedonia, Dalmatia, Dacia, Thrace, Moesia, Noricum, Illyria, etc.; these were the old classic names for the region now somewhat loosely known as the Balkans. Poor little Greece, a mere shadow of her old power and glory, at last rescued from Turkish vassalage, is today counted along with the Balkan units.

Is Hour of Roman Possibilities Near?

The forces that erstwhile threatened to bar every thought of an Eastern Empire to be built under the aegis of Italy have either been swept away or fatally weakened by the last war and its aftermath. The Austrian double-headed eagle is a symbol of a dead past, the Russian bear walks with a pronounced limp and the crescent (curious paradox) is on the wane. It seems like the hour of Roman possibilities. The Roman conquests and the ancient supremacy of Rome in the Balkans are attested by innumerable names and streets and old military roads, by the remains of arches and forums and amphitheaters in all the country between the Adriatic and the Black Seas.

Column of Trajan in Rome

Nor is the Eternal City without its monument to record the Roman triumphs across the Straits of Otranto. In what was once upon a time the heart of the imperial city there stands to this hour the column of Trajan, amid the noble ruins of its forum. On the sides of the majestic column, as well preserved as if they were still fresh, are found the sculptures in a winding series from top to bottom, all of them illustrating the victorious campaigns of the Roman legions along the Danube and the Carpathians.

All these conquests were completed and consolidated in the course of the first century of the Christian era. All these provinces remained under the jurisdiction of the Eastern empire until the crescent replaced the cross on the Bosporus.

Duce's Eyes Turn Eastward

Mussolini's admirers may well claim that he has the true Roman intuition, for all his foreign policy as far as it aims at expansion has looked steadily toward the East—down the noble Appian Way, the Queen of

Roads, with its majestic sweep to Brindisi, the ancient Brindisium, where the Roman legions embarked for conquest and where the Roman consuls and procurators followed in the wake of the eagles.

What lies opposite Brindisi, across the blue glittering Adriatic? Albania, the springboard from which, as Fascists fondly hope, Mussolini will, in the fullness of time, take his leap into the footsteps of the conquering Caesars. Durazzo, the ancient Dyrrhachium, perhaps the most important strategic point on the Eastern shore of the Adriatic, is today an Italian possession in all but the name, just as it was part of the ancient empire as far back as the days of Augustus.

It is, by the way, most interesting and surely not without significance, that Dante in recounting Caesar's rapid moves against his enemies, mentions Durazzo (poi ver Durazzo), implying its strategic value as the key to the Eastern possessions of the empire.

Italy's Penetration of the Balkans

No one who has not traveled in the Balkans within the last two or three years can form an adequate conception of the Italian penetration. The economic and commercial penetration has touched even Yugoslavia, where Italians constitute the obvious national pet aversion. Romania feels a Latin kinship with Rome, not without value as a factor in economic and political penetration. The dictator's recent flirtation with Rumania's most active enemies, the Hungarians, has somewhat chilled the pro-Italian sentiment, but that will pass, and no complete "alienation of affections" need be apprehended.

Italian Cash Welcome in Bulgaria

Bulgaria is poor and welcomes Italian capital, the dependence of Greece on Italy in commerce and politics is undeniable. Note, too, the recent rapprochement between young Turkey and fascist Italy. The great barrier is Yugoslavia. Hence the calculated efforts on the part of Mussolini to isolate the tri-partite kingdom; hence the stirring up of "irredenta" sentiments along the Dalmatian coast; hence the popular hatred all through Italy of the Yugoslavia state, and hence the frequent premature calls to arms issued by the extreme wing of the fascist press.

247

A Fertile Field for Intrigue

One must know the Balkans, the various nationalities and their courts, their character, their history, their economic conditions to realize what a fertile field it offers to political intriguers of the Mussolini type. Margherita G. Serfatti, a most loyal and flattering biographer of Mussolini, for whose book the dictator wrote a preface of approval ("my life is in this book") emphasizes on more than one page Mussolini's intense admiration for Machiavelli. The distinguished writer had worked side by side with Mussolini in many a hot radical campaign and in the offices of his newspaper. She was competent to X-ray him, but she only records the pleasant discoveries, or at least those she thinks to be pleasant, or creditable.

Mussolini's Eulogy of Machiavelli

She cites an article written by Mussolini in May, 1924 (a few weeks before the Matteotti murder) in the Fascist publication known as Gerarchia. It was called a "Foreword to Machiavelli's De Principe," the well-known book in which the Florentine statesman deals with what he conceives to be the duties of a modern ruler. It is a naked eulogy of the Florentine. After reading it one can well believe Signora Sarfatti when she assures the reader that Mussolini always called it the "handbook of a statesman." Mussolini strongly sustains the opinion that the principles of Machiavelli are as practicable and as applicable in 1924 as they were in the days of Cesare Borgia, who is another of Mussolini's highly limited number of idols.

According to the Machiavellian ethics such things as coercion, intimidation, bribery and indeed the plainest violations of the decalogue are not only permissible, but may in the wise practice of statecraft become highly commendable and meritorious actions. The ideal of Machiavelli was Cesare Borgia. One of the latter's vilest tricks, the deception and subsequent assassination of his captains, rouses Machiavelli to a frenzy of admiration. He calls the trick il bellissimoinganno—"the most beautiful deceit." For a page or two he just purrs over it.

So well known is Mussolini's devotion to the principles of Machiavellian statecraft that Nicholas Murray Butler, visiting Rome and paying his attentions to Mussolini, did not hesitate to say a lot of complimentary things about Machiavelli in a public address, in spite of his capacity as president of the Carnegie Peace Foundation.

Balkans Swarm With Agents of Duce

It is no secret in Italy, though the papers give no prominence to the fact, that the agents of Mussolini swarm in every casual of the Balkan States. The most ardent and most sincere workers for peace and understanding among nations might, on such soil and in such an environment, be drawn into the vortex of political intrigue and plots and conspiracies. Even fascism does not claim that the agents employed by Mussolini to further the interests of Italy and prepare the ground for the new empire give much of their time to efforts on behalf of a Balkan Locarno. They are guided by the good old Roman principle of "Divide and Conquer."

No extraordinary diplomatic gifts are needed to create dissensions, suspicions and quarrels among the nations living in the Balkan regions. Indeed, no stimulation is needed. The Mussolinian agents are not required to trouble the waters. If they know how to fish in the troubled waters they discharge their full duty. Mussolini has ample funds at his disposal for the propagation of fascism in foreign countries, but nowhere is the money spent more freely than in the Balkan States. These items or expenditure do not appear in the state budget except in the vaguest terms.

Pave Way for Imperial Projects

The sums spent in these regions are not intended to promote Italian culture but to pave the way for imperial projects of the future. Large amounts are judiciously distributed among the newspapers, and mostly to silence opposition. It has been revealed in the Balkans, as elsewhere in Europe, that the hottest pens often lie in the itching palms. The agents are told to play up the British backing of Mussolini and to heap ridicule on the League of Nations. Italy is described as the grand power of the future and the true protectress of the smaller states, historically, geographically and culturally their closest neighbor. The Little Entente is either ignored or scorned for its alleged impotence.

Mussolini Harbors No Delusions

Mussolini is under no delusions. He knows how arduous at best will be the ascent to imperial greatness. He may dress in the guise of patron and protector before he dons the purple of Caesar. These details will unfold themselves as the seeds of time will grow to blossom and maturity.

Of one thing he is sure. In his case the star of empire will travel east "against the motions of the heaven" (contro il corso del ciel, in the expressive words of the poet). He feels confident of beating down the resistance of the Yugoslavs, but back of the little kingdom looms the power which he accuses of having "betrayed Italy" and of having robbed her of her share in the spoils of the conquerors. France stands on the coast of Dalmatia just as she bars his way in North Africa. In a wider sense the struggle may turn into a battle between fascism and democracy, with the world for its arena.

Duce's Challenge Sure to Be Met

The challenge of Mussolini has not been met, but it is inconceivable that it shall not be met in due time. It is a challenge as old as imperial Rome and it was well expressed by Virgil, whom fascism now claims as its major ancient prophet. He anticipated the sentiments of "Rule Britannia Rule" in his immortal lines:

Tu regere imperio populos, Romano, memento
Hae tibi erunt artes, pacisque imponeremorem
Parcere subjectis et debellare superbos.

The last verse—sparing the subjected and making war upon the proud—sums up the Balkan program of Mussolini to a nicety.

Benito Mussolini--Immortal, and the World's Genius in State Making

The Times Dispatch/October 21, 1928

This is the last character analysis of the Twelve Immortals, selected by a group of prominent Americans and described by Dr. Archibald Henderson, professor at the University of North Carolina. In previous installments published in The Times-Dispatch, Dr. Henderson wrote of Edison, Mme, Curie, Jane Addams, the Wright Brothers, George Bernard Shaw, Marconi, Kipling, Paderewski, Ford, Einstein and Clemenceau. Today his final article is of "Il Duce."

The World War, to an extent not yet realized by the world released the creative instincts of mankind. Holding steadily in view the ideal of universal peace, Wilson imposed upon the world the creation of the League of Nations. Unshackled by tradition, Lenin engineered the downfall of Tsardom, and created a vast new experiment in government known as the Soviet Republic.

Taking advantage of conditions in Italy, the resolute Mussolini seized the reins of leadership with courageous decisiveness, organized an impressive demonstration of force and naive enthusiasm and dictated his own selection as premier and virtual ruler.

A famous pianist, with the world at his feet, closet his instrument; wins the support of Wilson, organizes the liberation of his country and becomes the first Prime Minister of the free Poland of today.

A studious and scholarly college professor gathers up the disjecta membra of countries and peoples and masterfully molds them into the new state of Czecho-Slovakia.

The dearth of genius, the decline of greatness, deplored today by the academic croakers, the dancing dervishes of dismay, are drastically belied by the arresting figures of Wilson, Lenin, Mussolini, Paderewski and Masaryk.

Oratorical in manner, melodramatic in pose, Mussolini has carried the vigorous methods of contemporary journalism into the parliament of statesmen and the palace of kings. This son of a blacksmith, with the torso of a giant and the head of a Roman emperor has the compressed lips

251

and compelling eyes of a ruler. Into the lists of a strictly realistic age has ridden this strange apparition, II Dedischado—this anti-Socialist—to win a spectacular victory over his erstwhile comrades of the red banner and to carry off the Grand Prize of Fascism.

This modern reincarnation of the Condottiere of romantic Italy gives the lie to the late Houston Chamberlain's observation that the type of the great Italians of the Renaissance is utterly extinct.

For all its melodramatic cast, the face of Mussolini, as reflected in the imaginative conceptions of painter and sculptor, inevitably summons fancies of the mighty days of Italy's past; of granite Rome, of turbulent Milan, of radiant Florence.

Mussolini, restless, seeking, ambitious, has lived a life rich in incident and variegate color. Born in the little hamlet of Varano di Costa, July 29, 1883, he was distinguished in childhood and youth for none of the conventional virtues embalmed in copy-book maxims.

Combative and sturdy, he won to friendship through honor able battles with his companions; and significance attachs to the symbols of "valor, courage and force" upon the heraldic device of some earlier Mussolini.

Under the direction of Valfredo Carducci at Forlirupopoli, he prosecuted his studies; and so same under the spiritual influence of his teacher's brother, the great poet, Giosue Carducci. After a year spent as a teacher at Gualtieri, he broke the irksome restraint and yielded to the invincible urge to escape.

During the Wanderjahre in Switzerland, he worked fiercely as a day laborer: developed his muscles as a stone mason: studied the sciences and exercised his mental faculties under the stimulating influence of Pareto at Lausanne. Instinctively he gravitated toward political gatherings, attracted the attention of the authorities in the form of expulsion from two cantons.

So back to Italy and home goes Mussolini-next to join the Bersaglieri regiment at Verona. Under military control he acquired the intense admiration for discipline and drill which today mark the leader of the Fascist state. A second attempt at teaching, this time at Opegalia, proved unsatisfying to this avid and restless spirit. The lure of journalism drew him to the famous socialist-patriot, Cesare Battisti, who afterwards became an Italian national hero. Expulsion from Austria quickly followed the publication of Mussolini's article, in which he declared that Ala was not located upon the true Italian border. Driven from Trento, he went to Forli, became the editor of a local Socialist newspaper, clamorously championed militant political action, and at the age of 29 was chosen director of the Avanti, published in Milan. By his vigorous efforts and inflammatory editorials, he soon pushed the Avanti up to a circulation of more than a hundred thousand. Mussolini had found his metier.

After two years of exciting life, varying the routine of the newspaper office with close study of Italian life, at that time volcanic with riots and upheavals, Mussolini was confronted with the crisis of the World War. The true genius of Mussolini, his profound political instinct, was first displayed in 1914, when he violently broke with his party, the Socialists, on the question of neutrality. It was flat reversal of the program and the policy he had long advocated, from innumerable platforms, and in countless editorials. He felt that the state was in danger; and like Lincoln in 1860, he was resolute to make any and all sacrifice to save the state. On October 10, 1914, Mussolini addressed this arresting query to his readers: "Do you believe that the state of tomorrow, Republican or Socialist-Republican, will not make war if historic necessities— internal or external—make it necessary? And who will guarantee you that the government resulting from the revolution will not have to seek precisely in a war its own baptism? And shall you be against a war which should safeguard your revolution, our revolution? To refuse to distinguish between war and war, and to presume to offer the same kind of opposition to all wars is to give proof of a stupidity bordering upon the imbecile." By upholding the national ideal, by gallant service at the front where he was grievously wounded, by later identifying resort to arms by the Fascists as the last hope for the maintenance of true nationalism. Mussolini exhibited an instinct for leadership and a profound political acumen which in time sat him upon a pinnacle towering high above his fellows.

The two years following the World War have been described by Mussolini as "the darkest and most painful period of Italian life." The miasma of a mistaken internationalism spread over the land. Italy's aspirations were thwarted at Paris; the death of six hundred thousand, the wounds of a million Italians were felt to have been offered in vain. Dalmatia was lost. Flume occupied by international troops. Processions of Socialists bore banners denouncing the war, and political leaders temporized with the situation by trying to persuade the people that everything it was possible to secure for Italy had been obtained at Versailles. As editor and founder of the Popolo d'Italia, Mussolini now waged a war of the most passionate polemics. On March 23, 1919, he opened at Milan the first meeting ever held of the Fasci di Combattimento—consisting of his former comrades in arms and his political sympathizers. At the end of two days of animated discussion, the signatories to the movement numbered exactly fifty-two! From this small germ was fecundated the liberation of Italy. In describing the fighting Fascist program, Mussolini has recently said: "It was not sufficient to create an anti-altar to the altar of Socialism. It was necessary to imagine a wholly new political conception, adequate to the living reality of the twentieth century, overcoming at the same time the ideological worship of liberalism, the limited horizons of various spent and exhausted democracies, and finally the violently Utopian spirit of Bolshevism." Now began the activities of the Fascisti—with a pitiful and inauspicious beginning in the overwhelming defeat of Mussolini as a candidate at the general elections in 1919. But the Fascisti went on undismayed— gradually building up an armed State within a state. "In America itself," as Mussolini's biographer. Antonio di Fiori, frankly states, "the Ku-Klux Klan of the reconstruction period and the Vigilantes of the Southwest employed methods similar to those of the Fascists, though their aims were different."

D'Annunzio's romantic seizure of Fiume, with the assistance of the most ardent of the Fascisti, was a dramatic gesture which furnished inspiration to Mussolini and his followers. The real enemy, however, was Bolshevism which was gradually enveloping the chief industrial centers of Italy. The Fascists entered upon a species of civil warfare against those whom they regarded as the enemies of Italy, and resorted to weapons ranging from the deadly revolver and the dreaded knife to the comic purgation of castor oil. In the internecine warfare of almost two and a half five thousand Fascist youths laid down their lives for the nation's redemption. So rapidly did the Fascist strength increase that by November, 1922, some four million men were enrolled. Mussolini's carefully matured coup d'etat went through like clockwork; Facta and Salandra crumpled up the moment pressure was applied; and the King ungrudgingly yielded to Italy's will, to prevent civil war. Fascisma was established in power by a bloodless revolution, and

Mussolini became the self-dictated Premier of Italy. He has made good the pledge of that historic hour, addressed to the Fascists and the people: "From this day you have not only a Cabinet, but a government."

Il Duce—the Chief—is a picturesque embodiment of the ideas of two of the most brilliant, acute and cynical thinkers of all time: Machiavelli and Nietzsche. Each was a master of subtle and seductive thought: each was without illusions regarding the virtues of humanity; each upheld an ideal of force. The popular conception of Mussolini as a ruthless despot, who strangles liberty with iron hand merely to perpetuate his own unstable position and imaginary grandeur, is a caricaturist's nightmare, a flagrant cartoon.

Even if his manner is haughty, even if it should be claimed that he flouts the ideals of democracy so dear to the human heart, even if he does trample upon liberty, even if he always speaks at the top of his voice. Mussolini is nevertheless a man of conviction and a statesman with a matured political philosophy molded by intense study and active participation in affairs.

The ideals of force, of the Will to Power, of the Superman, found realization in no Germanic leader—not in Kaiser Wilhelm II., scuttling fugitive to Holland in crucial hour of national debacle; not in Ludendorff, mighty organizer of armies, of transport, of material; not in stolid Hindenburg, Teutonic and massively martial, conservative president of a German republic.

Mussolini is the sole incarnation in national leadership today of the soaringly autocratic ideals of Friedrich Nietzsche.

No one who has given deep reflection and study to the phenomenon which is Mussolini can doubt that the strongest power ranged against democracy in the world today is not kings or emperors, monarchies or dynasties, but a single man of destiny—Il Duce. He is the avowed enemy of liberalism, the dearest foe of democracy, the unashamed champion of collective despotism under the name of Fascism.

Mussolini is first and foremost an opportunist. Nor is this characterization made in derogation. A man of violent passions, a being revealed in his own letter as one of the fiercest instincts when his anger is aroused, he has gone through life as a cynical experimentalist, a constitutional pragmatist. With an iron constitution, a relentless will, a passion for knowledge both of ideas and men, he never allowed himself to be diverted from one central line of pursuit, the search for power. Consistency, with him as with Emerson, is an obsession of weaklings, the ban of the trivial. This son of a blacksmith, who perhaps had in his vein the blood of one of the Mussolini of Bologna who in the great deals of the Italian Communes in the thirteenth century were Capitani del Popolo, has as his most striking characteristics audacity and self-reliance. There is something of the granite strength and fierce intolerance of Andrew Jackson, in this son of the people who now, at the dazzling height of his power, says with a sweeping gesture: "I take the responsibility for all."

Literature has had no small share in molding this grim, yet darkly gay, tribute of a new people. Hugo left upon him the imprint of ideals of sanity, virtue and fraternity. Stirner, Sorel and Nietzsche fired his soul with grandiose dreams of the autonomous individualist, beyond good and evil; with glowing visions of a great race, united in superhuman ideals of strength, discipline and self-reliance; with ambitions to realize upon this earthly stage a new Risorgimento of imperial Rome, titanic, majestic and august. Carducci, faithful companion of his darkest hours, surcharged his being with ardent and patriotic hopes, an indomitable passion to reinvigorate and reanimate the tottering figure of a decadent Italy. Above all, he owes his political philosophy to the great Segretario, Messer Niccolo Machiavelli, the much-maligned author of "The Prince." This book, which Mussolini honors with the title of "The Statesman's Vade-mecum," originated the well-established view of Machiavelli as a crafty trickster, an unscrupulous schemer, who believed in making any sacrifice to gain a desired end. In spite of all the modem trappings of federated syndicalism and state control, Fascism, with its despotic rule, its forcible and frequent infringements of personal liberty is but another name for Il Principe. "I affirm," said Mussolini in May, 1924, "that the doctrine of Machiavelli to more living today than it was four centuries ago, because, if the external aspects of our life are greatly changed, no profound modifications are perceptible in the merits of individuals or of races." Mussolini has no faith in human nature. He regards all men as his enemies until they have proved themselves his friends, and even then he doesn't trust them. He has a contempt for women as creatures merely invented for men's amusement in hours of relaxation—although he pays tribute to their moral courage, which he regards as superior to that of man. With approbation he quotes the devastatingly cynical words of Machiavelli: "As to demonstrated by all those who reason regarding civil life, and as all histories are full of examples to illustrate, it to necessary for him who has the directing of a republic and who has the ordering of its laws to presuppose all men to be bad and to exploit the evil qualities in their minds whenever suitable occasion offers. Men never effect good actions save from necessity; but where freedom abounds, and where license can come about, everything to filled immediately with confusion and disorder."

Italy today is not merely under the rule of a Fascist government it is a Fascist state. Mussolini has cut the red tape of bureaus and replaced the fumbling of liberalism with the decisive and detonating shibboleths: Order, Hierarchy, Discipline. In Italy now may dwell only Fascists, and non-Fascists who are loyal to the government: but anti-Fascists are exiled. The vigorous protests of Nitti and Salvemint against the despotism of Mussolini, the exposure of the workings of the military tribunals of Fascism which parallel the drastic dictates of the Soviet Chekha, the ghastly murder of Matteoti, the atrocities which preceded the establishment of Fascism, the exile of thousands of those who oppose Fascism to a group of small islands in the Tyrrhenian Sea, off Sicily— all testify to the darker side of Fascist rule. But it is futile to dispute the genius of Mussolini because he gained high place by a coup d'etat not lacking in the usual villainies; and retains that place and power by a rigid dictatorship backed by machine guns, which is the carrying over into peace times of the restrictive and despotic rule of the war period. Rejecting the Manchesterian industrial doctrine of laissez faire, Mussolini has begun the organization of capital in a new form: industrial co-operative syndicalism under state direction and control. Infringement of the liberty of the individual, curtailment of the liberty of the press, have gone hand in hand with the rehabilitation of national finance, the vigorous suppression of organized crime as embodied in the Mafia and other lawless groups, active stimulation of agriculture and industry and the organization of the Fascisti—from the youths of the Balilla to the veterans of the march to Rome— into a cohesive, enthusiastic loyal army: the supporters and champions of the state. The numerous attempts at his assassination give point to Mussolini's avowed motto, after Nietzsche: "To live dangerously!" The Fascist state is rapidly evolving under the directing hand of Mussolini. Italy is a new nation—with grievous faults, unpalatable tyrannies. But it is vastly superior to that mausoleum of pre-war days, Lamartine's "land of the dead."

Mussolini stands out today as the most stinking and arresting figure, holding the reins of government, in the world. Hated, feared and idolized, he holds in his hands an absolute power unparalleled in modem days. He is not, indeed, a modern, but a reincarnation of old Italy fortified by the resources of the new. His own idea of himself as the Man of Destiny has so impressed itself upon the world that should the history of Napoleon repeat itself in the form of Mussolini, there would be little astonishment. He has made of a small and weakened nation a great world power; and the fate of that nation, and it may well be, the fate of others, lies in the hands of this one man. And his philosophy of government he has stated in startling words in his magazine, Gerarchia, March, 1923:

"Fascism throws the noxious theories of liberalism upon the rubbish heap. When a group or a party is in power, it is its duty to fortify and defend itself against all. The truth, manifest henceforth to all whose eyes are not blinded by dogmatism, is that men are perhaps tired of liberty. They have had an orgy of it. Liberty today is no longer the chaste and severe virgin for whom fought and died the generations of the first half of the past century. For the youths of today, intrepid, eager, stern, who envisage the dawn of a new era, there are other words which exercise a more potent fascination and these words are: Order Hierarchy, Discipline

"Be it known, then, once and for all, that Fascism knows no idols, worships no fetishes. It has already stepped, and if need be, will quietly turn around and step once more, over the more or less putrid body of the Goddess Liberty"

Women Unfit for Politics
Salt Lake Telegram/November 4, 1928

"Il Duce" Stirs a Tempest Among Fair Sex by Declaration. They are "Mirrors to Men" and Should Stay at Home Minding Their Children— And Herewith a Spirited Reply From Dr. Leta S. Hollingworth

A Woman's Retort:

258

"Mussolini, in belittling women and their intellectual attainments, does so with a purpose: he wants women to be mothers only."

"He desires a large population in Italy for the purpose of self-aggrandizement."

"He knows that when a woman exercises her intellect and invades fields other than the home, it tends to restrict procreation."

"If the Italian dictator is sincere, he ought to broaden his knowledge regarding women."

"Mussolini has led too provincial a life: he needs world travel."

"Psychologically he has the marked idea of grandeur."

"The fair sex are confident, credulous little animals."

"Women have no wills of their own."

"A woman is like a mirror to a man; she reflects whatever he desires that she shall reflect."

"Women are amusing, sentimental and born romantic."

"Psychologically, women are unfit for politics."

"Women can imitate but not originate."

"I have never known a really practical woman."

"No man ever reached greatness because of the impelling power of a woman behind him."

"One has not far to look to see many examples of men who have fallen from power and popularity through the influence of some woman."

*"The greatest work that inheres in
woman is to stay in the home and attend to our children."*

—Extracts from recent magazine interview with Benito Mussolini.

When Mussolini, the Italian dictator, said disdainfully in a recent magazine article that "the fair sex are confident, credulous little animals," he might have known he would bring down a storm of protest around his head from all the "little animals" of the world. And when he further added, "I have always said that women are inferior to men" and that "women have wills of no their own," he must have suspected he was stirring up a fine kettle of spaghetti for himself.

But when he added injury to insult by remarking that "a woman is like a mirror to a man; she reflects whatever he desires that she shall reflect," he should have realized that he was starting a lot of shooting.

It is a lucky thing that Benito is far away in sunny Italy among his olive groves, or he might have an opportunity of feeling the sharp claws of the "little animals" whose ire he has aroused by his sneering analysis of their sex. They might look like a whole jungle of tigers to him if he had to face their wrath. For the bombs he has thrown into the feminist camps have exploded with a mighty detonation.

There is one American woman, however, who is not taking Benito seriously. She is a well-known New York educator and psychologist, Dr. Leta S. Hollingworth, associate professor of education of Columbia University. When she discussed the Italian premier's statements reflecting on the intellectual capacity of women she did so smilingly. And suavely. Not vehemently, by any means. For while Dr. Hollingworth is a feminist, she is not a flamboyant one, nor the kind who is always soapboxing around for women's rights.

Interviewed in her office in Teachers College, New York City, on the subject of Mussolini vs. Women, Dr. Hollingworth said:

"Mussolini doesn't mean all those uncomplimentary things he says about women. He is too smart to believe what he utters on that score. In belittling women and their intellectual attainments he does so with a purpose. The keynote lies in the commencement of his unflattering and disdainful appraisal of women, when he quotes Napoleon, another dictator, in his reply to his Empress: "Madame, I married you to give me children, not advice," and then confesses that he is in perfect sympathy with this very sage piece of counsel.

"Mussolini is desirous of a large population in Italy, and this primarily for the purpose of self- aggrandizement. Italy's overpopulation now is one of that country's greatest problems. But the larger the domain that Mussolini rules, the greater will be his glory and the greater number of vassals under his domination.

"He wants a very high birth rate. He well knows that when a woman invades other fields, escapes the close confines of the home and exercises her intellect, this tends to restrict procreation.

"The Italian dictator is far too bright to believe the startling and offensive things he says about and against women. These bolts which he shot, for instance:

"Women are amusing, sentimental and born romantic. It is the contrary with man. Women never created anything. Psychologically, women are unfit for politics. Women can imitate but not originate."

"His remarks are all offered with a distinct purpose, as I have said, and that is to continue to keep woman in the role of a producer of a brood.

"Granted, however, that the man is sincere and that he really believes all he says, then I would suggest for him a little world tour. He needs travel. He has lived too provincial a life and has not had the opportunity, through personal contact, to meet some of the great women of the world and to learn first-hand of their achievements. Perhaps he is too busy enlarging his ranks of personal followers to keep posted on what women are achieving in the great world outside his native country. Perhaps he has led too narrow an existence and needs a vacation.

"Before he leaves his country on this suggested tour of enlightenment, however, he ought to pay a little call on one of his own distinguished countrywomen, Signora Grazla Deledda, winner of the Nobel Prize in Literature. From there he might go to Paris and try to get an appointment with Mme. Curie, the discoverer of radium.

"From Paris he might go on to Vienna, and secure an interview with Prof. Charlotte Buhler, of the University of Vienna, the noted psychologist. Then he could take a little jaunt to Sweden and visit Selma Lagerlof, another woman who has captured the Nobel Prize. In America he might stop off to see Dr. Dick, the woman who discovered the scarlet-fever germ and its antitoxin, and call on Jane Addams and a host of other women.

"In the face of distinguished, accomplished and enlightened women he would meet all over the world on his tour he would have to retract what he said or be judged obtuse and mulish. Now there is some excuse for him because, apparently, he has confined his study of the fair sex to his native countrywomen. This is no reflection upon Italian women. It is simply that it is very apparent to the world at large that they have not been permitted to exercise their intellectual capacity or even test it. How can they, with a man who holds such views regarding womankind as Benito Mussolini at the helm?

Mussolini further says: 'Women are essential to life—but most certainly not to politics. Women will change their minds a half dozen times during the voting for a bill and are quite likely to vote in favor of a motion because the man backing it and trying to pass it has curly hair and nice eyes, and has at some time paid polite attentions to them.'

"When the Italian dictator expresses those absurd sentiments it proves again that he ought to come over to America and see our women politicians in action.

"Mussolini further asks: 'Have you ever known a really practical woman? and then answers his own question: 'I have not, with all due respects to my own family. Women are a blessing in life; they are the cushions of our primitive nature, and the greatest work that inheres in woman is to stay in the home, attend to our children and give us the womanly and spiritual guidance which all we men need. No man ever reached greatness because of the impelling power of a woman behind him. It may be that he has had a woman to sympathize with him and amuse him in his moments of relaxation but it has not been her direct influence that has made him reach his position.'

"When Mussolini speaks in that fashion he utters balderdash. He is living back in the Stone Age, when primitive women bore many children and were cushions of the primitive nature of man, using Mussolini's own phraseology.

"He talks like a man 300 years old. And what he says makes him appear an anachronism in this year 1928. Doesn't he know that woman has emerged from her serfdom and is no longer the chattel of man? Again I say that what he needs is to broaden his knowledge. He is unenlightened.

262

He has concentrated too much on self-aggrandizement to observe the world's progress. He has stuck his head in the sand, like an ostrich. It is up to him to study more intensively the so-called 'woman question,' which is and always has been simply this—how to reproduce the species and at the same time to win satisfaction of the human appetites for food, security, self-assertion, mastery, adventure and play?

"Men satisfied these cravings by competitive attack, both mental and physical, upon the environment.

"As compared with man, woman has always been in a cage, with these satisfactions outside her bars. The cage has been her cumbersome reproductive system. Years ago she did not attempt to secure public sympathy by an unbridled recital of woes that could not be eased. Primitive woman was engaged from youth in conceiving and bearing children, feeding, raising and burying them. Then the discovery of paternity affected woman's status. When men realized that they also were the creators of children, their attitude toward procreation was modified. And when they found that the mothers of their children depended on them for subsistence, it modified their attitude still more. This was a long stride in the evolution of the so called 'new woman.'

"Later, when childbearing was cut down a bit, women had more time to demonstrate that they have ability and aspirations, aspirations other than those represented by reproduction and manual work. Thus was proved that the element creating the woman question as distinguished from the thousands of simple human questions resided in human physiology.

"Some people blamed men as the trappers of women in those still unenlightened days, and the statements of Mussolini would almost tend to prove there was some truth in what they charged. But men are not and have never been the trappers of women. Woman has been caged by her own physiological nature. Woman realized this and so wrestled with her own problems, knowing that she and she alone could solve them. This she did, in a measure.

"But suppose we were to return to those days when each woman bore ten and fifteen children? Woman would be back in the cage. Science, however, has modified woman's environment, and she will never again return to those old days of slavery. She does not procreate as she did years ago, and new machinery and labor-saving devices have freed her from the necessity of spending all her hours in her home. She can exercise her

263

intellect as she sees fit. Now she is satisfying some of her human cravings, according to her individuality, as men do and have done.

"When I further read the derogatory remarks by Mussolini, I wonder exactly what his own countrywomen think of his attitude. What do they think of this: 'No man ever reached greatness because of the impelling power of a woman behind him, If one examines history one finds it is rather to the contrary. Many great men, emperors, kings and statesmen have owed their decline to some woman who has undermined the strong, resolute character and determination which it had taken years to build up. One has not far to look to see many examples of men who have fallen from power and popularity through the influence of some woman.'

"Where is the much-vaunted Latin gallantry and romance to be detected in this tirade? Italian men may know the game of courtship well, for they always boast of their prowess in this respect. But American men, though they may not be masters of the flowery phrase, the romantic gesture, the honeyed compliments, would never be guilty of uttering such opprobrious remarks about women as the Italian dictator broadcasts for a world of women to read.

"However, I must say again that I am convinced Benito Mussolini does not be believe the disdainful things he says about women. He is simply trying to exercise social control by upholding a stereotyped idea. If the Italian women want to be taken in by his tremendous urge for self-glorification and want to live a life whose sole function is to give more men and women for the kingdom of Mussolini, well and good: let them.

"But I am inclined to think they are too intelligent to pay any attention to him. By living close to him they undoubtedly have a better opportunity to observe and study him from the psychological viewpoint. No wonder he quotes his beloved Napoleon. He is Napoleonic in his outlook and his desires. His marked idea of grandeur and self aggrandizement is his chief aim in life."

from
The Archive of
American Journalism

Reporting: The Tulsa Riot/1921
ISBN: 978-0-9907137-5-3
List Price: $27.95
On June 1, 1921, an awkward encounter in a small elevator spiraled into the deadliest riot in American history. After two days of burning, looting, killing and mayhem in Tulsa, the reported death toll stood at "unknown (possibly hundreds)" and an entire neighborhood--Tulsa's prospering African-American enclave of Greenwood--had been looted, bombed, and reduced to smoldering ruins.

Published by The Archive of American Journalism, this collection of contemporary newspaper and magazine articles brings readers a street-level view of the events in Tulsa. The first volume in The Archive's unique Reporting series, it holds up a mirror to the city, its social and economic conflicts, and the wider rifts in American society.

Reporting: Immigrants
ISBN: 978-0-9907137-5-3
List Price: $27.95
Long before the Statue of Liberty was raised in New York harbor, the immigration debate was running hot in American newspapers, magazines and scholarly journals. Opponents of the new arrivals from Europe, Latin America and Asia saw them as a threat to the nation's cultural traditions, as well as wage-destroyers for "native" American laborers. Supporters believed immigrants were essential, contributing the labor necessary to build a continent-sized, "melting pot" nation and economic superpower.

The debate has never ended, or been resolved, and its familiar arguments can be traced through this new collection of historic articles written from both sides, and for newspapers and journals from every part of the country. The book includes a useful timeline of immigration laws and history, as well as listings of online resources and a bibliography of printed material. Students, teachers and scholars will find a wealth of background and context for any discussion, or argument, on the subject of immigration.

Damon Runyon: Articles/1915
ISBN: 978-0-9907137-8-4
List Price: $12.95

Starting out as a cub reporter in Colorado, Damon Runyon soon found the dusty sandlots of western semi-pro baseball an inadequate field for his major-league writing talent. Moving to New York City in 1910, he landed a beat at William Randolph Hearst's New York American, where he regaled readers with detailed, behind-the scenes tales of famous sportsmen such as Jack Johnson, Jess Willard, Grover Cleveland Alexander ("the Great"), and Babe Ruth. Runyon later moved on to short stories and Broadway plays, but real fascination in his writing can also be found in his clever sketching of talented and sympathetic men, simply climbing into a boxing ring, or trying to hit a small white ball.

This short collection of articles is the first of a multi-volume edition of Runyon's sportswriting presented by The Archive of American Journalism. Written with wit, insight, and literary flair, the stories have been gleaned from the pages of the Washington Herald, El Paso Herald, Omaha Daily Bee, Richmond Times-Dispatch and other papers. The articles are set out in chronological order, taking the reader through a dramatic year of baseball, boxing, college football, and wrestling from the Classical era of American sports.

Theodore Roosevelt: Wilderness, Vol. 1
ISBN: 978-0-9907137-1-5
List Price: $24.95

In the western states and territories a young Theodore Roosevelt found inspiring loneliness and a hunters' paradise. As "open season" on buffalo, antelope, mountain goat and white-tailed deer brought these species close to extinction, however, he began to understand the meaning and value of conservation—a progression expressed eloquently in the articles he penned for Century, The Outlook and other journals.

Richard Harding Davis: Journalism
ISBN: 978-0-9907137-4-6
List Price: $24.95

The year was 1897, and the place was the front page of Hearst's New York Journal. With "The Death of Adolfo Rodriguez," Richard Harding Davis created a sensation -- and public outrage that helped bring about the Spanish-American War. This collection of 25 original newspaper and magazine stories, complete and unabridged, offers the reader a front page seat to compelling events all over the globe, and newspaper reporting as done with literary skill, social conscience and a flair for the dramatic.

268

Nellie Bly: Undercover: Reporting for *The New York World* **1887-1894**
ISBN: 978-0-9907137-2-2

List Price: $24.95

Nellie Bly's convincing disguises gained her admission to oppressive sweatshops, underground gambling parlors, illicit adoption agencies and creepy mesmerists' parlors, all in the service of sensational headlines and the steadily rising circulation numbers boasted by the New York World. This fascinating collection of original, unabridged articles—compiled for the first time since their original publication--traces Bly's brief yet astounding career as an undercover journalist.

from
historicjournalism.com

"Apparently those in each boat were selected by lot . . .The only other persons originally in my boat were Red Cross nurses of the Post unit and infants. In trampling upon them to safety I foresaw no difficulty.

"But at the dress rehearsal the purser added six dark and dangerous-looking Spaniards. It developed later that by profession they were bull-fighters. Any man who is not afraid of a bull is entitled to respect. But being cast adrift with six did not appeal.

"One could not help wondering what would happen if we ran out of provisions and the bull-fighters grew hungry. I tore up my ticket and planned to swim."

Richard Harding Davis, "President Poincaré Thanks America"
The New York Times, November 6, 1916

"The rumor that a plot is on foot to dope Mr. John Johnson's tea was emphatically denied today by everybody connected with the affair, as it developed that Mr. Johnson does not drink tea. Another rumor that the fight is to be a fake was disproved in no time by your co-respondent, no less a person than Mr. Johnson himself stamping the story as a gross fabrication, wholly unjustified by the facts in the case. Mr. Johnson indignantly declared that he could not possibly lend himself to a cook-up unless the terms of his contract are made more advantageous.

"The champion looks well, and says he is confident as to the outcome of the battle. He confided exclusively to your co-respondent that he anticipates knocking Mr. Willard sub-conscious with a right hand uppercut to the maxilla at half past 4 o'clock in round 12, but he requests that the public regard this information as strictly confidential until the day after the fight, as it might get back to Mexico and affect the attendance. Mr. Johnson says that up to the knockout it may be a pretty good contest, but he does not want his friends to be too sanguine on that point . . ."

Damon Runyon, "Advance News of the Big Mill"
El Paso Herald, January 20, 1915

"**New York Noveletic:** Broadway is flooded with ambitious youth. Such were this stage-struck girl and newcomer-wrighter—ambitious in love . . . You can see hundreds of them in New York making park benches their thrones, holding hands in movie balconies or chop-suey joints— walking along the Drive, drinking in the moon and stars—not saying a word—while music runs through their veins and their hearts dance . . . All they hope, pray and hunger for is success. They want life to hug them and make their cheeks bloom . . . Two young people in a strange town finding a home in each other's memory. Well, one day she got a bit part in a show, clicked and was whisked off to Hollywood . . . He went into an ad agency.

"For a while love letters were swapped at a fast clip, then the traffic slowed down, limped along, and finally ceased . . . Love had "taken a powder" . . . A run-out . . . They were riding to the moon on their careers, they couldn't think of anything else. Soon, Christmas cards were their only contact. And now they both have everything they came to New York to get—dreams come true . . . But they are not as happy as they were when they had nothing—except each other."

Walter Winchell, "New York Heartbeat"
Spartanburg Herald, May 3, 1940

"For years and years California's position on the Chinese question has been conspicuously contemptible. We have been imploring Congress to save us from ourselves—to avert from our undeserving heads the consequences of our own selfishness. We have prayed that the Chinese might be kept away from us, in order that we might not hurt ourselves by employing them. Within the past fifteen years I have myself repeatedly submitted, with all due deference, that we need not employ them nor purchase of them if we did not wish, and that we merited no outside assistance so long as we did. Others spoke to the same effect, but we were a feeble and unheeded few.

"All eyes were turned to Washington, all hopes were centered in Congress. It is not surprising that the relief we got was grudgingly given, for our sincerity was open to disproof. If there had been no Congress to help us we should long ago have helped ourselves. But for our own apathy and greed there would not be today enough Chinamen in California to carry a lightweight Polish refugee into the Board of Education."

Ambrose Bierce, "Prattle"
The Wasp, April 3, 1886

"THAT is what it is, a royal sport for the natural kings of earth. The grass grows right down to the water at Waikiki beach, and within fifty feet of the everlasting sea. The trees also grow down to the salty edge of things, and one sits in their shade and looks seaward at a majestic surf thundering in on the beach to one's very feet. Half a mile out, where is the reef, the white-headed combers thrust suddenly skyward out of the placid turquoise-blue and come rolling in to shore. One after another they come, a mile long, with smoking crests, the white battalions of the infinite army of the sea. And one sits and listens to the perpetual roar, and watches the unending procession, and feels tiny and fragile before this tremendous force expressing itself in fury and foam and sound. Indeed, one feels microscopically small, and the thought that one may wrestle with this sea raises in one's imagination a thrill of apprehension, almost of fear.

Flying Through Air

"And suddenly, out there where a big smoker lifts skyward, rising like a sea-god from out of the welter of spume and churning white, on the giddy, toppling, overhanging and downfalling, precarious crest appears the dark head of a man. Swiftly he rises through the rushing white. His black shoulders, his chest, his loins, his limbs—all is abruptly projected on one's vision. Where but the moment before was only the ocean's wide desolation and invincible roar is now a man, erect, full-statured, not struggling frantically in that wild movement, not buried and crushed and buffeted by those mighty monsters, but standing above them all, calm and superb, poised on the giddy summit, his feet buried in the churning foam, the salt smoke rising to his knees, and all the rest of him in the free air and flashing sunlight, and he is flying through the air, flying forward, flying fast as the surge on which he stands. He is a Mercury—a black Mercury. His heels are winged, and in them is the swiftness of the sea. In truth, from out of the sea he has leaped upon the back of the sea, and he is riding the sea that roars and bellows and cannot shake him from its back. But no frantic out-reaching and balancing is his. He is impassive, motionless as a statue carved suddenly by some miracle out of the sea's depth from which he rose. And straight on toward shore he flies on his winged heels and the white crest of the breaker. There is a wild burst of foam, a long, tumultuous, rushing sound as the breaker falls futile and spent on the beach before you; and there, at your feet, steps calmly ashore at Kanaka, burnt black by the tropic sun. Several minutes ago he was a speck a quarter of a mile away. He has "bitted the bull-mouthed breaker" and ridden it in, and the pride in the feat shows in the carriage of his magnificent body as he glances for a moment carelessly at you who sit in the shade of the shore. He is a Kanaka—and more, he is a man, a natural king, a member of the kingly species that has mastered matter and the brutes and lorded it over creation."

Jack London, "The Joys of Surf Riding"
Pall Mall Magazine, September, 1908

www.ingramcontent.com/pod-product-compliance
Lightning Source LLC
Chambersburg PA
CBHW041624140626

46547CB00030B/814